Myron Smith Towne and the Meaning of Success, 1829–1918

MYRON SMITH TOWNE

AND THE MEANING OF SUCCESS

1829 - 1918

by

RUTH WARNER TOWNE

Library of Congress Cataloging-in-Publication Data

Towne, Ruth Warner
Myron Smith Towne and the meaning of success, 1829–1918 / by Ruth Warner Towne.
p. cm.
Includes bibliographical references and index.
ISBN 0-943549-50-7 (alk. paper)
1. Towne, Myron Smith, 1829–1918. 2. Pennsylvania—Biography. 3. Unionville (Mo.)—Biography. 4. United States—Social life and customs—19th century. 5. United States—History—Civil War, 1861–1865. 6. United States. Army of the Potomac—Biography. 7. Soldiers—Pennsylvania—Biography. I. Title.
CT275.T745T68 1997
977.8'232—dc21 97-26674
CIP

Published by Thomas Jefferson University Press at Truman State University in Kirksville, Missouri 63501 (*http://tjup.truman.edu*).

The paper in this publication meets or exceeds the minimum requirements of the American National Standard—Permanence of Paper for Printed Library Materials, ANSI Z39.48 (1984).

Contents

Acknowledgments vii
Preface ix

Chapter One
Youth in Pennsylvania 1

Chapter Two
Political Activity 12

Chapter Three
Pennsylvania Schoolmaster 18

Chapter Four
Marriage and Divorce 26

Chapter Five
Enlistment in the Union Army 40

Chapter Six
Chancellorsville and Gettysburg 53

Chapter Seven
Lull in the War in the East 68

Chapter Eight
Into the South 82

Chapter Nine
Camp William Penn 97

Chapter Ten
From Petersburg to Appomattox 108

Chapter Eleven
The Texas Border 129

Chapter Twelve
Starting a New Life 153

Chapter Thirteen
Death 172

Chapter Fourteen
A New Family 191

Chapter Fifteen
Life on the Dairy Farm 206

Chapter Sixteen
Politics and Public Service 222

Chapter Seventeen
The Great Venture 232

Chapter Eighteen
Shattered Dreams 244

Chapter Nineteen
The Last Days 254

Genealogy Chart 262
Endnotes 263
Bibliography 285
Index 290

Acknowledgments

To all the members of the Towne and Warner families of past generations whom I met in the proccss of researching this study. And to Kathryn L. Warner of Susquehanna County, a previously unknown third cousin. She gave me important assistance. I take the responsibility for any errors.

Preface

THIS IS INTENDED TO BE A SOCIAL BIOGRAPHY, a glimpse into the history of American society encompassing the nineteenth century and the first two decades of the twentieth century, told in relation to the life of one man. Since he did not materialize out of nothing, it was necessary to give a brief account of how he came to be born to the family in northeastern Pennsylvania, where he lived almost half of his life.

While Myron Smith Towne attained no high office, great wealth, or special renown, he had certain extraordinary qualities. He was both observant and reflective and he enjoyed recording his thoughts in letters, diaries, and stories he shared with his son and later his daughter-in-law. His long life spanned a time of many profound changes, which affected his own life and gave him much to recount. A theme seems to run through his life, one that is rather typical of Americans since Europeans arrived on these shores: the pursuit of success or higher social and economic status. In his lifetime the measurement for success changed; he tried to shift his quest in keeping with these changes, adjusting as best he might his activities to his situation. In this he was no different from others of his time. However, the goal curiously eluded him. It slipped out of his grasp time and again. Instead of complaining or abandoning his goal, he tried to refocus and approach it in a different way. When age and physical collapse gave him no alternative, he seems to have become curiously reconciled.

While I make no claim that Towne was typical, I do think that his life sheds light on the social history of the United States during the period in which he lived. Hence, this account is a social biography.

This work should not be dismissed as some kind of exercise in filiopiety simply because the author happens to have the same name as the subject and even appears briefly at the end of the subject's life. Rather it simply reflects the fact that the Towne papers are in my possession, and that I grew up hearing many stories about this man of whom I have no first-hand memory.

In part I chose to write this biography because I possess a wealth of materials that almost clutched me with the plea, "Write this story!" Towne had a strange sense of history which led him to save everything possible in the way of written records. His son, Frank W. Towne, was even more conscious of the importance of history, of which he was a student all of his life as an avocation, not profession. Therefore, he collected his father's records and brought them to his home in Kirksville. As his only heir, those papers came into my possession.

Finally, I grew up hearing many accounts, some told numerous times, about my grandfather. I know positively that Frank W. Towne, had a phenomenal memory. Persons in long contact with him professionally have testified to that fact. What he told me was reinforced by my mother, to whom her father-in-law told the same stories after she married into the family. I have used my own interpretations of many of these accounts as a consequence of other information I located.

Ruth Warner Towne
Truman State University

Chapter One

Youth in Pennsylvania

AT THE BEGINNING OF THE NINETEENTH CENTURY, northeastern Pennsylvania was still wilderness. Settlement had been delayed by a dispute over ownership of the land which was claimed by both Pennsylvania and Connecticut on the basis of their respective colonial charters. Pennsylvania did not receive title to its northern border until after the Revolution. Early settlers were daunted by the mountain range known as the Endless Mountains, which covered five counties in northeastern Pennsylvania. While not high, they challenged pioneer families traveling with livestock and wagons. In 1800 several men from western Massachusetts entered what was later named Susquehanna County and acquired land from a speculator named Robert Rose, who acquired a vast area consisting of 99,200 acres.

One of those men was Jehiel Warner of Granby, Massachusetts. He obtained title to many acres of gently rolling hills and fertile valleys. Much of the land was covered with timber: pine, hemlock, birch, cherry, maple, and chestnut. There were numerous brooks and creeks feeding into the Susquehanna River, which rose in southern New York, almost on the border of Pennsylvania, and swung in the Great Bend into the state where it rolled southward to enter the Chesapeake. The Susquehanna transected the eastern part of the county and Warner bought his land in the western portion. The land contained part of the Wyalusing, a major creek fed by numerous brooks rising from underground springs. Warner was an enterprising man; he saw the opportunities afforded by this region, and he capitalized upon them as fast as possible.

First, Warner built a log cabin, then he went back to Granby and on January 14, 1801, he and Phinis Moody, daughter of Elisha Moody, were married. As soon as spring returned, they traveled to Warner's log cabin, and he began to work. He raised wheat, barley, and oats and sold the surplus to newcomers who could not yet raise enough for themselves. He cultivated fruit trees and cut timber. Then he built a sawmill at the point where his brook joined the Wyalusing. Soon he prospered and in 1819 determined to

The house built in 1820 by Jehiel Warner (renovated 1970)

build a fine house (for that day and location) to prove his attainments. He was no architect, but he wisely used the lay of the land to control his design, particularly his monster of a foundation which was three feet thick and six to three feet high due to the slope of the land. It was built to withstand floods, earthquakes, and hurricanes, none of which he considered likely. He rolled massive boulders from his hillsides or the huge rocks he dug from the excavation for his cellar and piled them in such a way that they dovetailed in the time-honored fashion by which New Englanders had built fences since migrating to the rocky shores of Massachusetts. Upon this foundation Warner erected a two-and-a-half-story house with many large rooms. He used his own wood, sawed

Surviving stone wall from Warner mill

in his own mill, and achieved some beautiful interior effects with wall paneling and wide, smooth, shiny floors. He followed the New England pattern of attaching outbuildings to the rear of his house. There were two large sheds for tools, wagons, wood, and other items. Beyond the sheds, still under the same roof, were two small rooms.[1] Their intended purpose is unclear, but their actual use is well documented.

Warner built his home to accommodate himself; his wife; their four sons, Elisha Hubbard, Azor Moody, Seth, Eli; and their one daughter, Rachel. These New Englanders kept in close touch with their relatives in western Massachusetts, where most of the old families were interrelated. Therefore, when Jehiel and Phinis Moody Warner wrote to their kin, they were in effect telling their news to most of Northampton County, especially when it was such encouraging news about the opportunities for success in this newly opened region. One of those interested in these reports was John Smith Towne of Belchertown, youngest son of Amasa and Margaret Smith Towne. His sister just older than he, Mary, had married Quartus Moody, nephew of Phinis Warner.[2] John, as Mary knew, had learned the blacksmith's trade because farming opportunities were growing slim in the old states. So too were chances for young tradesmen; the time necessary to become a journeyman was too long for Americans, who were always in a hurry to achieve rapidly.

After some correspondence back and forth, first through the Moody connection and then directly between Warner and Towne, they came to an agreement. The new settlements in the western part of the county needed a blacksmith; therefore, Warner, who had prospered enough to be generous, would give Towne use of the two small rooms attached to the homestead. The first could be Towne's shop and the second, his living quarters. There was plenty of space before the big sheds to tie horses being shod or to back in wagons that needed new axles and so forth. This was indeed a fine prospect, so Towne agreed. He arrived in the community in 1824 at age twenty.[3]

At the time John Towne joined her extended family, Rachel Warner was seventeen. She may have been born in the proverbial log cabin, but she had been carefully reared to be a proper young woman. Naturally, she worked at household tasks, but she also had been educated as well as she could be. Her parents had few, but good, books which she read and reread; she learned to write attractive script and her grammar and spelling were both a part of the accepted standard at the turn of the century. As devout Congregationalists, she and her family read the Bible and tried to live by its rules.[4]

John Towne was brought up in a similar pattern despite having the advantage of the common schools in Massachusetts. Proximity in their isolated environment and their similar backgrounds and values soon led to the decision to join their lives together. On November 2, 1826, John S. Towne and Rachel Warner were married. At first they lived in the room adjacent to his shop, but with the birth of a daughter, Phinis Naoma, on January 17, 1828,[5] Towne determined to build their own home. He bought sixty-nine acres of land from Robert Rose, which ran, according to the deed, "from the southwest corner of Jehiel Warner's lot, a hemlock, thence south forty-three degrees west, fifty-eight perches to a post...."[6] Today's property descriptions are more exact, but somehow people in the original states managed to handle such imprecise and transitory demarcations.

At a point roughly one half mile from the Warner home, Towne erected a small one-story house with a garret. He made the house of neat clapboards and used small, four-paned windows of bottle glass, like that of the Warner homestead. He, his wife, and their little daughter moved into the new home well before the arrival of John and Rachel's second child, a boy, on October 13, 1829. They named him Myron Smith and determined that he completed their family. Towne liked to comment that a man should not have more children than he can adequately provide with not only the necessities, but better opportunities as they reached adulthood.

As Towne prospered, he bought more land so that he had room for pasture in addition to his barley and oats and he began to develop a herd of cattle. Fruit trees grew well on the sunny slopes, and he cultivated them carefully. He worked at his blacksmith shop in the early morning, after checking on his cattle, until the evening, when he left the shop and he hurried to the fields. Such hard work brought him greater returns, so he began to enlarge his house. He built a two-story addition, turning the original area into a kitchen and dining room. In the front he had a parlor, two downstairs bedrooms, and two upstairs bedrooms, so that each of his children had their own room.

Thanks to home training, Myron and Phinis learned to read well before they entered the district school located between their home and Grandpa Warner's, and they read adult books. Grandfather Warner had made it possible for his bright Towne grandchildren to read books not usually found in remote communities. In 1831 Warner invited residents of Middletown, for that township had not yet been divided to create Forest Lake, to meet in his home. There he proposed establishing a circulating library. Those present voted unanimously to form a library company. Towne then moved that each charter member contribute two dollars to buy books. A lower fee would be charged annually thereafter for each user. Towne set an example by laying two dollars on the table. His motion carried, and Warner offered to house the books in his home. He would build shelves to hold them and he would act as librarian.[8] These books provided much reading material for the Towne children. Their father's sisters, Mary Towne Moody and Lydia Towne Lyman, also augmented the Towne children's library by sending books to their niece and nephew at Christmas.[9]

The New Englanders of northern Pennsylvania believed strongly in the concept of tax-supported schools open to all children regardless of the wealth or poverty of the parents. Until the 1840s the New Englanders fought an uphill battle. Frugal

Germans of the limestone belt, the area west of Philadelphia, opposed paying taxes and allowing their children to mingle with others in public schools. German Lutheran pastors taught children of their flock on weekdays. Wealthy merchants of Philadelphia and its environs preferred private schools for their children and regarded schooling for the poor as depriving factories and mines of cheap labor. Nonetheless, as reform gained momentum, Pennsylvania voters in county after county provided for public schools, until the state legislature established the system statewide.[10]

Susquehanna County organized its school districts on a township basis. Each district would elect a three-member board of directors, who would determine the location of individual schools and be responsible for operating them. This entailed constructing the school houses, hiring the teachers, approving the curriculum, and selecting the textbooks. Voters took seriously the need for good men to carry out these multitudinous duties. People in the western part of the newly formed Forest Lake township determined that John Towne would be an excellent board member. They elected him school director year after year. Consequently, when his son and daughter entered the Forest Lake Centre School, they were under the watchful eye of their father in a more formal way than merely the parental interest displayed by other fathers.

That fact did not bother Phinis Towne; she was a bit prim and precocious around other children, although she and her brother could invent their share of mild mischief on occasion, and a few times they brought down their father's wrath for doing so.[11] However, Phinis was clearly John Towne's favorite. Perhaps he expected less of her, not that he by any means denigrated female intelligence. Quite the contrary; he regarded his wife as extra smart and he fully expected their daughter to be also. However, like his contemporaries, he assumed his daughter's intelligence would be expended in selecting a suitable mate, rearing fine children, and doing a variety of religious and charitable works.

Myron was different, and therein lay the root of the uneasy relationship between father and son. John Towne's goal was to see his son move into the professional class. Status-seeking was not particularity of John Towne's, but he seems to have developed a potent case of it. As the last of a large family, John had been relegated to being a tradesman of the humbler sort. By migrating to a sparsely settled area where land was still cheap, he had been able to combine farming with his trade. Financially John had prospered, and he felt that by the time his son was grown, John would be in a position to send Myron east to a good college or seminary where he could study for a profession.

When Towne said profession, he meant the ministry of the Methodist Episcopal Church. In 1832 one of the major experiences of John Towne's life occurred when John Griffing, a Methodist circuit rider, arrived in Forest Lake on a preaching mission. He must have been an able preacher, and he found willing ears for his message of free grace leading to personal salvation and to good works growing out of giving oneself to Christ and promising to walk in his ways. John and Rachel Towne were among those who became converts.[12] Although Towne had remained true to his stern Calvinist upbringing, he realized something was lacking. No one as self-confident as he or as determined to climb the socioeconomic ladder could quite accept predeterminism. In Methodism he found both piety and an emphasis on discipline, qualities he recognized as necessary for status. He also found an extra boon in the joyous singing of beautiful hymns written by the Wesley brothers and their followers in England. These hymns celebrated God's grace and the assurance of salvation. Towne discovered that he loved to sing and he had a fine voice that others praised.[13]

Griffing recognized leadership ability along with zeal and made Towne the class leader of the Forest Lake Centre Class. This was the way Methodism spread. Circuit riders made converts and formed classes; they left a class leader in charge of each class, whose task it was to hold services of Bible reading, discussion, and singing between the times when an ordained elder returned for another service. As he did with all obligations, Towne devoted much time and thought to his duties as class leader, a position he held until he left Forest Lake in 1873.

At first Towne's class met in the big dining-living room of the Warner homestead. As soon as Towne was able to enlarge his house, he added a parlor or front room large enough for the small group to hold its devotional services. He added a guest room so that he could host the circuit rider when he made his periodic visits. Towne intended for his house to be the "home of the itinerant minister always."[14]

As his charge grew, Towne determined it must have its own building. The class was designated by the 1840s as a regular preaching point on the Vestal Circuit. With encouragement from the pastor on that circuit in 1848, Rodney S. Rose, Towne organized the men and older boys of his class to erect a real house of God in a charming little dell on his land. He and his brother-in-law, Azor Warner, who, after Jehiel Warner's death, remained on the Warner place to operate the farm and the sawmill, donated timber and sawed it at the Warner mill. The building went up fast, and all that had to be purchased in Montrose were the windows, door knobs, hinges, and a few other niceties. The men even made the pews. The women helped with cleaning and putting everything in proper order once the structure had taken shape.

By harvest time, the church was ready for the formal dedication-consecration service. The Oneida Conference, in which the Vestal Circuit had been placed, dispatched D. A. Shepard, one of the leading pulpit orators in the conference, to preach the service.[15] Rose and the presiding elder were also in attendance, along with representatives from other stations in the circuit.

Forest Lake Centre Methodist Church in foreground, Forest Lake Center School in the middle, and Warner homestead above the school.

John Towne had made his son, Myron, then nineteen, song leader and had sent him to singing schools to learn more about music, for Myron, too, had a fine voice and clearly enjoyed singing. Aided by his uncle, the Reverend Josiah Towne, and his aunts, Lydia and Mary, Myron collected a few Methodist hymnals so that he had a larger variety of songs from which to choose.[16] He also bought a tuning fork in Montrose one day when he was there with his father. For this grand occasion, Myron had rehearsed the congregation thoroughly and the visitors offered compliments on the singing as well as the fine building for the small rural church. The Forest Lake Centre Methodist Episcopal Church was off to a great start.

Soon Towne had a Sunday School organized with two classes, one for adults which he taught, and the other for boys and girls, which he delegated his son to teach. By that time, Myron knew precisely his father's goal. He was determined that his son be a minister, a really good preacher, not a mere circuit rider. John Towne dreamed of his son winning thousands of souls in preaching missions from a large church in one of the growing cities on the northeastern seaboard. Towne promised to send Myron to a seminary in Massachusetts or New York to study for ordination.

Myron resisted his father's efforts, a matter that John Towne found hard to understand. Many years later, long after John's death, history repeated itself in a different fashion as Myron Towne more persuasively, but with as little success, tried to coax his son to attend the state university to study journalism so he could become a great editor-publisher, doing a noble work as well as gaining wealth.

Chapter Two

Political Activity

Myron Towne, like his father, began to engage in politics as a part of his strong relationship to the Methodist Episcopal Church. A cause that became increasingly important to Methodists in the 1840s was temperance. It was hardly a new idea for Methodists because John Wesley had preached in England against the evils of drunkenness and "trafficking in the spirituous liquors." His followers there and those in the United States understood him to mean distilled alcohol. Milder beverages were permissible if used in moderation, that is, temperately.

In northeastern Pennsylvania, more fruit was grown than could be consumed and it could be preserved only by drying or fermenting. Remoteness from mercantile centers made coffee and tea scarce. Therefore, brandies, cordials, and cider were the means by which hosts and hostesses expressed their hospitality. When the circuit rider arrived at Towne's house, John took charge of the rider's horse, he and the guest washed hands and face, while Rachel brought out her best peach brandy, blackberry cordial, or apple cider. Then they all sat in the parlor, sipped, and visited.

The more remote South and Middle West, where corn was the chief food crop, produced corn whiskey so potent that it led to the worst type of drunkenness—the drunken brawls and random shots. In the new industrial cities of the Northeast, workers arrived at work so inebriated that they endangered machinery, themselves, and fellow workers. When workers were paid, they spent their money in saloons and left their families destitute. Reformers eager to assist the poor determined to attack what seemed the root of the evil, whiskey.

Although the temperance movement that developed in the 1840s was interdenominational, it particularly appealed to the reform impulse so strong in Methodism. In 1836 the General Conference went on record as warning the faithful not to make or sell strong liquor. As time passed annual conferences and church editors began to encourage clergymen to form, or join in efforts to form, temperance societies.[1]

Once John Towne had his church building completed, he set about organizing a Forest Lake Temperance Society. On December 28, 1849, he invited the Baptists, who had a church near the lake itself, to meet in his church and form such an organization. In deference to his clerical status, the Baptist preacher, who signed the forms as "P. Frank" became president and Towne, L. M. Turrell, and John Strange held the vice-presidency jointly. They planned a general meeting with an imported temperance lecturer from a larger temperance society.[2] At this time those in attendance came forward to sign the pledge. If so minded the person might add "T" after the signature to signify total abstinence from the use of any alcohol, even the mildest forms. John Towne and his twenty-year old son put a "T" after their names, thus identifying themselves as "teetotalers." Rachel's brandies and cordials disappeared.[3] In his later years, when he established his own home, Myron Towne followed the same pattern and he brought up his son to feel the same strong repulsion to liquor, although neither imposed their feelings on their neighbors or friends.

Concern about education and the organization of school districts to serve the people of the township led John Towne to accept election as school director, and he served in that capacity for many years. This understandably carried no political label, nor did other positions in the township. When he was elected justice of the peace in the early 1850s, no one asked his party affiliation, and when he did change his party affiliation it made no difference to his position as the township justice of the peace. He held the office until he left Pennsylvania in 1873.[4]

As Myron Towne matured and became recognized for his superior education and sterling character, the township voters elected him clerk of the township year after year and later added the position of constable, until he left for military service.[5]

In actuality both father and son voted the Whig ticket in state and national elections. In John Towne's case his Whiggish tendencies were a result of his New England background. In his son's opinion a person of conscience could not be a Democrat because of that party's support of slavery. Rural Pennsylvanians of the northeastern corner of the state opposed slavery but without any fixed notion of how to eliminate it. Unlike the radical abolitionists, John Towne and his son could not advocate violence against anything that was legal. This rather tolerant stand changed in the 1840s.

Two events came together. The first occurred in 1844 when the General Conference of the Methodist Episcopal Church finally went back to the original Wesleyan rule that held slavery to be an "abomination" to be "exterpated." At least the action might be so interpreted. When a delegate called attention to the fact that a newly elected bishop from Georgia owned slaves and offered a resolution to the effect that the bishop should divest himself of such property before he could assume the episcopal office, the majority of the delegates approved the resolution. The Georgia delegation threatened to walk out unless the majority vote was rescinded. The majority refused to be threatened and stood firm. The entire southern group, those from all the slave states, withdrew. The seceders met in another location and announced the formation of the Methodist Episcopal Church, South.[6]

John Towne alternated between anger and pleasure as he read the news. He was furious at what he declared to be a violation of the basis of democracy: the rule that the majority determined what should be done. If one disagreed, he should work to convince the others that they were wrong. However, Towne was pleased about the northern majority at last standing for what was right. How could a true Methodist support anything so unchristian as a claim to own or encourage others to own human beings, God's creation? Towne moved closer to deciding that he must do something about this evil. His son did not need to be prodded to carry this thought even farther. The slaves must be freed, hopefully by some peaceful, legal means.

At that point the second event occurred that galvanized the Towne and Warner families along with their neighbors into making a major political change. At first a war with Mexico over Texas and California struck folks in Susquehanna County as foolish. It seemed too remote, but over time interest heightened as more information arrived about the remainder of the territory needed to give the United States a long stretch of the Pacific coast. Northeastern Pennsylvanians were beginning to realize what their parents and grandparents had discovered in New England, that there was no more wilderness left to provide an enterprising farmer the chance to improve his status. In this new territory far to the west there seemed to be ample land for new pioneering ventures.

There was one flaw in this otherwise rosy future, and that was the determination of southerners to force slavery into all of the new area. Easterners felt equally determined to keep out what they regarded as the unequal competition of slaveowners, who held huge uncleared areas for the day when the cotton culture had so eroded the old lands that they were no longer able to support the cotton-slave style of agriculture. The people of Susquehanna County looked to their representative in Congress. He was David

Wilmot, a Democrat, who saw the war as an opportunity to begin the process of ending slavery.

In 1846, while Congress considered the appropriation bill to permit the Army to spend more money to fight the war against Mexico, Wilmot offered an amendment stating that any territory acquired by the United States as a result of the war would be closed to slavery. The House of Representatives adopted the amendment; the Senate refused and passed the bill without the amendment. From that time until 1850 Wilmot and others added this proviso to all sorts of bills. The House voted for the amendment repeatedly and the Senate continued to vote against it. The action clearly spoke volumes for the demographics of the nation and the census of 1850 supported it. The urban northeast and the diversified and increasingly commercialized agricultural Old Northwest were growing much faster in population and wealth than the cotton South.

John Towne and his son, who reached voting age in 1850, remained Whigs despite their admiration for and support of Wilmot and his free soil principle. They only deplored the bad company in which he found himself as a Democrat.

The Compromise of 1850 shifted the decision from Congress to the territories in the second phase of territorial government. The Compromise provided for a new idea of popular sovereignty; that is it, let the voters of a territory decide whether or not slavery would be legal. When they elected a territorial legislature they would choose representatives in accord with their views on slavery. This potentially opened all territories to slavery if the territorial legislatures chose, and it was dramatically opposed to Wilmot's idea of closing all territories so slavery would eventually die. People in the Northeast, even if strong Whigs, felt unhappy that Whigs had joined with Democrats to put across this omnibus measure. However, it took the Kansas-Nebraska bill to complete the disillusionment of John and Myron Towne and other die-hard

Whigs. When the Whigs in Congress crumpled before the determined coalition that, as they saw it, pushing slavery into Kansas, they were through with Whiggery.

The Old Northwest, now in many ways the equal of the Northeast, acted first. Meetings took place in Wisconsin, Illinois, and spread quickly to Pennsylvania. Wilmot chose not to run for Congress again so he could devote his time to organizing the newly formed Republican party, as the Anti-Nebraska Democrats and Conscience Whigs called their new organization. The short-lived Free Soil Party joined forces and a formidable combination ensued.[7]

Wilmot scheduled a series of meetings in his old Congressional District, one close enough to Forest Lake that John and Myron Towne joined a small delegation to hear Wilmot, and in almost the same pattern as a temperance meeting, signed the lengthy list of those enrolling in the Republican Party. From that time until his death John Towne remained a firm supporter of the party. Myron Towne too considered himself a Republican until all the great causes—Union, freedom, and equal rights for all men—had become a part of the Constitution.[8] As other issues developed, his Republican affiliation finally came to an end, but that lay far in the future. Meanwhile, he had to begin his career.

Chapter Three

Pennsylvania Schoolmaster

AFTER CONSIDERABLE GRUMBLING AND SOUL-SEARCHING, John Towne concluded that his son might as well become a teacher. Although it was a substitute for the ministry which John Towne coveted as a career for his son, it also represented a way to assign an adequately prepared instructor to one of the township schools for which John was responsible as school director. He knew that he had done as much as possible, under the circumstances, to see that Myron had a better than average education. Therefore, as school director, John would not hesitate to recommend his son to the fellow directors. The father did not see any ethical conflict in such action, nor did his colleagues. On the contrary, they probably saw their action as both good for the schools in their system and a means to regain some of the cost of educating one young man who had attended more terms than most. Nepotism was no crime in small rural communities; indeed it was considered a positive good if it truly was advantageous to all concerned.

In November 1848 the directors engaged Myron S. Towne to teach in the common schools of Forest Lake and assigned him to the McKelvey School.[1] Many years later he told his daughter-in-law, "Father hired me out to teach a school under his direction when I was nineteen."[2] Although she assumed this statement represented a complaint, that does not accord with the record. Myron was not averse to teaching, and he continued in the profession for twelve years. From many accounts told to his son by Towne and from the way the he educated the boy, one can see that Myron enjoyed the years he taught. Following the standard procedure, Myron Towne taught only the winter term each year. For the remainder of the year, he farmed, ran a small business, or both. The district, like others, hired young women to teach the summer sessions when older boys would be working in the fields and not in school. Supposedly, young women could not cope with the conduct of the bigger boys. The district also saved, money for females could be paid less since they worked only until marriage, such was the attitude of the day.

Myron Towne took pleasure in offering an enriched curriculum for his upper section students: he added lessons in history, geography, and literature, as well as elements of science or natural philosophy, as scientific studies were termed. He also delighted in the music lessons he offered daily. They provided both teacher and pupils a welcome treat from the often monotonous giving and hearing of recitations, and he used singing as a reward for good behavior and success in mastering particular aspects of each day's lessons. He obtained satisfaction from honing his skills in neatness by keeping the records prescribed by law. In a clear script he entered the name of each pupil, tiny marks for each day in attendance to be totaled at the end of the term, and the number of times each pupil stood at the head of his or her class in any given subject. These records went to the school directors of the town, but out of some sense of caution or even a perverse desire to be able to "show up the directors" should they lose track of his number of terms taught, which figured into salary calculations, Myron made another copy of each page to keep for himself.[3]

As he moved about the township teaching in different schools, Towne's self-assurance grew, and he became more adept at presenting materials. In later years he liked to say that he had never had trouble with discipline, but that he achieved it by positive means. He eschewed corporal punishment except on a few rare occasions when all else had failed and a mild paddling was the last alternative. He refused to use ridicule such as dressing a boy in a simulation of girl's garb or the commonplace dunce cap of the time. He claimed that he had seen too much of that sort of thing, which created more trouble than it cured.[4]

In his second year of teaching Towne faced an interesting challenge: he was assigned to his home school. There he was under the direct scrutiny of father, uncles, and neighbors, and eight of his thirty students were Warner cousins. His cousins knew Myron in an entirely different way from the role he held as their teacher. Would they understand that before the other pupils both he and they must preserve a posture different from that practiced at a big family gathering at the homestead? He resolved to institute the new order quickly; he had no difficulty with the younger children, but he had to be quite distant with the older ones until they got accustomed to saying "Mr. Towne" during school hours.[5]

Two years at his home school, one at the Turrell School, and one at Forest Lake were followed by one more at Forest Lake Centre in 1853–1854.[6] By that time Towne had accumulated enough money to buy a farm. Improved land was by the middle of the nineteenth century all that was available; therefore, the cost was much higher than when it had been virgin land. Consequently, Towne followed the well-established practice of mortgaging the property to buy it. He farmed the land in the summer, taught school in the winter, and used the proceeds from his farm and his teacher's salary to make the interest payments.[7]

While he was scarcely prospering as he desired, Towne had enough money to satisfy another goal, which was to gain more education. Advanced schooling had reached a turning point by the middle of the nineteenth century. Traditional liberal arts subjects remained the basis for theology and law, but what about new occupations such as teaching, business, or commerce? Mushrooming public schools in the United States trying to cope with a new concept of educating the masses latched onto the European theories of pedagogy. Connecticut and Massachusetts established schools for teachers under the name "normal schools" to indicate the concept of a norm or a standard way to train teachers. In Pennsylvania the legislature refused to establish a state normal school or college as the pioneer New England states had done. Instead, it passed enabling legislation by which a county could vote to operate a normal school or the county superintendent of schools, a newly created office, could hold an institute for teachers. County normal schools offered one six-to-eight-week term once or twice a year. The institute was a gathering of teachers, already licensed, to help them refresh their skills or learn any new developments in teaching. The institute lasted no more than one week and often less time. A still different approach appeared at some small liberal arts colleges when they added a "Normal Department," which consisted of a few courses on education, to the traditional liberal arts classes.

In Susquehanna County, near the village of Harford, there was an academy which had opened in the 1820s; by 1850 it had adopted the pretentious title of Harford University. This the trustees might justify due to the fact that the school had adopted a combination of traditional liberal arts, modified by adding modern languages to Latin and Greek, and a normal department. The latter was designed to permit a teacher or one preparing to teach to take the how-to courses superimposed on some or all of the regular liberal arts subjects. It was to this school that Towne directed his attention.

Harford's proximity, its modest fees, and its convenient calendar consisting of three sessions, one beginning in April and ending in July, were obvious attractions.[8] Towne completed the winter term of school, put in his crop, and, left a part-time hired hand to look after things, under the watchful eye of his father, for

Myron Towne's land lay just behind his father's farm. Then Myron enrolled at Harford for the summer term of 1854.[9] There he matriculated in a science course that combined geology, botany, a smattering of paleontology and astronomy; a composition and public speaking class which required membership in one of the two debating societies in which men engaged in weekly disputations on selected topics; a class in geography-history; and a French class. He lived in one of the dormitories for men located next to the classroom building.[10] He bought several volumes for each class, and he carefully incorporated them in his library, which he moved with his other possessions as he changed residence later in life.[11]

Towne liked his instructors, largely members of the Richardson family. He took natural philosophy and mathematics taught by the president, the Reverend Lyman Richardson; French from Maria Richardson, the president's niece; and the geography-history course plus the English composition and public speaking class from Willard Richardson, a nephew. The younger Richardson particularly appealed to Towne for as head of the normal department, Richardson tried to integrate theories of teacher training with traditional and practical subject matter. He would pause during discussion in a class that dealt with history in its geographic setting to illustrate points that could make study of that subject more meaningful to students in the sixth reader, for example.[12]

Towne enjoyed the Lyceum lectures presented at the school. Speakers on a variety of topics arrived at the campus on almost a weekly basis, and Towne eagerly attended their lectures. A chemist discussed elements and compounds, with an array of test tubes and other apparatus to illustrate his points. A phrenologist explained human behavior in terms of the bumps on a person's skull, and that by rubbing bumps of different types in special fashion, behavior could be modified.[13] The notion filled Towne with secret mirth. He dismissed phrenology as a pseudoscience, as it soon came to be classified by all but a few devotees.

The Lyceum lecture that made the greatest impression on Towne was presented by an astronomer. Towne's science class had studied a chart of the heavens as seen in the northern hemisphere so he had some background besides the obvious points rural people observed and noted as they did nightly chores. However, under the stimulus of the Lyceum speaker and the section in science on astronomy, Towne developed a life-long interest in amateur stargazing. Years later on his farm at the edge of Unionville, Missouri, he took his son to the highest point on their land and taught the boy to locate major constellations and the planets visible to the naked eye. One crisp, bitterly cold, clear winter evening he directed the boy to wrap up well and come with him. After they were away from the house and its grove of trees, Towne pointed to a brilliant pattern of lights rising and falling along the northern horizon. He informed the youngster that these were the aurora borealis. He explained the atmospheric conditions that rendered the startling display visible on certain nights even in northern Missouri's latitude.[14]

Towne felt his months at the college had been quite productive. He looked forward to returning the next summer, but for various reasons he did not do so. However, he did return to Harford sooner than anticipated. As improvement in public education came to hold an increasingly high priority in the reform agenda, teachers in the northeastern states organized and used the potential political clout they obtained to pressure legislators to enact certain laws calculated to improve the common schools. In Pennsylvania, teachers' associations sprang up in urban areas then gradually spread to rural counties where organization, out of necessity, tended to be countywide. Rather quickly these groups banded together at Harrisburg to exert pressure on the legislators.

One demand was to establish a county superintendent of schools. The second demand was for means to train teachers, which at first meant a state-supported normal school, something that the state superintendent of common schools had asked the legislature to accomplish in his annual reports beginning in the 1840s. This never became a reality, however.

Therefore, the teachers decided on the teachers' institute, which might take the form of a week in which teachers throughout a county gathered for a concentrated training session. Someone already trained would, through lectures and demonstrations, show how to teach basic subjects. An alternative was a six-week term in a county normal school. The latter provided time for more subjects to be covered and more practice. Furthermore, it was not necessary to be licensed to teach in order to attend the normal institutes as was true for the one-week teachers' institutes. In 1853 the Pennsylvania legislature combined the two basic proposals by permitting the election of a county superintendent by the combined boards of directors of the townships in each county. This official was authorized to hold a teachers' institute at the time or place he designated.[15]

The Susquehanna County teachers formed their association on December 11, 1853. They also voted for a teachers' institute. In the summer of 1854, the directors chose Willard Richardson, head of the normal department at Harford University, to be the county superintendent of Susquehanna County. His first action was to schedule an institute to be held in Harford shortly before the opening of the winter term.[16] Towne quickly enrolled in the institute. Over one hundred teachers in the county did likewise.

Richardson, as Towne knew from the classes he had taken in the summer, held ideas later to be termed progressive, about learning by doing. Rather than bring in specialists to speak to the participants as they sat passively, Richardson divided the teachers into groups for discussions and demonstrations of topics he outlined at the opening of each session. Each participant served on one such group and they all took turns acting as leader. They pretended one was the teacher and the other pupils and they each critiqued the others' presentations to find new ways to fit what were believed to be normal learning patterns. Towne liked to try new ideas in his own teaching so he participated with enthusiasm in these activities. He felt that he was not likely to engage the students with rote memorization of answers to questions posed by standard texts.[17]

Each evening the professor of vocal music led the singing of rounds and medleys suited to varied patterns and demonstrated ways to present them in singing schools so popular in the area. This also helped Towne, for he offered singing schools for any district school interested in opening its doors to him, which provided a small supplement to his income.[18]

The only objection Towne had to the teaching profession was that it did not provide an adequate income for a man; it had to be supplemented by some other occupation. Farming was the obvious answer, but Towne had more aspirations than to settle for life as a farmer.

Chapter Four

Marriage and Divorce

Myron Towne had a strong incentive for improving his income. He had begun to court a young lady by the name of Sarah M. Wright. Prior to 1855 he had displayed no serious interest in anyone. Although Towne first encountered Sarah when he taught the 1852–1853 term for the Forest Lake School, she made little impression on him. She had already finished the common school, but her younger sister and two nephews were among Towne's students. Therefore, he no doubt knew who she was, or at least he knew his pupils had an older sister or aunt.

One factor turning Towne's thoughts toward marriage was the decision of Phinis to marry John Deuel in 1853. Deuel came from a large family in Middletown. Unfortunately, he did not appear to be a good choice in the eyes of Phinis' family. When someone tried to defend him by saying he was a "good boy," John Towne snorted "Good for nothing!" Myron was in full agreement with his father. No one was likely to appear good enough for Phinis in the eyes of her father and brother. History appeared to support their case against Deuel. After the couple were married by the Methodist preacher in a ceremony held in the Towne home,[1] she and Deuel went to his parents' house to live along with younger brothers and sisters still at home. In little more than ten months a son arrived, who was given the name Wellington Bonaparte. Myron gasped and asked his sister what she meant by such an incongruous name. She dodged the issue by saying she would call the baby, "Welly." Myron secretly regarded this as evidence that the marriage indeed represented a "Waterloo" for Phinis Deuel. The child lived less than a year, but on June 27, 1856, a daughter was born. This time Phinis named the child, and she called the girl Lydia Rachel.[2]

With Phinis no longer at home, Myron felt lonely; he missed his trusted companion so he began to think of starting his own family. Previous to his sister's marriage, Myron Towne had purchased a farm, and now he moved to the house located on the land. He had selected his land carefully with several thoughts in mind. It lay just south of his parents' farm, which meant he knew the possibilities it offered for some tillage and for cattle. It was only a short walk from his place to his old home, the church, and the school. More to the point, the land he purchased lay on the Middle Branch of the Wyalusing; indeed the address, if one could call it that, was Creek Road, since the road paralleled the creek. Farther up on the Wyalusing, Towne's grandfather and later his uncle had long operated the Warner Mill. Azor now opened the mill only haphazardly, mainly when someone insisted upon getting some timber sawed. Therefore, Towne reasoned, there was room for another sawmill that operated steadily, and the fact that his land lay farther downstream meant the current would be swifter and would provide more power. Thus Towne's plan was to build and operate a sawmill.[3]

In 1855 Towne repaid the first debt he had assumed to buy his farm and immediately borrowed again to build his mill. He also planned to add to his small house. He felt that then he would be in a position to provide for a wife. Myron Towne reflected a tendency already noticeable by the 1850s. Young people seemed unwilling to start at the bottom of the middle class and work their way upward as Jehiel Warner's or John Towne's generations had done. Evidences of amazing progress in industry and transportation were visible even in rural areas. Myron Towne and others of his period were in a hurry to enjoy the fruits.

Meanwhile, Towne farmed, taught school, and held singing schools to accumulate funds toward his projected enterprise. It was in a singing school he offered at Forest Lake during the winter of 1855 that he met and fell in love with Sarah Wright. She attended the singing school with her younger sister, Miriam. Sarah was two months shy of nineteen, with fair skin, blue eyes, and light brown hair that she drew smoothly back from a center part into a heavy chignon at the back.

From all indications Sarah Wright made a deep impression. Towne saw her as beautiful, sweet, generous, firm, and courageous. Perhaps a smitten man sees what he desires, and clearly Towne desired Sarah for his wife. Yet having read too many of the romantic novels of Sir Walter Scott, Towne feared that pitfalls lay ahead. Reflecting perhaps more of his father than he realized, Towne felt he must have more income or at least potential funds to marry the delectable Sarah. He also knew that her father, Chauncey Wright, might be a stumbling block.

Wright was a New Englander; he came from Connecticut and he was of good Congregational faith. Like John Towne, Wright had abandoned the religion of his fathers after coming to the wilderness of northeastern Susquehanna County in 1815: he became a Baptist. Like John Towne, Wright was pious and a strong supporter of his church, and Wright also practiced a trade along with farming. He was a fuller, who operated a fulling mill in Choconut Township for a time before moving to Forest Lake where he bought land near the lake and built a large house. It was not as pretentious as the Warner place farther to the west, but it showed that Wright had prospered. He opened a grist mill on his land near Forest Lake, and he developed a reputation as a sharp man who drove a hard bargain.

Whether Towne discovered more obstacles involving Sarah's father cannot be determined today, but of Wright's five daughters, two never married,[4] and he clearly was reluctant to consent to Sarah's marriage. Subsequent events show that he tried to break up the relationship soon after consenting. He attempted to do this by playing on a fundamental difference in temperament between husband and wife. Myron had developed into a studious, rather solemn man with little time for or inclination toward frivolity. His idea of recreation was reading and he continued to be active in the church where he taught a Sunday School class for youngsters, led the singing in worship, and assisted in the church library.

Sarah preferred the company of young people her own age rather than the older people or school children who were her husband's friends. She desired some merry-making, as Myron finally learned. As for further education, Sarah seemed indifferent. She wrote a graceful hand, but she became bored by discussion of books and seemed to think that when she completed the eighth reader, she had read enough. However, as their romance developed neither seemed to notice differences in interests or background. They had fallen in love according to the romantic concept then prevailing in middle class circles. Both were eager for marriage, but her father's initial reaction was to forbid any such notions.

Towne felt he must make money quickly to overcome what he perceived to be Wright's objection. While Towne prepared for the sawmill, he also applied for a postmastership. In1843 when Amasa Chase closed the post office he had operated for nine years, Forest Lake Centre citizens had to get their mail from one of the other post offices in the township, the closest of which was four and a half miles away. Towne proposed to operate an office in his home on Creek Road, and he supported his idea with a small diagram drawn to scale which showed the proximity of the Forest Lake Centre Methodist Episcopal Church and the Forest Lake Centre

School. With arrows and mileage he supported the claim of inconvenience to citizens of this part of the township who had to travel too far to get their mail. His last recommendation was that the new office be called the Forest Lake Centre Post Office.[5]

The choice of name indicated that Towne kept abreast of current developments in the postal service. By midcentury stations' names generally represented their location, not the person who kept the office. Although postmasterships in major towns or cities were awarded as favors to those who belonged to the political party victorious in the last election, Forest Lake Centre was not important enough to constitute a political plum. Therefore, the fact that Towne was a free soil Republican did not deter the Postmaster General, James Campbell of the Democratic Pierce administration, from making the appointment. Expansion of the system with the growth of population was a nonpartisan question.

On May 9, 1856, Campbell named Myron S. Towne postmaster of the newly created office, although at first the department referred to it as a revival of the Chase office. Towne had to post bond before the appointment could become official, but that was no problem. On July 21, 1856, his commission arrived conferring upon him "all the powers, privileges, and emoluments" pertaining to the office "during the pleasure of the Postmaster General" whose signature adorned the document.[6]

Whether it was the post office, John Towne's standing in the township, or Sarah's persuasiveness is not known, but Wright consented to the marriage, and the young couple set the date for the marriage as September 3 at the Wright home. All of her numerous family members were in attendance, while Myron had only John and Rachel Towne and Phinis Deuel to witness for him. However, the Towne family, particularly John, prevailed in one detail; the Methodist minister of the Vestal Circuit performed the ceremony.[7]

Following a wedding feast, the bride and groom departed for their home. Everything was ready for them to begin housekeeping. Several days prior to the wedding Miriam and the two older Wright brothers brought a load of furniture, linens, Sarah's clothing, and other articles to the house. Not to let Chauncey Wright outdo them, John Towne and Rachel selected some items to add to what Myron had taken with him when he first left home.

On the following day, John and Rachel Towne came to the newlyweds' house and took them in the buggy to Montrose so that they could have pictures made. A daguerreotypist named W. B. Deans had established a studio over the Bentley and Read Store. There the two couples repaired for individual portraits, each to be framed in ornamental boxes lined with velvet. In their wedding finery or Sunday best, in the case of the groom's parents, the sitters represented those who had achieved a stable place on the status ladder. Although the daguerreotype had certain definite limitations and was soon to be superseded, it did permit a skilled operator to bring out many nuances that gave indications of character.[8]

Undoubtedly, while in Montrose, the two generations of the Towne family toured the newly completed Susquehanna County Courthouse. Built in the prevailing Greek Revival style with Ionic columns supporting the portico and a domed cupola, it was reached by a long flight of graceful steps from a cloister separated from the street by arches. The cupola had a clock, the gift of the citizens of Montrose. For its dedication some self-styled poet wrote a rhyme, which was printed in the Montrose paper. Towne read it and laughed, but the words stayed in his memory. Hence, he could recite it for his wife's and mother's amusement:

> Where to the North and the South, to the East and West,
> It points with its hands to the minutes as they fly;
> While, with slow-measured stroke, it wakes a sad unrest,
> To hear its midnight toll on the winds as they sigh.[9]

Meanwhile, whether it could be viewed as a portent of things to come, evidence that times were changing, or simply proof that the Towne family did in truth have a streak of "otherwise-mindedness" in the congenital make-up of its members, who can say? But Phinis brought her baby daughter to her parents' home and asked permission to move back into her old room which had been left much as it was when she vacated it. The parents somehow had anticipated a crisis to be brewing, so they assured Phinis she was more than welcome. They both adored little Lydia and had worried greatly that their only daughter and granddaughter were being deprived of the chance for a good life in the Deuel household.

Phinis never explained fully what had happened; she only said that John had left to go elsewhere to look for work and that she refused to stay longer with his family. She displayed no grief or expectation of his return. From that day to the end of her life she had no further contact with him. Many years later after moving to Illinois, she styled herself "Widow" on the church records, but that was simply the easiest way to deal with the anomaly of being a mother and grandmother without a husband. The evidence indicates that she had no knowledge of his demise or of his whereabouts.[10]

Myron did not teach in the winter following his marriage; he was too occupied with preparations for the sawmill, which he hoped to open in the spring or early summer. Construction began in the spring of 1857. The next winter he taught at the Birchardville School and in 1858–1859 he taught at the Stone School. He had negotiated another loan to put the sawmill in operation, and he felt he must earn every cent possible to pay the debts. So he farmed, ran the sawmill, taught school, and operated the post office. This meant he was away from home many hours of the day, leaving Sarah alone. His family tried to look after her; John Towne would go to her door to see if she needed anything, such as wood or water, before he brought his cattle in from the pasture in the evening. Sarah always thanked him but assured him that Myron had left her well supplied. Phinis came frequently, often urging her sister-in-law to come to the house, where Rachel would make the afternoon go fast with quilting, fancy work, and pleasant conversation. Sarah went occasionally but did not seem to be very enthusiastic about such efforts to ease her loneliness.

Instead, Sarah would tell Myron when he came home at night that her father or one of her brothers would come for her the next day and she would go "home" for a few days, likely a week. Myron agreed and even felt relieved for he worried about her evident loneliness and boredom. Regularly, he promised her they would take life easier as soon as he made enough money. He even offered her what he dreamed of, travel to strange places, places of note, say Harrisburg or into New York, but he could not tell if that really interested her. She obviously did want to go up to Forest Lake so he encouraged such expeditions. As time went by, the trips became more frequent and people in the neighborhood began to whisper comments behind his back, which some person always managed to let him know about to his annoyance and vague anxiety.[11]

By the spring of 1859, Sarah's visits to Forest Lake became more frequent and prolonged. What precisely triggered Towne to become convinced that she was tired of the marriage and wished to be the wife of another man is not clear. One plausible explanation is that he may have thought to surprise her by going to the Wright home to take her back with the promise of some special celebration they could enjoy now that the school term had ended, the crops were planted, and the sawmill was operating at capacity. If so, like many other well-meant surprises over the years, he may have been the one astounded.

Far from assisting her mother, as Sarah had frequently excused her absences, Towne found she had been enjoying parties or dances, termed by the Baptists as "play-party games," as though she was an unmarried woman. Towne's world must have crashed about his ears. Sarah did accompany him home, but apparently they each made charges and countercharges, which both could not or would not forgive. In the succeeding days neither was able to see the other's distress as each nourished his or her own pain. Both equated wounded pride with dead love. In blind despair Myron uttered the fatal words, "If we cannot feel as we once did toward each other the sooner we separate the better."[12]

A few days later he arrived home with the three mill hands who had been taking their noon meal at the mill owner's table, only to find no meal ready and no sign of his wife. A glance at their bedroom showed that she had taken all of her clothing and other items she had brought with her when they were married. Later, his father told him that he had seen Chauncey Wright with Sarah in Wright's buggy on the road that led past the blacksmith shop to Forest Lake. A wagon followed, loaded with things John guessed to be furniture and other items belonging to Sarah.[13]

Early in July a letter arrived in Sarah's neat handwriting. It had been posted in New Milford, where one of her older sisters lived. She wrote:

> *Dear Myron,*
>
> *I would gladly spare myself the pain of writing this letter, and you the pain of receiving it, if I could do it and be true to myself. I have thought calmly and candidly of our living together and I feel convinced that we can never again be happy together. My heart aches while I write for I feel crushed and the future looks bleak and dreary, but I know we shall live happier apart and I think you feel the same. . . .*
>
> *God knows my heart, I have tried to faithfully perform every duty I owed you and I have not been untrue.*

I feel no hardness towards you and while I live, you shall have a friend, but more than that, I can never be to you. I thank you for all your kindness to me. I shall never forget it. You do not know how it pained me to write this, but I felt that I ought not to hesitate longer—this is my decision.

May you be happy—Farewell.

Sarah Towne[14]

Towne carefully filed the letter in his secretary where he kept important legal papers. He would have use for it later. His immediate task was to engage a housekeeper, and he knew exactly whom he wanted. He promptly walked to his father's home and found his sister fortunately alone in the kitchen. He offered her the position as a business proposition, telling her he would pay the going wage plus a room for herself and Lydia and all their meals as part of the contract. She was to operate the house as if it were her own. Whatever she did, he knew, would suit him perfectly. The only extra obligation would be the noon meal for the mill hands as long as that was part of their pay. Phinis could hardly believe her ears, for this solved a problem for her as well as her brother. Their parents had made Phinis and Lydia more than welcome; they were unmistakably happy to have their daughter and granddaughter with them. However, Phinis was distressed, feeling that she had not only returned home for her father to support after a failed marriage, but had added another person to the burden. John and Rachel Towne had reared their children; it was not right to expect them to raise another generation. Nonetheless, Phinis had one qualm, so she inquired of Myron how long she could expect this arrangement to last. His answer reassured her; he made it clear it was for as long as she desired for Sarah had left him.[15] That was all he ever told anyone in the family or later in a court of law.

Thereafter, life moved on in a pleasant, uneventful fashion. Phinis kept the house spotless, she had well-prepared meals ready on time, and Lydia was a joy. Myron Towne became a kind of surrogate father along with his role as the indulgent uncle. In fact, he grew so comfortable in his new situation, that he seemed content to let things continue without interruption. He had no contact with Sarah from the time he received her farewell letter. On two occasions, when he needed her signature on a deed to land he was selling, he mailed the forms to her, and she signed and returned them. Since John Towne was the justice of the peace, he notarized them without the formality of her "appearing before me" as the line above the justice's signature mandated.[16]

In the summer of 1861 Myron Towne received what seemed to be a roundabout message from Chauncey Wright. A neighbor, Warren T. White, came into the mill one day; after transacting his business he hung around making small talk, as though summoning courage to say what he had come to tell Towne. Finally, he prefaced it by saying that he had seen Wright the day before and that Wright had said he knew "in all reason" that his daughter would "never go back to live...." Knowing full well that the subject was one Towne had never permitted anyone to discuss in his presence, White gulped and left his last words unsaid, but Towne filed the report in his mind. That night he told Phinis, and they agreed it was perhaps time to take action.

In July, Towne went to Montrose to the office of Albert Chamberlain, a lawyer. Towne directed the attorney to draft a petition to the Court of Common Pleas requesting a decree "divorcing Myron S. Towne from the bonds of matrimony as if he had never been married." He gave the cause for such action as "desertion." Sarah M. Towne had absented herself from the "habitation" of the petitioner without any "reasonable cause" and such desertion had persisted for "the term of two years and upward."

Not long thereafter, Towne was notified to appear on July 24 in the court presided over by Charles F. Reed, one of the associate judges. There he swore that the facts stated in the libel were true to the best of his "knowledge and belief." On the following day the presiding judge, Ulysses Mercur, issued a summons to Sarah M. Towne to appear on the third Monday of August to answer the charges and show why "Myron S. Towne should not be divorced from the bonds of matrimony." On the back of the summons she wrote, "I hereby accept service of the written writ. Sarah M. Wright Towne."[17] She made no effort to contest the case.

The wheels of the law ground onward. Chamberlain filed depositions on October 21 from John S. Towne, Phinis N. Deuel, Warren T. White, Orange Mott, Jr., Jeremiah Baldwin, and R. L. Gordon. John Towne and his daughter testified to the basic facts. Both stressed their observation from frequent visits that Myron S. Towne treated his wife "well," in John Towne's words, and "kindly," as Phinis expressed it. She added, "I never heard her complain of him or find a word of fault." Nor had Myron Towne uttered any complaint against his wife. Both identified "exhibit A," the letter, as written in Sarah's handwriting, with which they were quite familiar.

Baldwin, Mott, and Gordon agreed with the testimony of the other witnesses. They went to the house of Myron Towne on a regular schedule to pick up or deposit mail. They testified that Sarah Towne had never been there since departing in June 1859. White corroborated their testimony and added that Chauncey Wright had said his daughter "would never go back and live with him."[18]

A copy of the evidence was dispatched by the court to the defendant. As before, Sarah wrote on the receipt accompanying the package, "RE'd. copy Oct. 22nd 1861. Sarah M. Wright Towne." On November 18, 1861, the court in the case of *Myron S. Towne v. Sarah M. Towne* decreed a divorce.[19] In the eyes of the law it was as if the marriage had never occurred. Perhaps in time, the principals themselves came to believe that. Sarah M. Wright dropped "Towne" from her name and listed herself as "unmarried." She never remarried, but she was in no way a recluse; she lived an active life until her death on March 9, 1892.[20]

Towne did not hide the fact of his divorce; both of his subsequent spouses knew about it. One did not seem to care and the third wife only threw it up to him occasionally, when she wanted to be spiteful. His older son not only knew of it, but also knew the name of the woman involved.[21] One day, Towne commented to his daughter-in-law, "If Sally had behaved herself, we would have been married fifty years today." It was September 3, 1906, so the fact that it was his wedding date fifty years before had apparently been on his mind.[22] He said no more, and Mary Towne was so astonished she asked no questions until she and her husband returned to their home in Unionville.

Myron's remark, like many others in his later years, was subject to confused interpretations. Mary concentrated on the implication of immoral conduct as she viewed it. She had adopted the position that all married persons must emulate Caesar's wife. Such an interpretation ignores the evidence. Whatever the cause of their original quarrel, Myron never charged Sarah with unfaithfulness. He let the letter she wrote denying any possible wrongdoing stand with no hint of rebuttal. Furthermore, the remark was inaccurate because Sarah Wright had been dead for fourteen years, a fact he used in his application for a pension.[23] Lastly, except for this oblique reference, there seems no evidence that he had called his first wife, "Sally." He frequently criticized the habit of using nicknames, and Sarah had signed her full name in her letter as well as on the legal transactions.

A more significant question is why the marriages of both Myron and Phinis Towne failed. One fact is clear: neither behaved as the mores of midnineteenth century dictated. According to the code, a wife who objected to her husband's decision that they were to live with his family was supposed to endure her discomfort. She did not take her child, go to her parents, and ask them to shelter her until she could start a new life; but Phinis did just that. Later, she moved from her brother's paid housekeeper to postmaster and then small loan operator.

A man who fancied himself wronged, or at least his pride injured by his wife's conduct, or who more likely concluded that he and his wife had irreconcilable temperaments, was not supposed to suggest separation and then begin divorce proceedings in a manner that hinted of collusion. In both Phinis' and Myron's cases, however, a woman and a man of the Towne family transcended some of society's behavioral standards.

Nor did Sarah Wright fully accept her proper role. She left her husband after a quarrel, went to her parents, made no objection to divorce, and resumed using her family name. True, unlike Phinis, Sarah remained at home with her family and engaged in "suitable" women's work. She taught a Sunday school class, visited the sick, and took offerings to the needy.[24] However, by adding all of these elements together one can conclude that Victorian family life did not always accord with the supposed norms, even in a remote corner of rural Pennsylvania.

Chapter Five

Enlistment in the Union Army

A FATEFUL SERIES OF EVENTS rent the Democratic Party into quarrelling factions on the eve of the presidential election of 1860. Two candidates ran as Democrats and a third, representing fence-sitters, chose a different name. The chances of the Republican Party looked bright. Republican leaders wrote a platform with appeal to a variety of northern interests and chose a compromise candidate rather than one of the more controversial hopefuls. Along with this expedient course, Republicans held firmly to their original stand against the extension of slavery. A majority of voters in the more populous northern states gave the Republican candidate their vote, which ensured an electoral majority. Abraham Lincoln, the Republican candidate, was elected President.

As a result, South Carolina's legislature promptly voted secession and by inaugural day six other slave states joined South Carolina to form what they styled the Confederate States of America. Many northerners, among them John and Myron Towne, saw this as a denial of both the fundamental law of the land and the democratic principle of majority rule. By combining the popular vote of Lincoln and Stephen A. Douglas one could see that 69.3 percent of the voters cast their ballots for candidates who opposed the expansion of slavery into the territories, although by different means.[1]

Once he assumed the presidency, Lincoln declared he would enforce federal law and retain Union property in the seceding states. Unfortunately, most of the latter had been surrendered by former President Buchanan. Only Fort Sumter in Charleston harbor remained, and South Carolina militia, now termed Confederate troops, held Sumter's garrison under siege. When Lincoln announced his plan to send a relief mission, the besiegers opened fire and forced the garrison to surrender. This was an overt act of treason as defined by the Constitution. Lincoln responded by calling 75,000 volunteers to augment the regulars in suppressing the rebellion.

Response to Lincoln's call was enthusiastic. A wave of patriotism aroused by firing on the flag was further fanned by the decision of four additional slave states to join the Confederacy on the pretext that the federal government had no right to coerce a state. Students of the Constitution like Myron Towne pointed to the provision authorizing presidential use of troops to enforce the law where courts and civil authorities were unable to do so in the face of widespread resistance. Nonetheless, from the President to the average citizen, there was a serious misevaluation. The confident expectation that the rebellion could be crushed in three months, the time for which the special volunteers enlisted, was harshly disabused by mid-summer. Most legislatures in the loyal states began to empower recruiters to raise state regiments, composed of volunteers, for three years.

As soon as Lincoln issued his call, Myron Towne felt a strong urge to respond, but that sense of caution which had held him back from precipitate action more than once before operated again. Whether this was a negative response to his father's pushing or evidence that upbringing had taught him to be careful is immaterial. He needed to make certain decisions before he enlisted. He was a man past thirty who owned a business and had certain family obligations, unlike the youths in their late teens or early twenties who were a large part of the first group of volunteers.

Myron's finances remained somewhat uncertain. In January of 1861 he had sold thirteen and seven-tenths acres to Warren T. White, who needed the land in order to run a connection between Creek Road and Warner Road. Towne shrewdly charged $1,300 for the right-of-way, thereby settling some of the debts incurred in building the sawmill.[2] He debated what to do with the mill and finally decided to lease it with an option to purchase later. Levi Lincoln was the lessee.[3] To allow himself the freedom to leave in the coming year if he so decided, Towne did not contract to teach another term after he completed that of 1860–1861.

Consideration of military service was one of the factors which led Towne to resolve the status of his marriage. More difficult to resolve was his concern for his sister's future. He understood how much being his professional housekeeper meant to Phinis. It gave her a sense of independence and self-worth. Not only could she provide for herself and her daughter, but she held a position in the community. She was Mrs. Phinis N. Deuel, not just the daughter of Mr. and Mrs. John S. Towne. Myron refused to send Phinis back to their parents after promising her that she would be his housekeeper as long as she desired the position. He had an idea that was taking shape in his keen mind, but he needed time to make sure it was feasible.

Fortunately, a pleasant respite came in the late summer of 1861, when the Vestal Circuit elected to hold a camp meeting at Vestal in September. Methodists, contrary to commonly accepted notions, neither originated camp meetings nor gave them blanket endorsement. They were born on the frontier, where they served a definite social as well as religious purpose, but they often led to what eastern Methodists, where the leadership of the connectional system held sway, felt to be unseemly conduct. Excesses too often plagued the camp meetings in the Trans-Appalachian region.

However, leaders of the strongly Unionist Methodist Episcopal Church in this rather remote corner of northeastern Pennsylvania and southeastern New York considered the situation of the nation so dangerous in the late summer of 1861, that only a revival of godliness could strengthen the President and all those who were striving to keep the Union intact. The Wyoming Conference, of which the Vestal Circuit was then a part, approved the project with the stipulation that there must be careful planning and policing of the campgrounds to prevent any suggestion of irregular conduct.[4]

With all of these assessments John Towne heartily agreed and his son concurred. The elder Towne urged his flock to join the cavalcade to Vestal, and almost all of them did.[5] Much preparation went into attendance at a protracted meeting. Phinis, her mother, and her daughter cooked and baked. They washed and packed clothing, towels, and other necessities for approximately a week's stay. The Towne men strung boards to make cots with straw-filled mattresses. Then, the family loaded a big wagon and made ready for predawn departure on the morning before the religious gathering would begin. After traveling all day over rutted roads, they arrived just before sunset.

The Vestal congregation had laid out a miniature "city" with "streets" separating the spaces designated for each wagon where the occupants could pitch their tents and build their campfires. The Vestal hosts had thoughtfully provided "little houses" in a concealed section, with those for each sex carefully separated. Choconut Creek, which flowed beside the campground, provided water for cooking, drinking, and washing of hands, face, and dishes. A great bell mounted near the open space designed for preaching services summoned campers to the morning, afternoon, and evening services.

One of the characteristics of the camp meetings, joyous singing, was associated with Methodism.[6] However, when adapted to the East the hymns were the standard Wesleyan hymns rather than the white spirituals of Trans-Appalachia. As the son of the well-known John Towne of Towne's Church, Myron Towne was asked to lead the singing at several services. In fact, he was kept busy, for it quickly could be seen by those not familiar with the station in Forest Lake, Pennsylvania, that he was unusually skillful. He managed to make the woods surrounding the clearing echo with such favorites as "There is a Fountain Filled With Blood" and "Jesus, Lover of My Soul."[7]

Soon it was time to go home. While his family took care of most of the details, John Towne conferred with the circuit pastor and the presiding elder. He proposed a revival at his church to be preached by Richard Van Valkenburg, one of the best preachers at the Vestal meeting. With everyone's consent, a date in October was chosen. Naturally Myron, as the church's song leader, spent considerable time selecting hymns and rehearsing his congregation prior to the opening of the nightly services for the gathering. During the revival Van Valkenburg must have been a mighty exhorter; he won forty-five converts to bring the membership of the Forest Lake Centre Methodist Episcopal Church to its all-time high.[8]

These church gatherings occupied so much of Myron Towne's time that he put his future out of his mind, except for trips to Montrose in connection with the divorce proceedings. Once the decree was final Myron felt at liberty to serve in the Union Army, He broached his ideas to Phinis. He suggested that he would resign his commission as postmaster and she would simultaneously apply for the position. Since he would rent his house with his farm, she would need to move back to her old home, but she would have an important position in the community. With their father's consent, they would enclose the back porch of the house except for a half door on the side facing the road. On post mornings she could have the mail ready for the rider to pick up and he could throw her bag into her porch-office as he galloped past. It might even shorten the distance for the post-rider since his next stop was Friendsville and Warner Road was perhaps a bit shorter distance than Creek Road. The distance was almost precisely the same for patrons because Myron's house was only a half mile from his father's.[9]

Phinis was delighted and her parents were equally enthusiastic about having their daughter and granddaughter back with them. When Rachel announced that it would be lonesome with Myron gone to war, which she obviously regarded as his duty, her husband uttered a kind of muted agreement. To conceal any possible lapse into emotion he quickly began to measure the back porch and estimate the amount of lumber needed to enclose it to make a post office. Rachel with equal efficiency started planning the rearrangement of the two large upstairs rooms, so that Myron could bring home his things from his house and put them in his old room.

With everything arranged to his satisfaction, Myron Towne dispatched his resignation as postmaster along with Phinis' application to take over the office. On January 7, 1862, Postmaster General Montgomery Blair commissioned Phinis N. Deuel as the postmaster of Forest Lake Centre.[10] However, Towne's enlistment was delayed by events in Washington. As widespread corruption in the War Department came to light, Lincoln removed the Secretary of War, and replaced him with Edwin M. Stanton. Then the President permitted Stanton to halt recruitment and dismantle federal recruiting machinery. Presumably, this decision rested on the assumption that the projected Peninsular Campaign would bring quick victory. Once more, hopes were dashed.

In the summer of 1862 Lincoln was forced to issue another call for volunteers, this time for 300,000 to be prorated among the loyal states. Governor Andrew Curtin of Pennsylvania responded with a tour of large population centers where, in patriotic speeches, he urged his fellow citizens to fill the state's quota quickly. Local leaders took it upon themselves to recruit with the incentive that these leaders would become captain of a company if they filled it. John C. Morris of Middletown began such a campaign in Susquehanna County, starting with his own and neighboring Forest Lake townships.[11] This company would join with other companies from Susquehanna and neighboring counties of Luzerne, Lycoming, and Wyoming to form a regiment from the mountains of northern Pennsylvania.

When Towne learned that Morris would be at Friendsville in mid-August, he announced to the family that he would go there and enlist. Two of Azor Warner's sons, Asa and Stanley, asked to accompany their older cousin and former teacher. On August 16, the three went to Friendsville and completed the necessary formalities. It was really quite simple, Towne discovered; he filled out a form which asked for obvious things. He listed has age as 32, his occupation as "teacher," and his marital status as "unmarried."[12] That he did not use either farmer or mill owner-operator to describe his occupation suggests that he had in mind to do more than carry a rifle. Once a man signed his form he was an enlistee, but not yet in the army. Those signing up at Friendsville were ordered to return to the same place on August 31. From Friendsville they would go to Harrisburg to be mustered.

Towne drafted a petition after he returned home. Then he went to Montrose to confer with Fred P. Hollister, the county sheriff with whom Towne had worked if need arose while he served as constable of Forest Lake. He showed Hollister the petition and found the sheriff most willing to cooperate. In fact, he offered to sponsor it and while Towne was in the office to copy the petition. Hollister then signed the petition and Towne's copy. From Hollister's office, Towne visited various other officials in the courthouse or in nearby offices. Before going back to Forest Lake Centre, he secured signatures from the county clerk, a county commissioner, the judge in the preliminary hearing on the divorce case, the county bridge inspector, the lawyer who handled the divorce petition, and the trustees of the Rose estate from whom he had purchased his land. The substance of the endorsement was that the "undersigned" believed Myron S. Towne to be a "man of strict integrity and sobriety" and that his "educational and business qualification eminently" fitted him for "any official station in the company of Captain John C. Morris," and they duly recommended him for such a position.

In the next few days Towne traveled to certain spots in the township where he secured signatures from two physicians, an innkeeper, and two neighbors, one of whom was also a former county commissioner. Towne had an impressive list of endorsements.[13] He felt satisfied that he had done all that was possible, so he carefully put the petition with the few other belongings he was permitted to take with him. Then, his father took him and the two Warner boys to Friendsville.

Following more formalities, including the election of officers, the men headed for Montrose where they were told to assemble at the courthouse on the morning of September 3. After roll call they were ordered to march to the railroad station eight miles away at Montrose Junction, where they would board a train for Harrisburg. The raw recruits stumbled awkwardly into what they fancied was proper formation and began the trip. A large crowd of well-wishers had assembled and many walked along beside them, while others lined the streets calling greetings and good wishes. However, there were a few dissenters. One whom Towne dubbed a "copperhead," yelled, "What a pity these fine boys are going down South to be killed for the niggers; they ain't worth it." Rumors of Lincoln's plan to issue a statement about freeing the slaves were afloat, and this man was venting his spleen about such a prospect.

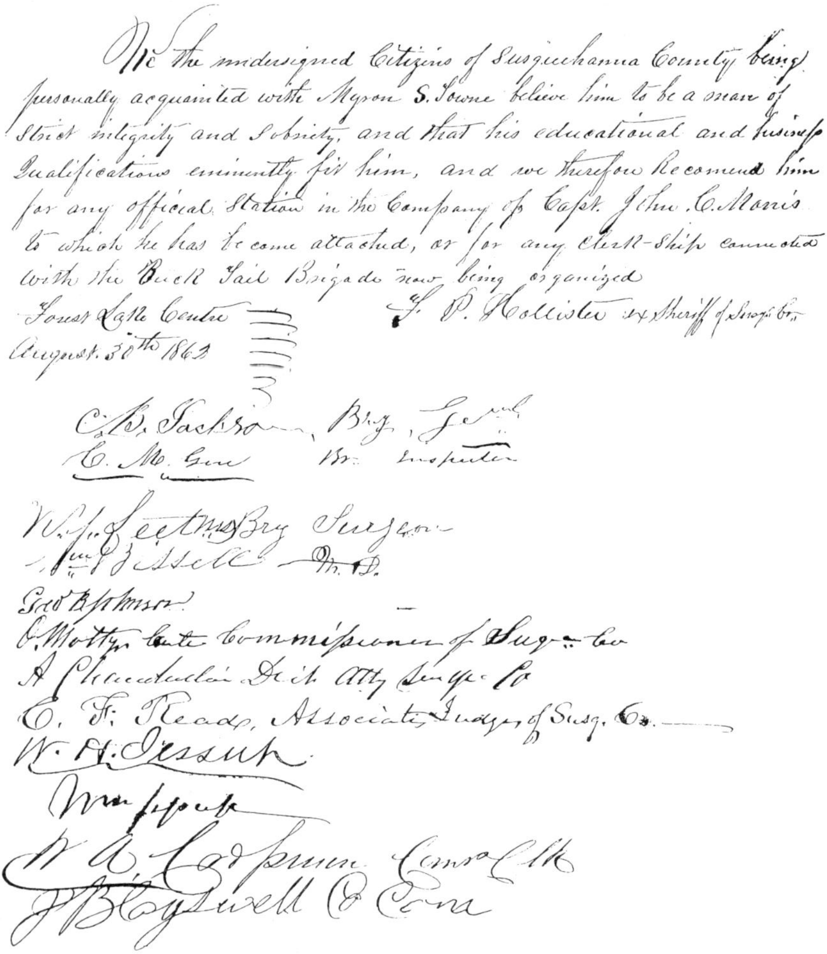

We the undersigned Citizens of Susquehanna County being personally acquainted with Myron S. Towne believe him to be a man of strict integrity and Sobriety, and that his educational and business Qualifications eminently fit him, and we therefore Recommend him for any official Station in the Company of Capt. John C. Morris to which he has become attached, or for any Clerk-Ship connected with the Buck Tail Brigade now being organized

Forest Lake Centre
August 30th 1862

F. P. Hollister ex Sheriff of Susq. Co.

C. L. Jackson, Brig. Genl.
C. M. Gere Br. Inspector

W. J. Leet [illegible] Brig Surgeon
Wm Bissell M.D.

Geo B. Johnson
O. Mott late Commissioner of Susq. Co
A Chamberlain Dist. Atty Susq. Co
C. F. Read, Associate Judge of Susq. Co.
W. H. Jessup
Wm [illegible]
W. A. Crossmon Comrs Clk
J. B[illegible] Co Comr

The recommendation drafted by Towne and signed by county officials

Towne was angry, but he was more concerned about the possible effect on the younger men, several of whom were his former students. They tended to look to him for interpretation of such occurrences, so he denounced the onlooker for having no concern that the Union was being destroyed; this seemed to satisfy the younger men.[14]

On September 6, the company was formally mustered into service in Harrisburg and issued Enfield rifles. It began training there while it awaited the arrival of other companies for the still unnumbered regiment. After two months the order came to entrain again, this time for Washington, D.C.[15] Towne could not quite restrain his excitement; he had long dreamed of travel and had vaguely thought of Harrisburg as a possible future destination, but he hardly dared to imagine going to the nation's capital.

Another train ride was in itself a novelty. For most of the men from the Endless Mountains the trip into Harrisburg was their first experience with rail travel; now they would travel a bigger rail, the Baltimore and Ohio, which operated the only line into Washington, D.C. A little engine with a smokestack almost bigger than the boiler pulled a string of cars loaded with men in new navyblue uniforms. Smoke and cinders belched from the train as it chugged slowly, stopping every few miles to permit sergeants to board and check for possible unauthorized persons. Guards stood at intervals along the tracks, for rebel sympathizers in Maryland might try to destroy the railroad connecting Washington to the loyal states. Lincoln had in the first months of the war taken unprecedented measures to keep Maryland in the Union. Some of these measures were still in place, as Towne could see.[16] He concluded that Washington had the appearance of a city under siege. At last the troop train edged into the Washington station. Peremptory orders told the men to fasten their full complement of gear on their backs and debark quickly to march to a camp outside the city.

The men obeyed, but their eyes moved this way and that to see as much as possible, and Towne admitted to the same desire. However, one of the first sights was less than reassuring. A veritable army of wounded filled the depot and spilled over into benches along the platform and sidewalk. Bandaged heads, patches over eye sockets, empty sleeves pinned across jackets, and trouser legs pinned to upper garments gave evidence of what bullets did to human flesh and bones. The newcomers to the capital soon learned that most of the Union wounded were brought to Washington to hospitals hastily erected on the vast open spaces remaining in the intricately planned capital. Long, low, whitewashed buildings housed the wounded and sick from the armies of the East.[17]

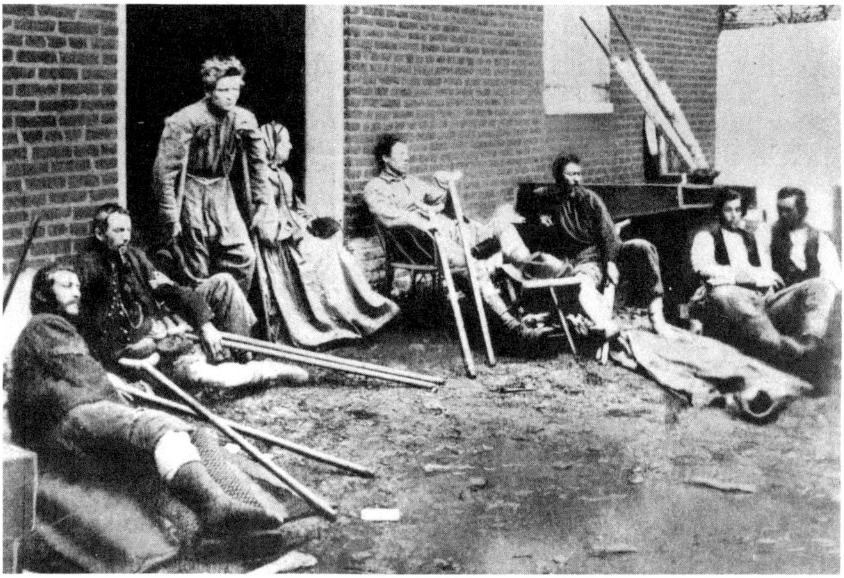

Wounded Union army soldiers similar to ones seen by Towne in Washington, D.C.

The Pennsylvania volunteers went to Camp Seward. Duty consisted of endless drilling that soon became monotonous. Towne utilized every chance he could to apply for a pass to allow him to spend as many hours as possible in the city. He toured public buildings, most of which he found still under construction. The Capitol in particular seemed almost comical with a derrick standing inside the hole where the dome was to be added. Debris that littered the grounds included everything from columns to statuary.[18]

In camp, Towne watched carefully and noted the wasteful, careless way that supplies were handled. He felt he could do a better job, if he had a chance, of bringing order out of the chaotic inefficiency. Now that the regiment finally had been designated the 143rd Pennsylvania Volunteers, Towne concluded the time had come to present his petition for a clerical position. He directed it to Morris and received a summons sooner than he had expected. Morris, after a few questions about Towne's education and experience, said he would recommend Towne for commissary sergeant. Towne knew that each regiment had a quartermaster of supplies and that the commissary sergeant was the quartermaster's assistant. The official promotion did not come until January 1, 1863, but in December he was detailed to work in the commissary department.[19]

At first, Towne found the work to consist mainly of counting, weighing, measuring, and itemizing incoming supplies which included all food, clothing, and utensils carried by the men. After supplies were received, they were stored to be issued as needed. Finally, reports had to be sent to the Quartermaster General's office each month to account for all supplies. The long columns with their tiny spaces for figures reminded Towne of his public school reports. He took the same kind of curious pride in filling the columns with neat, accurate figures. Soon, the regimental quartermaster, Lieutenant Milton Dana, relied on Towne to prepare the reports.

January 1, 1863, had a greater significance than Towne's promotion for on that day Lincoln's proclamation for emancipation, announced on September 22, 1862, went into effect. Years later, Towne continued to see this edict not only as right, but as an effective tool of victory for the Union cause.[20] Emancipation, whether an immediate reality or not, had become a goal of the Federals, and it thereby transformed the war from one for an abstract ideal to one for a tangible goal. Towne had no difficulty fighting for the Union, but he realized that it involved other questions about the nature of the Union. An end to slavery, on the other hand, put matters into human terms. Slaves were people with hopes and ambitions; if liberated, enlistment of members of the subjected race into Union armies offered a tangible means for the bondsmen to prove their worth. Possibly the first glimmer of his own role in uplifting those who had been enslaved entered Towne's mind. He knew that not everyone in the loyal states felt as he did, but he anticipated that as the war progressed and colored soldiers displayed their talents and abilities, sentiment would change.[21]

Towne did not have long to ponder these events for on February 17, the regiment was ordered to break camp and march to Belle Plain, Maryland. There it joined the 149th and 150th Pennsylvania Regiments to form the Second Brigade under command of Colonel Roy Stone. The brigade was incorporated into the Third Division of the First Army Corps. General Abner Doubleday commanded the Third Division and General John F. Reynolds of Pennsylvania was the corps commander.[22] A spring offensive was about to open, which the men in the eastern army, now known as the Army of the Potomac, anticipated would bring an end to the rebellion.

Chapter Six

Chancellorsville and Gettysburg

FOLLOWING THE APPOINTMENT of Joseph Hooker to the position of commander of the Army of the Potomac, the sense that victory was at last within grasp once more infected military and civilian personnel alike. "Fightin' Joe" would live up to his nickname and not retreat in the face of one reverse. Officials in Washington, D.C., representing both the Commander-in-Chief and the Chief of Staff, had drawn up a plan of operation for Hooker that seemed to almost guarantee success. It called for the cavalry to cross the Rappahannock River and cut the lines of communication and supply between Lee's army and the seat of Confederate government at Richmond, Virginia. Hooker, with the infantry and artillery, would then cross farther downstream and make a surprise attack on R. H. Anderson's division at Chancellorsville. When the rebel unit collapsed, Lee, in desperation, would rush into combat without adequate knowledge of where the Federals were and be decisively defeated. This was the broad outline of the strategy. It was so simple that sharper privates or noncommissioned officers like Towne could deduce it.

Two factors, not yet apparent, destroyed whatever possibilities the scheme possessed. The first was the heavy rainfall characteristic of the tidewater, in April. Torrential rains day after day brought the Rappahannock River and its companion streams to flood stage and land not covered by rising water turned into seas of mud. Foot soldiers sank into the mud to the tops of their boots, and for the cavalry the situation was hopeless. There was no way that horsemen could send their steeds into the roaring waters of the swollen river and rider or animal reach the other shore. The general in charge of Union cavalry for the Army of the Potomac made the point clear to Hooker. He must wait for dry weather and a drop in the level of river must occur.

At this point, the second element developed. Hooker's patience snapped, and he went straight to the second phase of the undertaking. He decided to cross with his infantry at Ely's Ford. He made one curious exception to this movement; he ordered Reynolds' First Corps to stay on the north bank and march down stream to Pollock's Mill. There it was to remain as a reserve force.[1] This was a crack unit proud of its history and potential to do even greater things; hence, the order brought a certain amount of grumbling from both men and officers. That, however, was a minor factor in the final fiasco. Without his cavalry, it was Hooker who was operating blindly. Lee, not worried about Union cavalry, could rush reinforcements to Anderson while the latter had time to put up barricades and fortifications to protect his location.

To make matters even worse, Hooker permitted no wagon trains to accompany his troops on the march. They must carry eight days' rations with them. As Towne and others in the quartermaster-commissary department read these orders, they exploded. Towne tried to preserve the proper deference due superiors, but even his mild temper frayed. He uttered a savage growl along with a cry of anguish at what he must do to his men. Did not this mysterious official, who made such a decision and sold it to the top commander, have any conception of what a foot soldier regularly carried? A rifle, sixty rounds of ammunition, tent-blanket-poncho roll, cooking equipment, and sundry other items constituted enough weight without adding eight days' rations. Hard bread, dried vegetables, dried beef, or salt pork were all Towne drew besides the ubiquitous coffee. Had he not issued huge amounts of coffee there would have been a mutiny on the spot. At every halt in a march or wait for another group to go around or some such delay, the men lit fires, and the coffee pots came out of knapsacks while some member of the platoon got water and everyone filled his tin cup to be fortified for another march.

However, Towne knew something else that made the situation more absurd. Not even "desiccated" potatoes and beans, as the men termed dried vegetables, or salt pork and dried beef would survive for eight days in the heat of the Virginia lowlands. Spoilage was inevitable; so too was the propensity of the average soldier to solve the problem of heavy loads by dumping part of what he carried. This meant loss of equipment as well as food. Mud added to these factors. The men of the First Corps christened the march of more than twenty miles down the shore of the Rappahannock River the "mud march." The weight of their loads sunk the men farther into the mire. Shoes and boots stuck in the mud and the men got out by leaving footwear behind. Then there were howls from company commanders for instant compliance with requisitions for apparel. To irate captains in the 143rd, Towne could only point to the fact that he was in the same position; he was the same distance from a supply base and he was without wagons to go back and forth to bring back needed items.[2]

Towne's superior, Lieutenant Milton Dana, the regimental quartermaster, went directly to Colonel Edmund Dana, who not only offered sympathy and understanding, but in his formal report to his superiors courageously expressed his opposition to the policy. "The experience of the late movement," Dana wrote in his summary of the Chancellorsville campaign, "if I may be permitted to remark, furnishes strong evidence that ... men should not be compelled to carry, in addition to their usual equipment, including sixty rounds of cartridges, eight days' rations."[3]

Following the mud march, the First Corps waited to see what its role would be. Men and commanders alike assumed their movement had served as a screen to cover the crossing of the main army. If that indeed had been the purpose, it was rendered futile by Lee's ability to send scouts to locate the Federals. Furthermore, Hooker either became confused or changed his strategy without making that decision clear, for he issued another order directing Reynolds to cross the Rappahannock by way of the United States Ford, march back to Ely's Ford, and wait there.[4] Grumbling and complaining became louder.

Compounding his rash action in going ahead without waiting for his cavalry, Hooker delayed attack until the second of May. That evening, when the First Corps reached its destination, the sound of gunfire was relatively close. After preparing a defense line, the men were told to sleep so they would be fresh for battle the following morning.[5] However, they were aroused soon after darkness and told to march forward to fill a gap created when the Eleventh Corps was routed. Groggy but determined, the men of Doubleday's division heading the march went forward through a heavily wooded area. Soon they met demoralized soldiers fleeing to the rear. The half-crazed men who had been caught in a trap due to the confused strategy of the high command, shouted to the relief force that they would only be killed if they continued toward the front.

Doubleday was fearful because panic could be contagious, but he soon realized his men were resolute. The drummers struck their instruments to the time of the favorite marching song, and soon the men were singing lustily. Towne shouted the words perhaps with a bit more tune but equal vigor:

> John Brown's body lies a-mouldering in the grave;
> John Brown's body lies a-mouldering in the grave;
> John Brown's body lies a-mouldering in the grave;
> But his soul is marching on.
> Glory, glory, hallelujah!

Glory, glory, hallelujah!
Glory, glory, hallelujah!
His soul is marching on.[6]

Once more Hooker changed his mind and refused to order the First and the Fifth Corps he had also held in reserve to join the attack. He rejected the advice of the council of corps commanders that he had summoned to use all of the army save the demoralized Eleventh Corps in one massive strike. This, the commanders theorized, would catch the rebels off guard, for they confidently anticipated a retreat in the face of one loss in the pattern of Hooker's predecessors.

Bitter over what they viewed as a lost opportunity, Reynolds and his personal friend Doubleday plotted their own stratagem. Scouts and pickets reported that the First Corps was not far from what seemed the weakest point in the Confederate line. A brigade from the Second Division would creep forward and when close to that point the rebel pickets would sound the alarm, an engagement would ensue, and Reynolds would rush all of his forces to support the infiltrators and they would break through. This would surely renew Hooker's flagging nerve, and Chancellorsville would be a great Union victory.

Whether this plan was as hopeful of success as Reynolds and Doubleday thought is open to question. However, it was doomed by its own cleverness. First, Doubleday selected Stone's brigade because the three Pennsylvania regiments which composed it were well trained, eager, and resolute. Doubleday's orders to Stone had to be circumspect. Inferior commanders cannot openly countermand their superior. Hence, Stone was told to lead his men on a reconnaissance mission. Because the men from Stone down to the lowest private knew that absolute silence was essential, they crept forward with extreme caution. Soon they were close enough to hear the sound of hammers and saws. Johnny was building fortifications. Those sounds would cover closer approach. When construction ceased, Stone's men were close enough to listen to evening roll call; they took note of the name of the unit, the numbers, and the fact that fortifications were not yet formidable. This was indeed a weak point in the Confederate line. Feeling very good about what they had learned, Stone gave the word to withdraw as silently as they had gone forward. He sent back his report to Doubleday with praise for how well his men had performed. Doubleday had to compliment the Second Brigade, even as he and Reynolds rued their failure.[7] Not until many years later, when he read Abner Doubleday's memoirs, did Towne realize that the stakes that night had been far higher than he or his officers and comrades had imagined.

Hooker ordered withdrawal, and the Army of the Potomac started back in more heavy rain. Once more a Union general had been defeated, not by superior force, but by his own poor tactics and indecision. Perhaps the value of the Chancellorsville campaign was that it seasoned the Army of the Potomac. Colonel Edmund Dana evaluated the 143rd Pennsylvania this way; the men, he said, performed with the "coolness and self-possession" of "veteran troops."[8] This was well for they were about to be called upon to face the greatest engagement of the war.

In June, Lee began a move to invade Pennsylvania and thereby cut communications between Washington, D.C. and the large populous areas of the Northeast. In view of the fact that the Army of the Potomac far outnumbered Lee's army, one may consider that he made a mistake. Hooker had recovered his wits and took sensible steps. He closed the supply bases at Aquia Creek and Belle Plains and marched his troops at an exhausting pace of twenty-eight to thirty-three miles per day over roads now ankle-deep in dust under a scorching sun. Many men became so exhausted they dropped by the roadside to rest and then had to walk half the night to overtake their unit.

Towne credited his wiry frame and his ability to concentrate his thoughts on the task at hand for the fact that he was able to keep going. For one thing he was thankful: the men were required to carry only a days' rations. Each evening Towne and other commissary sergeants went to the wagon train traveling behind the main line of the march and picked up the supplies for their respective regiments. The sergeants hauled the rations forward and their men came to the commissary to receive their items for the next day. This prevented considerable waste and spoilage, and it served as an incentive to stragglers to arrive as fast as possible to get their quota of food. Towne's men learned that he would be available also before the next day's march began to check for late arrivals who had missed the issue of the previous night.[9]

While camped on the outskirts of Frederick on the night of June 28, the Army of the Potomac received the not entirely surprising news that Hooker had resigned and been replaced by George G. Meade. The frequency with which the carousel, equipped with commanding generals, rode in and out of the Army of the Potomac had left the veterans at the point where they paid little attention. They hoped the new commander would not lead them into traps or order impossible assaults. At least Meade seemed "safe"; his record did not indicate that he was likely to do anything rash. The men had concluded they could do their job largely on their own.[10]

More to the point, Lee was already in Pennsylvania, apparently headed toward Harrisburg. So too, was the Army of the Potomac. Reynolds swung his corps toward Emmitsburg, Pennsylvania, and made contact with General John Buford's cavalry, which had taken a position on the heights overlooking the little town of Gettysburg. Its chief significance was its position as the terminus of the rail line to Harrisburg. Reynolds decided that this was a good spot from which to stop Lee's advance. Reynolds also recognized the significance of the rifled musket, which extended the range of a bullet four times that of the smooth-bore gun. Armed with rifles, a smaller defense force could overpower a considerably larger force that attempted to charge a fortified position. So, Reynolds directed Buford to fortify his position and await the arrival of more Union troops marching rapidly northward.

On the morning of July 1, 1863 one of those flukes of fate intervened to disrupt Reynolds' well-planned strategy. A small group of men from A. P. Hill's Confederate corps romped into Gettysburg bent on nothing more than breaking into the town's shoe factory to get all the shoes in its inventory. Already, rebel forces suffered from shortages of clothing, especially footwear. Other raiding parties were garnering food from gardens, hen houses, and homes. To their surprise, the group bent on shoes found Buford's cavalry instead.[11] As Buford's guns went into action, the raiding expedition became the opening round of one of the greatest battles of the war.

Hearing the sound of gunfire, Hill converged his main corps on Gettysburg, and Reynolds rushed toward the town. Hill arrived first, and Buford sent a frantic plea to Reynolds to get there quickly. After ordering Doubleday and James S. Wadsworth to take their divisions forward immediately, Reynolds rode ahead to direct defense operations.[12] He selected the so-called Iron Brigade, (called that because the men came from Wisconsin and Michigan, at that time principal sources of iron) from Wadworth's division, and the Second Brigade from Doubleday's to hold the woods between the Fairfield and Chambersburg roads. As the Iron Brigade marched around Doubleday's men, he entreated the westerners to hold the position "to the last extremity." The men shouted back, "If we can't hold, where will you find men who can?"[13] They were cocky, but he liked that.

Stone's men had been held back about a half-mile from the woods, but by midmorning it became obvious they were needed immediately. Towne afterward recalled how they threw knapsacks and blanket rolls to the ground and advanced at the double quick to an incline where the Iron Brigade struggled with masses of enemy. Doubleday, who had succeeded to the command of the Corps when Reynolds was killed soon after reaching Gettysburg, also exhorted the Pennsylvania group to make great sacrifices for their homeland. He never forgot their response. They cried almost as one man, "We have come to stay!" In his memoirs Doubleday sadly observed, "The greater portion did stay, laying down their lives there for the cause they loved so well."[14] They exerted an almost superhuman effort to keep the enemy from breaking through, but they were too few in number for the defensive position to be advantageous. In his official report Doubleday asserted, "My confidence in this noble body of men was not displaced...."[15]

The Second Brigade took such a toll on the rebels that the Confederates were forced to give ground. Just as Stone's men rushed forward to claim a fencerow that would serve as some defense, Confederate batteries on a higher ridge opened fire, and more Confederates swung to the point to retake the fence, climbed it, and hand-to-hand combat ensued. Towne recalled later that he used his bayonet, stabbing viciously, then whirling to shoot others trying to scale the fence while he struggled to keep his footing on the "rocky slope rendered slippery" by the "blood and brains" of the fallen. To his dismay, he realized when it was over, that he had behaved like a "savage, killing with abandon." He concluded that war produced a reversion to barbarism, which he deplored. Years later, he snorted in disgust at Theodore Roosevelt's fulsome glorification of war as bringing out the true "manly spirit." Towne confessed that at Gettysburg he was more concerned about self-defense in the heat of the battle. Confederates were trying to kill him just as he tried to kill them. However, he did not pride himself on his survival; it was not fitness as much as luck that determined who lived and who died.[16]

By four o'clock in the afternoon, the men who had been in mortal combat since midmorning were too exhausted to continue; they must be sent to the rear, but, Doubleday did not have reserves to replace them and he was forced to order retreat. This seemed to disconcert the men who had given their word to stay there, so they were reluctant to obey the order. Stone declared, "It was as if each man felt that upon his arm hung the fate of the day and the nation."[17] When they did give ground they did it slowly, stopping to turn and fire repeatedly. They saw Confederates race to seize the big guns of the artillery, but the men of the Second Brigade were determined not to let that happen. They dropped to the ground, firing and yelling wildly as if they numbered in the thousands instead of a mere hundred or so, while a few nimble souls ran to drag the guns back manually.[18] This frustration seemed to enrage the rebels, who badly needed artillery, so they redoubled their efforts to catch the perpetrators of this enormity.

The 143rd was the last unit to fall back, so its men were in grave danger. Their officers kept urging a faster retreat. To make matters worse, many of the men had exhausted their ammunition. Towne and a few others who could run faster paused long enough to grab the cartridge belts of dead or dying comrades and then raced to overtake their companions. As long as ammunition lasted, the men of the 143rd periodically turned and fired at their pursuers. Finally, as both cartridges and time went against them, they fell back. All except the color-bearer, Sergeant Ben Crippin. Finding he had no ammunition, he threw caution to the winds and stood upright to face the enemy, shaking his fist in rage. A perfect target, he fell before a torrent of bullets. The Confederates pounced at the flag, just as Major C. M. Conyngham gave the cry, "One Hundred Forty-Third, rally on your colors." Almost as one man, the members of the regiment whirled, grasped the flag, and bore it to safety. In the history of the regiment compiled for the reunion held at Gettysburg in 1883, the historian proudly listed the successes it enjoyed on the first day of the great battle: first, saving the artillery pieces, and second, preventing the enemy from gaining the coveted flag. Such was the protocol of this last war to be fought according to rules. However, they were already wearing thin, and before the war ended many frills and flourishes would be abandoned. Nonetheless, the 143rd had its hero. When the regiment chose its monument for the national park made on the battlefield, the statue of Ben Crippen clutching his flag in one hand and shaking the other at his pursuers represented the regiment.[19]

The second day of battle was largely uneventful for the Third Division. Not until late afternoon did it engage in combat and then only briefly. Meade called upon Doubleday's unit to bolster a weak point in the Federal line that seemed on the point of crumpling. The division not only saved it, but retook four big guns that the Confederates had captured. Saving artillery pieces had become a specialty of the Third Division's Second Brigade, which also claimed credit for this action. Then the unit, still reeling from the first day's engagement, was sent back to the comparative safety of the cemetery and told to sleep, for every man in the army would be needed by the next day.[20]

Generally soldiers found it easy to fall asleep anywhere they were given the chance, but that night most of the men found rest impossible. The scene itself was eerie; one did not need to be superstitious to feel that strange shapes moved about in the shadows of the tombstones under the light of a waning moon. The night was breathlessly hot, and most of the men quickly consumed all of the water in their canteens. Almost steadily, it seemed, there was the muffled tread of the stretcher-bearers either moving in search of the fallen or returning with those who might be saved by the surgeons.[21]

Towne awakened with a burning thirst, and he slipped cautiously down the slope to find a spring that he thought he had spotted earlier. He was right; there was a pool of what once had

Union dead at Gettysburg

been water, now reduced to a mudhole by the many who had preceded him. He explored as much as he dared and located a canteen under the body of a dead soldier, who apparently had died before he could quite get his water out of his knapsack. In death he had rolled onto the container so that the looters who had already raided his knapsack had missed the canteen. With a whispered apology to his dead comrade, Towne confiscated the canteen and gulped the last water in it. Its taste was sickeningly hot and brackish, but he tried to tell himself that his imagination was running away and he must not pursue it.

Everyone anticipated that the third day would be decisive. With renewed vigor the Army of the Potomac pushed themselves in hope that their effort would end the conflict. Doubleday again rode about, carefully placing the First Corps in the second line of Union defense at about midpoint, always the crucial area. He knew his men and had great confidence in them. Meade had directed all the corps commanders to erect strong barricades of stone and rails, both plentiful in this area. Once in place, the men lay flat on the ground as the rebel artillery opened fire, bombarding the Union line with one crash after another. Union gunners answered until the earth trembled, and Towne and his fellows behind the breastworks coughed and choked from the sulfuric fumes that settled over the field. He decided that Dante must have conceived his *Inferno* from some glimpse into the future which portrayed this scene.

Suddenly, the firing ceased. For a moment, their ears still deafened by the awful noise, the men could hardly believe it. Towne cautiously turned over until he could see the gunners behind him bringing out more guns to replace the damaged ones that could be repaired or the few caissons that had exploded. The gun crews were working frantically to cool the big guns, but the gunners seemed almost as hot. Sweat poured off their bodies stripped to the waist in a vain attempt to be cooler. Others brought up wagonloads of shells to arrange in order, solid shot to be used first, then shells, and last, canister.[22]

Then, all eyes of the defenders focused on the signal station and soon they spied the wigwagged message; "They are coming." Squinting through holes in the breastworks, the men watched in growing disbelief an unforgettable sight. From a point, which many years later Towne would explain to his son was "about as far away as our south forty from where we now stand,"[23] came a large force of Confederate infantry. The men marched forward in perfect formation as though on parade. They were out in an open field, unprotected by any natural shelter; their artillerymen had ceased firing from either the mistaken notion that they had silenced the Union guns or fear of killing their own men.

If Pickett's charge was supposed to overwhelm ungenteel Yankees with awe from the open contempt for them that the proudest of the southern aristocracy displayed, it had no such effect. Union defenders saw not proud glory, but amazing stupidity on the part of the commander who decreed such a suicidal assault on a heavily fortified line. They felt sorry for the men who were the victims, but that did not preclude Union defenders from an almost fiendish resolve to kill every charger and end the rebellion at once.

Union artillery opened fire, blasting great gaps in the approaching column. The Confederates closed ranks and marched on, veering only slightly to the left of Doubleday's men. That merely gave Union gunners time to switch to shells. They fired with such accuracy that each shell brought down as many as ten attackers. As the marchers came closer, the gun crews loaded their weapons with canister and further thinned the rebel line. The gunners then stopped; now it was time for the rifles behind the breastworks to finish the day. The powerful and deadly rifled bullets now tore into flesh and bone. In one segment of the Union line the rifles kept firing faster than even the most skilled shotgunner could reload, further dazing the assaulters.

No one knew at the time, except those given the new guns, that one corps had been issued the new breech loading Springfield, the repeating rifle, on a trial basis. Ordnance was skeptical of its accuracy and continued to be so even after the successful experiment at Gettysburg. In short order, however, the repeating rifle would further revolutionize military strategy. It was not decisive at Gettysburg, but it was significant as a new kind of weapon.[24]

A few determined Confederates reached the Union lines. Leaping to their feet, Federal soldiers swore and yelled as they shot, bayoneted, and used knives in hand-to-hand combat, killing or maiming those who managed to storm the barricades. By that time most of the rebels had decided that retreat was the only escape from death, some concluded even that was not an alternative.They threw down their guns and raised their arms in surrender. Those who were far enough in the rear, fled as fast as their legs could take them. Lee agreed and ordered withdrawal across the boundary into Maryland.

However, the Confederate rear guard and stragglers found a new menace. Pennsylvania farmers in the southern counties, many of frugal German ancestry, were enraged by the depredation to their crops, gardens, orchards, and livestock by the invaders. These farmers decided to fight their own engagement. Armed with pitchforks, axes, and hunting weapons, they intercepted fleeing rebels, tied them up like cattle, and drove them to Union lines, where crews were already busy processing prisoners.[25] The ignomy of the rebels made its own statement, as if in retort to contemptuous southern attitudes toward the plebeian "Pennsylvania Dutch," as these farmers had long been termed. It also suggested an American trait, which had affected even the Germans who prided themselves on nonassimilation, to turn high tragedy into comedy. While later the episode provoked mirth, as it did at the time, it also may have further delayed Meade, who was already receiving adverse comment for his delay in pursuing Lee.

seemed normal with the military, Towne's orders were slow in coming. Meanwhile, he was able to write to his family and relieve the anxiety his parents and sister had endured since receipt of Asa's letter. As he laconically hinted at prevailing conditions in General Hospital, they reacted as countless persons in the North were doing. They were already contributing to the work of the Sanitary Commission, but in response to the very personal connection now existing, as well as the directives of the Wyoming Annual Conference, the ladies of Towne's church took it upon themselves to organize a unit of the Ladies' Aid Society.

Later historians would note the break from the past as women throughout the Northeast organized massive efforts to provide necessities and delicacies for their men at the front. Men directed the Sanitary Commission and the Christian Commission, already in existence, and they told the women what they were to do. Gettysburg was not necessarily the impetus, but it served as a dividing mark in respect to aid for the army, as it did for other aspects of the war. Women began to form Soldiers' Aid Societies, as they were first termed. Since it seemed that women were determined, worked energetically, and accomplished wonders, the men blessed the "ladies' work." The Methodist Episcopal denomination not only urged local charges to undertake such endeavors, but christened the organization the Ladies' Aid Societies, and the term quickly superseded the earlier name.

When Towne received letters from home, they were filled with accounts by his mother or Phinis about how they spent much of the mornings cooking, drying, canning, and turning fruits into jellies and preserves. In the afternoon they met with Orange Mott's wife, Bertha Warner, and other women of the church at different homes to knit, make bandages, shred old sheets into lint for surgical dressings, and sew hospital attire and bedding.[5] As Towne saw barrels of such items come into the hospital after he was able to walk about and to use his knowledge of supply to gain him

Union soldiers getting mail

admittance to warehouses behind the hospital, he fancied he saw some of the items from home. Because he had always regarded his sister as a most capable woman, his superior in many ways, he had no thought that this was a departure from the norm.

After what seemed too long a time, Towne received the necessary papers discharging him from the hospital and ordering him to report to his regiment, then on duty at Bealton Station. He headed southward promptly and on September 9 reported for duty.[6] After two months it was good to be back. He felt pleased by the greetings of comrades and their apparent delight that he had recovered. The best was Milton Dana's greeting. After Towne gave the customary salute, Dana dropped protocol, shook hands, waved at a stack of reports, and told the sergeant the forms were his. Some men might have resented this type of welcome, but Towne attacked the job happily, thinking it was good to be missed. He also believed it boded well for another project he had considered carefully while staring at the whitewashed walls of the hospital ward; however, he decided, it must wait until other things had been clarified in his mind and in the situation of the army.

On September 12, John Newton, the commanding general of the First Corps, received orders to be ready to move at short notice. This meant extra work for the quartermasters and their staffs. They discovered a new problem, or more precisely, one stemming from Gettysburg that had not been corrected: there was a shortage of wagons. To handle the great number of casualties the ambulance corps had commandeered supply wagons. Those left had to carry heavier loads, which meant they moved slowly; often the drivers had difficulty keeping up with the infantry. The densely wooded terrain and narrow winding roads of northern Virginia added to the problem. If that were not enough, contradictory orders intensified the confusion. Sometimes the wagons were traveling in opposite directions from the troops. At other times, one part of the wagon train met another part, each going in opposite directions.[7] It must have been comical to some imaginary watcher in the sky viewing the scene below; however, those responsible for the supply train or those with the duty of supplying the marchers were not amused. Later, Towne could joke about it, but not in 1863.

Despite all of the frustrations, the Federals occupied Warrenton without opposition on October 20. However, they discovered the rebels had destroyed the Orange and Alexandria Railroad from Bristoe Station to the Rappahannock River. Meade ordered the line rebuilt, and Colonel Daniel C. McCullum, Superintendent of Military Railroads, began the task. The First Corps was detailed to guard the operation. The troops camped at Bristoe Station, but those in supply spent most of their time at whatever was the farthest point that the track had been laid. Towne had discovered upon rejoining his regiment that Gettysburg roughly marked another shift; the quartermasters and their commissary sergeants had become almost a separate unit in the corps. The commissionary sergeants stayed with their wagons and each evening they drew food and other necessary equipment that they had requisitioned. Next, they made the trip to their respective regiments to issue rations or other items as needed. Daily, as a long train of cars moved up the line to deposit their goods, McCullum's crews were building. Then, the train backed to a siding where it could gradually maneuver the turnaround to return to Alexandria, the great Union supply base. Thus, Towne had a vantage point from which to watch the efficient railroad crews in operation.

Towne applauded the speed and efficiency with which the construction force built the bridge over Kettle Run and moved on to construct a depot and sidetracks to facilitate the train's departure after unloading. When the last tie was laid and the spike driven into place, the builders waved the train waiting up the line to come into the yards. Those in supply began to cheer even as they drove their wagons to the station to load the supplies marked for each division, brigade, and regiment.[8] Towne and his colleagues already knew the significance of the railroads to Union victory. The rails formed the link between the superior productive capacity of the North, as compared to the South.

Fighting largely ended in December, and both sides settled into winter quarters. The Army of the Potomac established itself around Culpeper, Virginia. At year's end the men of the 143rd and their comrades were beginning to settle into camp routine after months in the field. Towne worked to requisition winter clothing and camp needs as well as daily rations. Once the army was in winter quarters, the advantage of the rail line to Washington became more apparent. Better transportation combined with higher standards pushed by the Sanitary Commission enabled Towne to receive food that provided a more palatable and varied diet. He included sugar, soft bread, fresh beef, potatoes, and beans in New Year's Day rations to which he added a ration of whiskey so the men could celebrate the arrival of 1864.[9] He had no problem offering whisky to his men. As a temperance man he would not indulge himself or "serve" it in his house, but this was a different situation. Towne had learned that war and civilian life were totally different.

A sharp wind caused the men to hasten making their quarters as warm as possible. In between work relating to his regimental duties, Towne joined the men armed with axes as they attacked the dense woods surrounding Culpeper. They erected miniature cabins or shacks. Towne used his building skills and his ingenuity to make his almost comfortable. He put up siding, plastered it with mud, and hung a door. Inside, he set up his cot and draped his poncho over it to protect it from rain that might seep through the roof or blow in through the walls. Another luxury was the opportunity to wash and mend his garments. He took advantage of the first Sunday after he completed his cabin to do his laundry and mending.[10]

By the middle of January, Towne finished the returns for November. During the next four days, when heavy rains and chilling winds made staying indoors the order "of the day," he completed December's reports. He congratulated himself that he was at last "caught up" and could "take it easy." His first indulgence was to write letters to his family. Much of the time during the fall he had been so rushed that his letters home were brief notes scrawled as he sat in his wagon a waiting his turn to move forward to receive supplies. Now, he wrote a longer letter that included comments about winter camp. Later, he wrote to his cousin Ruth Warner, who had recently married Edwin Wallace Taylor and gone to California to make their home, traveling in a covered wagon. Such a mode of travel seemed strange to her relatives in Susquehanna County, and California struck them as the end of the world. When Phinis wrote to her brother about Ruth's odyssey, his curiosity was aroused. With his early interest in the land added to the nation in the 1840s, he wanted Ruth to tell him her impressions, not only of California, but the land between the Mississippi and the Pacific coast.[11] After completing his letter writing, Towne read several city papers.

Another pleasant aspect of winter camp was the arrival of newspapers from major eastern cities. Vendors, who set up their little shops near the campsite, offered papers for sale. Towne gladly spent a few pennies for a paper, read it, and exchanged with a buddy who had purchased a different paper. Thus, he was able to read the *Philadelphia Enquirer,* the *Washington Chronicle,* and the *New York Tribune* on a leisurely Sunday afternoon. He enjoyed himself so much that he decided to postpone his washing until Monday, which, as he well knew, was the proper wash day for housekeepers of Forest Lake like his mother and sister.[12]

Heavy fog and more rain kept most of the men indoors in early February. Towne was clearly not the only one writing letters now that there was time and mail moved in and out of the camp readily, so he requisitioned stationery for his regiment, along with candles for work indoors and soap so the men could do laundry. He issued some of these items to himself as well. He spent considerable time invoicing camp and garrison equipment and clothing he had received in January, for he hoped to have his January returns ready by mid-February. Food supplies continued to improve, and he added apples and rice to rations he issued.[13]

For some time Towne had considered a major step, that is, to volunteer for service with the growing number of units in the branch designated as the United States Colored Troops. He knew there were strong feelings, even among Unionists, about the wisdom of arming ex-slaves or even free persons of color. Some white soldiers felt a people so long subjected could not fight effectively or might run amuck when they encountered southerners who had long mistreated Negroes. Other people, Towne learned from the papers and journals he was now reading more frequently, saw enrolling Negro troops as a device for limiting the number of white northerners who would be conscripted. Towne dismissed all such notions as lacking any validity; he regarded military service as part of citizenship. Once slavery was outlawed forever, the former bondsmen must be accorded full citizenship rights. However, he did accept the concept of white officers for the colored units as a temporary expedient until Negroes reached a sufficient level of education. The army could serve as a school for basic literacy as well as military tactics, and officers should serve as schoolmasters for both.

Some minds in Washington, D.C. operated from similar premises. Word had gone to soldiers in volunteer regiments that applications for officer positions could be made, and if a person's application sounded hopeful, the board of examiners would summon the person to Washington for examination. Towne felt that he had good qualifications. Twelve years of teaching with some normal training seemed rather impressive. However, he had another goal; his experience as a regimental commissary sergeant, during which time he had done most of the work of a quartermaster, suggested that in a new regiment he might as well have commensurate rank and pay.

On February 21, 1864, Towne mailed a letter to Charles W. Foster, head of the Bureau of Colored Troops. Towne stated his general qualifications, referred to his service in supply, and gave Lieutenant Milton Dana as a reference. Having done all that he could for the moment, Towne resumed work on his vouchers. On the first Sunday in March he attended church services held in camp; then he read, wrote his regular Sunday letter to his family, and began a systematic study of tactics. Evidently, he had received a favorable reply from Washington and he was preparing for the examination.[14]

March weather on the Virginia tidewater proved unpredictable with a sudden snowstorm on the twenty-fifth which was accompanied by strong winds, so Towne kept to his quarters. He completed the February reports and studied tactics further.[15] He, like his comrades, kept an eye on shifts in command as they were announced. On March 9, President Lincoln named Ulysses S. Grant to the newly created rank of Lieutenant General with command of all Union armies. Grant would join those in the East. Although Meade remained technically the commander of the Army of the Potomac, it was clear that Grant would plan strategy and Meade would simply execute his assignments.

Meade had already decreed a reorganization which Grant approved. This eliminated the First and Third Corps, both of which had suffered irreparable damage at Gettysburg. They were proud units and the order was disappointing when first read, but the 143rd and its companion regiments in the brigade, commanded by Roy Stone, were kept together. The units were only augmented by two other regiments and placed in the Fifth Corps with Stone still in command. The numbering occasioned some laughter and wisecracks from the men since they were now in the Third Brigade of the Fourth Division of the Fifth Corps.[16]

More exciting was the news that Grant would arrive on March 29 to inspect the Army of the Potomac. He told Meade that he did not desire a formal review; he only asked that the men be lined up in front of their respective corps encampments. He would ride about the camp and look at the various units. A heavy rain fell that day. Towne was too busy drawing and issuing rations to do more than slip into place with his regiment just prior to Grant's appearance. Towne, trying to form an opinion, looked closely at the new commander. At first glance, he saw a man who did not seem prepossessing and apparently made no attempt to do so. Grant wore a private's coat and trousers with only the shoulder straps denoting his rank. He wore a slouch hat which he had pushed sideways so that he could better view the men, and he gave an almost uncanny illusion of looking at each one as he rode along.

What most impressed Towne was the easy, confident way Grant sat on his horse. Grant appeared to give it a command and then leave matters to the mount. Having grown up in the household of a man who had a similar manner with horses, Towne could appreciate Grant's attitude.[17] The horse walked sedately ahead while the General devoted his full attention to the men who were now the soldiers with whom he would try to accomplish the long awaited victory.

Spring seemed slow to arrive in northern Virginia. On April 4, heavy snow began and developed during the night into a nasty storm that produced mounds of snow around all the cabins. Rising temperature on the fifth turned the snow to rain and melted snow piles. Rain and melting snow made the camp into a series of islands set in the midst of lakes and rivers. Another storm on Sunday added to the misery.[18] Towne watched the weather anxiously because he had been notified to report to the Board of Examiners on April 16.

Towne applied for and received a furlough to go to Washington, D.C. Before he left he secured a letter from Milton Dana. It contained a warm endorsement of Towne for the position of regimental quartermaster in one of the new regiments being recruited. Dana pointed to the fact that Towne had performed the duties of commissary sergeant and quartermaster's clerk in the 143rd Pennsylvania for a year-and-a-half. Therefore, he was able to handle all details of the office. Furthermore, he was "thoroughly familiar with English branches and arithmetic" from his years as a schoolteacher.[19]

On April 13, Towne washed his underwear, bathed, and trimmed his hair and beard as best he could. Before going to bed he brushed his uniform to make himself as presentable as possible. He traveled with the wagon train to the Culpeper depot where

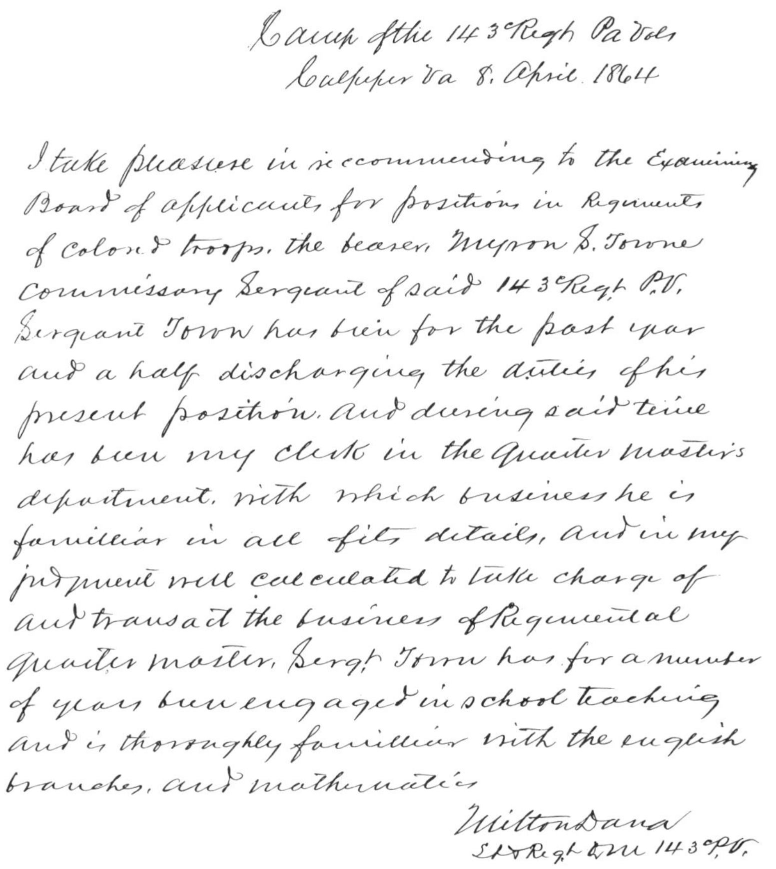
Camp of the 143d Regt Pa Vols
Culpeper Va 8. April. 1864

I take pleasure in recommending to the Examining Board of applicants for positions in Regiments of Color'd troops, the bearer, Myron S. Towne Commissary Sergeant of said 143d Regt P.V. Sergeant Town has been for the past year and a half discharging the duties of his present position. and during said time has been my clerk in the Quarter master's department. with which business he is familliar in all of its details, and in my judgment well calculated to take charge of and transact the business of Regimental Quarter master. Sergt Town has for a number of years been engaged in school teaching and is thoroughly familliar with the english branches, and mathematics

Milton Dana
Lt & Regt QM 143d P.V.

Towne's letter of recommendation from Milton Dana

he boarded the train. As he boarded, a guard checked Towne's pass: "Age, 34; height, five foot seven and a half inches; complexion and hair, light; eyes, blue" and waved him on.[20]

The crews of the United States Military Railroads had done their work well. Towne admired the smooth track, which permitted the train to puff along at a faster pace than any train he had ridden thus far. At Alexandria there was a long stop to take on supplies and leave orders for others to be filled and ready to load

Sergeant Towne in his dress uniform

when the train came back from the Capital. It was night when the train pulled into Washington, D.C., but Towne and his fellow passengers in the city, briefly on business or taking other trains out of Washington the next day, knew what to do. They headed to a large building near the depot which was known variously as the Soldier's Retreat, Soldier's Rest, or Soldier's Lodge. It provided clean, decent lodging and meals for soldiers temporarily in the Capital.[21]

On Friday, Towne reported to the examining board and learned the precise hour to return on Saturday for the examination. At that time he took the written portion of the test, which was easy for him in view of his education and years of teaching, plus his careful review of Casey's *Manual of Tactics.* Following the written exercise, he was interviewed by the board. They accepted Dana's letter of recommendation as sufficient evidence of Towne's ability to handle the duties of quartermaster. In his application, Towne had stated his membership in the Anti-Slavery Society and Methodist Episcopal Church; that seemed to satisfy any thought that he was insincere in his desire to serve with colored troops. As the interview closed, he was told that he had passed and would be recommended for First Lieutenant and regimental quartermaster.[22] The examiners directed him to J. B. Young, recorder for the board, who would sign a statement to the effect that Towne had been examined as his pass stipulated and therefore was to rejoin his regiment without delay.[23]

Early on Sunday morning, Towne enjoyed a good breakfast at the lodge, reflecting that it was probably the best meal he would encounter for a long time. After an uneventful train ride he hurried to his post where he discovered that orders had come to prepare for breaking camp. The long awaited spring campaign was about to begin.

Chapter Eight

Into the South

UPON HIS RETURN FROM WASHINGTON, D.C., Towne undertook the tasks associated with preparations for a campaign. He ordered additional supplies, repaired wagons, and checked draft animals for those needing new shoes or harness. He had learned from experience that clerical work could not be accomplished in the field, so he worked diligently to complete his March returns, and he began those for April. He had not finished them when orders came that the troops would leave at 1:00 a.m. on May 4.

Because Towne's regiment was on picket duty until 9:00 p.m. on May 3, he had to await their return to issue marching rations to the men. Consequently, he worked almost until the departure and then spent the remaining time making a final survey of the loads in each wagon and their teams. Although "really tired out" from a sleepless night, Towne had the satisfaction of reporting all in readiness as the wagon train departed in the wake of the infantry.[1]

The Fifth Corps led the way across the Rapidan at Germanna Ford and into a thick forest of cedar and pine meshed together by a tangle of bushes and vines. Ravines and knolls, crisscrossed by numerous streams and interspersed with marshes, completed the terrain into which the Army of the Potomac plunged. Towne quickly concluded that Virginians who named the region The Wilderness had aptly described it. Unfortunately, they knew the trails through the area while the invaders did not.

In the dark tangled woods Union soldiers became confused, lost their sense of direction and wandered in circles. They betrayed their presence with swaying trees and breaking brush, which enabled the defenders to focus a barrage of bullets that set fire to leaves and bushes. Stone's brigade strayed into a swamp where the men wallowed waist deep in mud. At the time it seemed a hopeless situation, but it likely saved many lives because it placed their heads below bullet range and stopped the progress of the fires.[2]

When they finally pulled themselves out of the mud, the men of the brigade began to search for each other; regiments had become so confused and the men were so coated in mud that it was impossible to tell friend from foe. In fact, some men literally blundered into enemy hands. Colonel Dana of the 143rd almost made that mistake. As he tried to round up his men, he saw a band of soldiers on a nearby knoll. Another soldier, who looked vaguely familiar despite his muddy face, was running toward Colonel Dana. The colonel finally recognized the runner as Sergeant Dempsey and called out to him, "What troops are those?" Dempsey replied, "Rebs, and you'd better get away fast." Dana snorted in disbelief for he could not grasp that the two armies were actually that close together. In response to this the other retorted, "All right, Colonel, if you want to get captured stay here, but…I'm getting out…" and he departed in haste with Dana following. His guide seemed to have an idea of where some of the men of the 143rd might go when they crawled out of the giant mud hole. Gradually, a semblance of order was restored, but Towne and those with the wagon train simply gave up the search. Even if he could locate his charges, it would do no good to issue rations because they dared not make fires to boil coffee, much less stew dried vegetables, dried beef, and hard bread.[3]

With daybreak, fighting resumed, but Confederate reinforcements had rendered their defense too strong for any hope of breaking through. The engagement in The Wilderness had produced the heaviest toll in the shortest space of time of any engagement thus far for the Army of the Potomac. Nonetheless, a new spirit prevailed. When orders to march on May 7 arrived, it was quickly apparent that there was no retreat; instead, orders stated the troops were to go left toward Spotsylvania. Far from the demoralization Lee had anticipated, the men seemed to have caught a contagion from the new commander. When Grant rode by on his big horse to take his place at the head of the march, the infantry serenaded him with a new song, "Ain't I glad to get out of the wilderness!"[4] Like him, they were not thinking of turning back. They inferred something of the General's goal: to force Lee out of his trenches. Unfortunately, the plan for a surprise assault on the Confederate earthworks before Spotsylvania Court House failed from a combination of factors. Rain produced a dark night and more mud. Meade decided that the trains of the Fifth Corps should follow the infantry, cavalry, and artillery of that corps, then would come the trains of the Sixth Corps. It would bring up the rear of the leading units, the prime attackers, in other words.

Towne issued his rations, went back to the main wagon train, which, as directed rolled into position behind the marchers. Then Warren ordered the wagons back for they were "greatly in the way." This created another example of wagons meeting each other in endless confusion. If Warren had simply followed Meade's orders, which Towne estimated had come from Grant, things could not have been so bad, but the confusion caused delays, which destroyed the surprise element. When Warren finally reached Spotsylvania, his troops were too exhausted to undertake an assault. Grant immediately demonstrated his flexibility by substituting constant reconnoitering and skirmishing to probe the Confederate line for weak spots.[5]

Meantime, Grant ordered the Quartermaster's Department to establish a supply base at Aquia Creek. He repeated his directive that wagons be integrated with marching columns. Another order called for sturdier wagons and more careful packaging. Towne reflected that it paid to have a commander who understood supply from his own experience as a quartermaster.

Towne found himself called upon more often to do extra duty. His calmness, dependability, and efficiency became more apparent as supply grew in importance in the eyes of staff officers. On May 9, as he started forward with his wagons, orders came for him to report to the brigade commissary. He was put in charge of sorting, labeling, and recording materials that had been received from Aquia Creek. It was late afternoon before he was released to take his wagons forward for evening distribution of rations. He parked at a relatively safe distance from the fighting, unloaded his supplies and dragged them forward to locate his men. To his dismay only 250 men appeared by nightfall.[6] When soldiers did not show up for food, they were either dead, wounded, or so exhausted they had fallen asleep in any hole into which they stumbled. By morning, he located the latter, but learned there had been another heavy toll of the former.

Towne was not exactly sheltered even though he was behind the lines much of the time, and he had a number of close calls. One night, as he tried to locate the 143rd, he emulated his commander: he almost blundered into a rebel detachment and was "near being captured," he recorded. An engagement, which "opened furiously" May 12, came dangerously close to where he had parked his wagons. A shell hit one wagon, killing the driver, a horse, and a mule. That required hasty movement farther to the rear, which meant a longer distance to walk and carry or pull his supplies. The following day, as he crept along the line handing rations to his men, an enemy sharpshooter spotted Towne, and a bullet zipped close to his ear. As he put it, rebel sharpshooters fired at "anyone who shows his head."[7]

Quartermasters were responsible for transporting wounded to the hospitals or at least were required to provide the wagons. The mounting number of casualties taxed the number of wagons designated as ambulances. Therefore, the chief medical officer ordered that empty wagons held by supply should be turned over to the medical corps.

The problem was that there were no surplus wagons. Any that were empty were simply those that had discharged supplies and were going back to Aquia Creek for more provisions. Quartermasters and their commissary sergeants came together and solved the dilemma, illustrating the fact that the men in the lower staff levels had learned to handle misunderstandings on the part of the top commanders. The Army of the Potomac had become a first-class professional organization. Once more the quartermasters of the brigade looked to Towne and gave him the task; he was detailed to take all of the empty wagons of the Third Brigade to the field hospital.

There Towne assisted in loading the wounded to be transported by the medical corpsmen to the hospital at Fredericksburg. They would bring the wagons back to the field hospital as soon as empty and he would take them back to the supply base. Thus, wagons were rotated to serve all needs. While he waited, Towne joined hospital crews who were trying to clean up the "mess" that Confederate shelling had created in the hospital so it would be ready to receive more wounded.[8] On other trips he looked for men from his regiment who had been brought in, for he was responsible for whatever provisions they required until they went to a major hospital.

After days of constant fighting, May 20 brought a lull during which details from both armies, under flags of truce, searched for the dead and buried them. Others enjoyed a day of rest. General Warren commandeered the Beverly House, a large plantation, for his headquarters. He ordered the commissary and ordinance wagons to park in a grove of trees near the big house. Towne directed his teamsters to unhitch the draft animals and tether them to the trees with enough leeway to graze on the lush grass. He dismissed the drivers until late afternoon, and he himself left for a tour of the holdings of the Beverly family.[9]

Towne desired to see what a tidewater plantation was really like. He climbed a low hill, from which he had a good view of the house, which he termed "quite grand."[10] However, he did not stay long on the hill due to a familiar sound that caught his attention and filled him with delight. There was a brook close at hand. Recalling the happy hours he had spent in his childhood playing along the brook on his Grandfather Warner's farm, Towne unhesitatingly followed the sound until he reached the bank. He walked beside the stream a short distance, scanning it and noting the difference the Tidewater terrain made from the mountains and hills of northeastern Pennsylvania. This brook did not babble like the Warner brook, nor was its current swift. The stream on the Beverly plantation gently murmured as it moved sedately. Nonetheless, it was fed by an underground spring so the water was cool and refreshing. After a long drink, he filled his canteen.

Towne had another thought about this little natural treasure. He stripped quickly and grabbed a cake of soap from his knapsack. Then he soaped his underwear heavily and held the garments into the current of the stream, letting it swirl the dirt out of them. After repeated dousings to rinse the clothing, he spread each item carefully on the bank where it could get sun. Next, he waded out into the middle of the stream and rubbed soap over his body. As he squatted in the water, he scraped caked mud off his legs. They felt sore and painful, but he thought little of it at the time. Only later did he connect that with the varicose veins that became a problem before the end of the campaign. He soaped his head and face and splashed water over hair and beard which sadly needed trimming. He tried to use the scissors from his sack, but the brook made an uncertain mirror. When he climbed back to the bank, he sat in the sun and dried himself. By the time he was ready to dress, his garments were dry, so he dressed and left the brook where he had spent a strangely peaceful afternoon in the midst of a grueling campaign of warfare.[11] Then, it was back to his wagons and the preparation for an early morning march.

The Fifth Corps moved out on the morning of May 21. As it prepared to march, Warren raised the issue once more of the place of the wagon train. The reply came quickly, "The trains that are authorized to be with the troops will move with them." This seemed logical, but as Towne had observed, that was the difference between Grant and his predecessors. He did what was sensible and feasible regardless of precedent.

Grant continued to demonstrate his knowledge of supply and recognition of its importance. As the army moved southward, he ordered the base at Aquia Creek closed and a new one opened at Port Royal on the Rappahannock River. Moving the main supply base meant shorter distances for wagons to travel, faster turnaround time, and thus more effective use of wagons and teams. It also permitted more fresh goods to be included in the rations than had been possible in the field.[12] Towne's confidence in Grant grew steadily. He was not alone; many of the men in the eastern armies had become convinced that Grant would at last lead them to the long-awaited victory.

As the army moved deeper into the South, Towne admired the land. It was "fine country," he said. As his unit passed a plantation, many slaves hung on the fence to watch the troops pass. He sensed that the men in their dusty, faded, worn blue uniforms were viewed by the bondsmen as liberators. He called out greetings, as did others. He asked what the slaves knew of enemy movements, and they responded quickly "they went by last night; they be just over there." This was somewhat vague, but Towne thought it represented the fact that slaves were seldom allowed to leave the plantation or were allowed to go but a short distance if given a pass for some errand.[13]

The slaves were right, however; by 4:30 that afternoon Union skirmishers struck a sizable contingent of the Confederate rear guard, and a sharp fight ensued. Union artillery drove the rebels back. When Towne returned to the place where he had parked his wagons while he took rations to the regiment, he found that a horse had been stolen. Rebel deserters or stragglers were nearby. He notified other commissaries in the brigade to be alert and to leave a guard with their wagons while in park.[14]

Each succeeding day found the Army of the Potomac plodding farther south in a zigzag pattern dictated in part by the lay of the land and in part by Grant's strategy. Almost daily encounters with the enemy required constant vigilance. On the first of June, Union troops hit the enemy at a place called Cold Harbor. There the Confederates had strongly entrenched and they seemed to be well supplied with artillery capable of sweeping the open field before the trenches. Nevertheless, Warren attempted an attack which resulted in severe losses. As the Union troops fell back, the men took matters in their own hands and dug trenches themselves. For five days the two sides stayed in their trenches with almost continuous fire from batteries and sharpshooters. On the fifth day, Warren attempted another assault with similar murderous results.

During this engagement Towne's wagons came under fire, forcing him to move to what he deemed a safer spot. Then, worn out with moving heavy loads and calming frightened animals, he followed the rule that every veteran knew: "If there is a lull, go to sleep; it may be the only chance for a long time." He woke to discover that he was in the midst of a "big battle." A shell struck one of the ammunition wagons, which burned to the accompaniment of a series of explosions. Another shell struck a caisson and it also exploded. Concluding that the spot was "too hot," Towne moved his wagons still farther to the rear. That put him four miles from where his regiment was engaged. To deliver the evening supplies, he had to load them into one wagon, leave guards with the others, drive part of the way to the front, and leave that wagon with the driver while he walked and carried the rest. A shell burst within two feet temporarily deafening him in one ear. More disconcerting was the fact that relatively few men appeared to receive their rations. Those who did locate him had sad accounts of comrades dead, wounded, or missing.[15]

Following Cold Harbor another reorganization of the Fifth Corps occurred, but the men paid little attention. More significant was the fact that they were on the march again. This time Grant swung his army toward the coast. As the movement began, the quartermasters and commissary sergeants received the good news that the main supply base was moving, too. It was now located at White House on the Pamunkey River. Although not entirely clear then, Towne could see in retrospect what Grant had in mind. He was the first Union commander to comprehend that to crush the rebellion it was necessary to destroy the main army of the Confederacy, Lee's Army of Northern Virginia. The effort to capture Richmond, so long the goal of commanders of the Army of the Potomac, was a will-of-the-wisp. Grant easily had command of greater manpower and far better supplies and transportation, but Lee had the advantage of fighting a defensive war. He had only to hold on long enough to sap the patience of Union supporters. They would, hopefully, in the November election turn Lincoln and the Republicans out of power and elect a peace Democrat who would recognize the Confederacy. The Union must win soon to prevent its own destruction.

Grant, like his men, understood that the rifled bullet had virtually ended the value of frontal assaults. Trenches were the answer to sensible defense, but trench warfare dragged on interminably thereby bringing Grant back to his initial problem. The only solution was to force Lee out of his trenches. Grant's understanding of supply reinforced his goal. He had excellent resources and a good rail system able to deliver all he needed to his army daily. Lee had far fewer resources. The South's agriculture consisted mainly of cotton, corn, and hogs, but even the last two were inadequate to feed an army in the field and cotton was of no value at all. The Union blockade had virtually ended its effort to pay for imports, which could only enter in small quantities brought by blockade runners. Grant's campaign in the West had curtailed supplies from the best source of foodstuffs with the closing of the Mississippi. Southern industry was in its infancy and the railroads of the South consisted largely of a few short lines, often with no connections and largely obsolete equipment. Lee's army had to depend on two main sources of supply: the Shenandoah Valley, the chief wheat-producing region in the seceded states, and some supplies coming up the coast from the deep South by a railroad to Petersburg, downstream from Richmond. Grant proposed to send hard-hitting cavalry to sweep the Shenandoah Valley clean while the main army encircled Petersburg, Virginia, and cut the railroad. Lee, in desperation, would have to come out of his trenches. Then, Grant's superiority in manpower and materials would be sufficient to destroy the rebel army.[16]

At one stop Towne took advantage of his proximity to the main supply base to indulge the men in a little treat. He drew ten and two-thirds canteens of whiskey and doled it out to 325 men. He had no problem finding recipients. As he passed down the line, he was greeted by cheers and laughter when the men saw what he had brought.[17] On June 13, the army crossed the Chickahominy River and headed toward the James River. That night they were so close to the river that Towne heard a steamboat, another thing he had not previously encountered. Despite the dangers and hardships, he enjoyed these new experiences.

The troops were to cross the James on transports. As the boats plied back and forth, men waiting on the banks pulled off their clothes and jumped into the river and romped about like schoolboys playing hooky. Towne laughed as he watched them from the bank where he waited to issue rations when the men emerged from the water. The wagons would cross on a pontoon bridge a mile farther downstream. Once he arrived there, Towne decided, he would have a swim himself. As soon as the 143rd boarded a transport, Towne and his teamsters drove the mile to the point where the engineers were completing the bridge. Towne and his crew shed their garments and took their swim. Towne splashed about hoping the big river would cleanse him somewhat despite his lack of soap and clean garments. He felt refreshed and it allowed him to record another new experience: he had gone swimming in the James River. By the time he donned his clothes, the engineers signaled the wagons to fall in line to cross.[18]

After crossing the James the Army moved quickly to Petersburg. On June 17 and 18, Grant tried two assaults in an effort to probe for a weak place in Lee's defense line. When this effort failed, he put the Army of the Potomac into trenches also. The result was daily skirmishing with periodic exchanges of gunfire by artillery and sharpshooters. It became so commonplace that Towne stopped giving details in his diary beyond the phrase "about the usual fighting" or "shelling as usual."[19]

What did attract Towne's closer attention was his own experiences with supply. With his army before Petersburg, Grant moved the major supply depot to City Point on the confluence of the Appomattox and the James. Rather than attempt to put up a railroad bridge at this point, Grant utilized steamboats. A steamer left City Point in the morning and reached Washington, D.C. by the following morning, but somewhere en route, it passed its companion making the return trip. This provided daily delivery of food, further enlarging the range of offerings. Towne was able to include such items as cabbage, sauerkraut, onions, and vinegar to the customary rations. He also began to receive items from the

Ladies' Aid Societies shipped by the Sanitary Commission. From that source came peaches, cucumbers, pickles, and tomatoes. One day when he discovered that part of the pork was spoiled, he refused to accept it.[20] Things had definitely improved when a regimental commissary could reject an item.

After two months of strenuous marching and fighting most of the men's uniforms and undergarments were virtually rags; hence, company commanders began petitioning supply for clothing. In recognition of the need, clerks at City Point ordered a large quantity of clothing so it that would be ready when the commissaries brought their requisitions. As he worked on his quartermaster's returns for May and June, Towne prepared clothing and camp equipment forms to get the necessary signatures to take with him when he made his daily trip to City Point.[21]

On the last Sunday in June, Towne went to one of the numerous creeks near the camp, bathed, and washed his garments. Whereas he had simply enjoyed himself in good cleansing on the Beverly plantation and in the fun swim in the James, he now examined his legs as he scraped the dirt from them. He quickly ascertained the reason for the soreness; the veins in the calves of both legs were knotted and swollen. He shrugged the matter aside; there was nothing he could do about it now. He merely filed the time of discovery in his mind for future reference, if needed. For the time being he simply appreciated the opportunity to reestablish a measure of respectability by at-least-weekly bathing and laundry.[22]

Part of Towne's haste to get all reports ready up through July and to dispatch them to headquarters was the fact that notification had come that his new assignment had been approved and orders were on their way. On July 16, 1864, his commission as First Lieutenant, Forty-Fifth United States Colored Troops arrived, properly signed by Edwin M. Stanton, Secretary of War, and C. W. Foster, assistant adjutant general in charge of the recruitment and assignment of officers and men of the colored troops. Accompanying the commission was an order for the honorable discharge of "Commissary Sergeant Myron S. Towne" and another directing him to report in person to the commanding officer of Camp William Penn, near Philadelphia.[23]

Towne went immediately to regimental headquarters, where he received his formal discharge and was mustered for six months pay.[24] One thing had not improved: soldiers' wages continued to be inexcusably delayed. After the formalities, Milton Dana and other officers came to offer congratulations and best wishes in an improvised send-off. He was able to tell Dana that he had everything ready up to the middle of July.

On the morning of July 17, Towne completed his usual duties, told "the boys good-bye," and went with the main train to City Point in the usual fashion. There he arranged for passage on the steamer bound for Washington, D.C., scheduled to sail at 10:00 a.m. the following day. That accomplished, he located Walter Jenner and asked to spend the night with him.[25] Jenner was from Forest Lake and had joined the 143rd at the same time as Towne. Jenner, probably upon Towne's recommendation, had been detailed to work in supply and Towne had trained Jenner in the rudiments of the work. After the big base was opened at City Point, Jenner was detailed to work there. They had tented together in the winter of 1864.

While Towne and Jenner reminisced about their experiences, Towne pulled up his pants legs to show Jenner the broken veins and commented on their soreness.[26] Towne had a legalistic turn of mind, and he intended to be ready if he should need a witness to the fact that this ailment arose from conditions in the service. He did not know what might develop with respect to pensions or other emoluments for those with good service records, but he determined to prepare a possible case. However, that was for the future; now he was heading for a new form of service, social as well as military, he hoped.

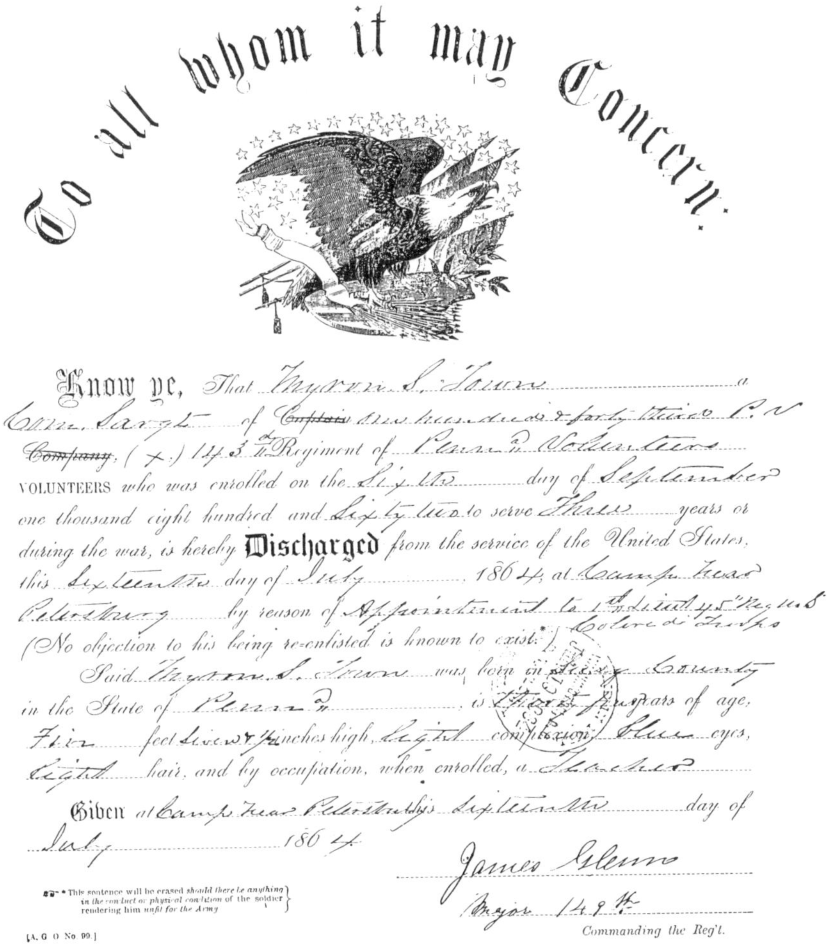

To all whom it may Concern:

Know ye, That Myron S. Towne a Com. Sergt. of ~~Captain~~ One hundred & forty third P.V. ~~Company~~, (✗) 143rd Regiment of Penna Volunteers VOLUNTEERS who was enrolled on the Sixth day of September one thousand eight hundred and sixty two to serve Three years or during the war, is hereby **Discharged** from the service of the United States, this Sixteenth day of July, 1864, at Camp near Petersburg by reason of Appointment to 1st Lieut 45th Reg. U.S. Colored Troops (No objection to his being re-enlisted is known to exist.*)

Said Myron S. Towne was born in [illegible] County in the State of Penna, is [illegible] years of age, Five feet Seven & 1/2 inches high, Light complexion, Blue eyes, Light hair, and by occupation, when enrolled, a Teacher.

Given at Camp near Petersburg this Sixteenth day of July 1864.

James Glenn
Major 149th
Commanding the Reg't.

*This sentence will be erased should there be anything in the conduct or physical condition of the soldier rendering him unfit for the Army.

[A. G. O. No. 99.]

Towne's discharge

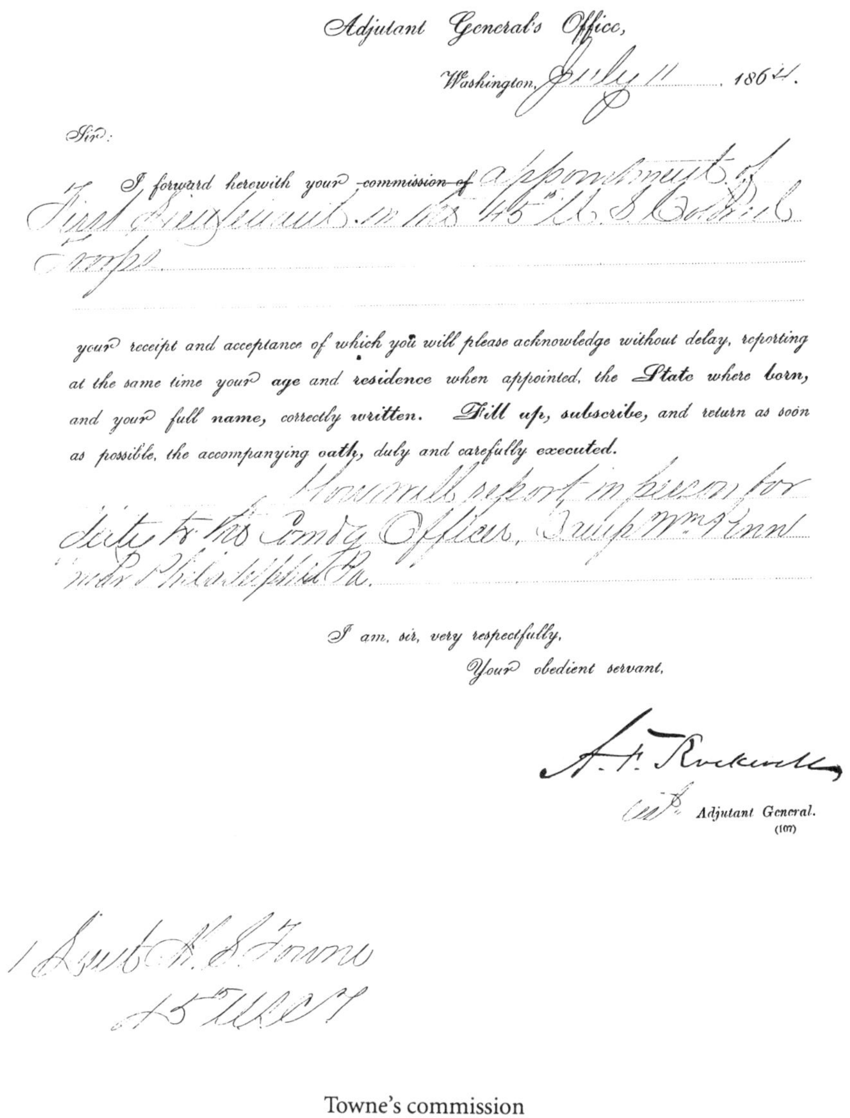

Adjutant General's Office,

Washington, July 11 1864.

Sir:

I forward herewith your ~~commission of~~ appointment of First Lieutenant in the 45th U.S. Colored Troops

your receipt and acceptance of which you will please acknowledge without delay, reporting at the same time your age and residence when appointed, the State where born, and your full name, correctly written. Fill up, subscribe, and return as soon as possible, the accompanying oath, duly and carefully executed.

You will report in person for duty to the Comdg Officer, Camp Wm Penn near Philadelphia Pa.

I am, sir, very respectfully,

Your obedient servant,

A. F. Rockwell

Asst. Adjutant General.

(107)

1 Lieut H. S. Towne

45 USCT

Towne's commission

Chapter Nine

Camp William Penn

At 10:00 a.m., July 18, Towne boarded the daily steamer at City Point bound for Washington, D.C. This was his first experience on a steamboat, and he was determined to learn all that he could and enjoy himself. After the proper officer checked his pass, Towne located a steward and purchased a ticket authorizing him to bunk in a tiny cubicle rather than doing as most of the soldiers did, sleep on the deck. As the soldiers did on marches, they used their blankets, rubber ponchos, and knapsacks as bedding. Towne had done that as well, or slept in his supply wagon, but now he felt entitled to splurge. His new rank and prospect of a better salary encouraged him. That detail accomplished, Towne found a good spot on the deck where he could observe the river and shoreline. The James was wide and muddy from the load of silt accumulated on its way to the sea. Tall pines lined the banks, affording the same air of mystery that he had first noted in The Wilderness.

Next, Towne explored the boat. Newspaper correspondents complained frequently about dirty conditions and unpleasant smells, but to a soldier just out of the trenches, the ship seemed very satisfactory. With his experiences in the commissary department in mind, Towne looked into the dining room. Satisfied that he had seen as much as he could below, he returned to the deck to survey the scenery as it unfolded. At 4:00 p.m., the ship reached Fortress Monroe, where the James emptied into the sea. To

Towne's landlubber eyes the harbor looked large; many boats were docked or moved in or out of the basin. The fort topped a cliff, its row of guns commanding the harbor.

The steamer did not tarry, but swung up the Chesapeake Bay just as the bell sounded to signal the supper hour. Passengers crowded into the dining area for a meal that Towne found quite good, despite criticisms he had read. Compared to what the men in the trenches ate, the ship's food was delicious. As soon as daylight began to fade, he went below to his bunk and enjoyed a restful sleep. Altogether, he characterized it as "a fine night's sail."[1]

The steamboat docked at seven o'clock the next morning. He went to the United States Hotel, another hostelry for soldiers, and obtained a room where he could deposit his gear, clean up, and eat breakfast before starting on his rounds. He presented his pay voucher to Major Taylor, a paymaster in the Adjutant General's Office, who handed over the $143.15 due Towne. No doubt feeling rather good with that much money in his possession, Towne went to Finley Hospital to see his cousin Stanley Warner. Stanley reported that the surgeon had recommended a medical discharge. Towne's next stop was at Carver Hospital where Robert West, another Forest Lake Centre Methodist wounded in The Wilderness, was a patient.[2] Later, Towne took a fast tour of the Capital, noting how the city seemed even more bustling than it was in April. People hurried about bent upon private business and pleasure; one would have fancied the war was over except for the many men in blue uniforms. It was obvious Washington was no longer a city under siege.

Towne boarded a train on the morning of July 20 for Philadelphia. The train began the trip at 7:30 in the morning and arrived at its destination at 1:00 p.m. He went directly to Camp William Penn, as his orders specified. The camp was only a short distance from the city, and the military had built an interurban line to permit easy access, because new recruits came to the camp almost daily. He found that the train stopped directly at the main gate, so he got off, passed the sentry on duty, and went to the commanding officer to report. An aide took down Towne's name, rank, and so forth, and returned shortly to inform him that he was free to go back to the city and spend the night. He should report again early the following morning.[3]

By the time Towne caught the return train to the city, evening was near; therefore, he again went to the United States Hotel, where he obtained lodging and breakfast. At 9:00 a.m. he was officially mustered, assigned to Company F, and told that he was free for the remainder of the day, but to return to William Penn before nightfall. The remainder of the day he spent in Philadelphia. There he made a few purchases and enjoyed seeing the sights of this historic city. He was back in camp in late afternoon and joined the officers at the mess for the first time. There he became acquainted with the men with whom he would be closely associated for a year and a half.[4]

Towne spent his first full day at William Penn familiarizing himself with camp procedures and learning the names and backgrounds of the men in his company. He had understood from the time he volunteered for this particular service that each officer was responsible for training a company. He was then issued a new edition of Casey's *Manual of Tactics.* Towne turned through it quickly because a fellow officer said he thought that it had been edited for the use of colored troops. Towne could not understand why that would be done. True, many of the colored soldiers were illiterate or poorly educated, but tactics had to be taught to any soldiers by example and endless drill. Highly technical manuals were not readable to the average soldier of any color. After a quick perusal Towne concluded the new manual was little different from the one he had studied prior to going to Washington to take the test for his new assignment.

Most of the men of the Forty-Fifth were from Pennsylvania, Maryland, and Virginia.[6] Although, some of the recruits were reluctant to admit it, probably most of those from the slave states were bondsmen. On the other hand, those from Pennsylvania were second or third-generation freemen. However, Towne also soon learned that recruiters would randomly write down a state as the home of a person the recruiters were signing for service. In fact, he hated to admit it, but recruiters from Towne's own state were likely to list as many from Pennsylvania as possible to count against the state's quota under the 1863 conscription law. In any case, Towne felt sure the men would need more time in such details as learning to handle their guns, for "persons of color" as the law classified Negroes, had no right to possess weapons, even if they were not slaves. Part of the freemen might have had some schooling, but those who had been slaves would not. Towne ached to begin classes in the core subjects, but he realized that his immediate task was to teach the tools of war.

Time was at a premium. Victory needed to come soon, since 1864 was the year for presidential elections. Without some indication of success in crushing the rebellion, the electorate would probably replace Lincoln with a so-called "Peace Democrat." Many persons, including Towne and the Army's new commander, General Grant, viewed the unit of United States Colored Troops as the decisive factor. They believed Negroes would be excellent soldiers, if for no other reason than a burning desire to prove their right to freedom and respect as equals.[7]

As he learned camp rules, Towne liked the approach being used by those in charge. For example, the policy required each man as he completed guard duty to discharge his musket at a target. The best shot of the week received a forty-eight-hour pass. In drill competition, the company deemed to have performed best each week was awarded a small rosette for each man in the company, to wear on his breast pocket for the following week. These devices fostered team spirit and served as positive inducements.[8] As a teacher, Towne had preferred rewards to punishments so he applauded these regulations.

Colonel Ulysses Doubleday, brother of General Abner Doubleday, was to command the Forty-Fifth U.S. Colored Troops, but he had not yet arrived at camp when Towne reached William Penn. Lieutenant Colonel Edward Thorn was serving as acting commander. However, Major James T. Bates was the man to see for most things that Towne needed, he discovered. Towne's formal appointment as regimental quartermaster had not yet been made official, but Bates assured Towne that he was to undertake the duties of that officer immediately. That he had complete familiarity with all of the details struck Bates—and he appeared to speak for other officers—as providential. He shoved a mass of requisitions toward Towne and told him to begin ordering.[9]

At that point, Towne discovered he had no commissary sergeant or even an informal assistant to whom he could turn over the detailed clerical work. He must, in effect, be Lieutenant Dana and Sergeant Towne in one. There was no man with the background of higher education, school teacher, and small businessman to be detailed to assist the quartermaster and then promoted to commissary sergeant. The men of his new regiment were poorly educated, if not illiterate. He would watch for those who might be able, with special training, to assist in the office, but for the time being he must do everything himself during the night and off-duty hours. Mornings and much of the afternoons had to be spent in drilling Company F.[10]

If matters were not already complicated enough, Towne found he had to familiarize himself with the protocol of the officer corps. On his first Saturday in camp, he was detailed as Officer of the Day. He consulted his new officer's manual, complete with pictures and diagrams showing how the Officer of the Day wore his sash. To denote his position, he must wear it in scarf style across the right shoulder to the left hip, where it was tied so that the ends extended no more than eighteen inches below the knee. Towne did the best he could, without a mirror, to satisfy the formula, but after his stint ended on Sunday morning, he felt more relaxed. He made the "grand rounds" of inspection and brought out his "raw boys," before being relieved at 10:30 a.m. He went to church in the afternoon to fortify his spirit perhaps for the work before him, but he enjoyed the service tremendously.[11] He was impressed by one significant difference from the men of the regular army. Relatively few of them, even in winter quarters, were likely to attend church services, which were held irregularly because there never seemed to be enough chaplains. The Negro soldiers, Towne realized, literally celebrated the Lord's Day. They sang with a will and voiced emphatic "Amens" to prayers or echoes of what the chaplain said. Those who could, read from the Bible and those who could not, listened closely to Scripture reading on the Sundays when no formal service took place.

At the end of his second week, Towne paid his mess bill, which amounted to $5.04. This in itself was not so much, but it signified that his pay increase as an officer was illusory. Now, he received sixty dollars a month compared to twenty-one as a commissary sergeant, but he must pay for his own food and buy his uniforms.[12] Nevertheless, he did not regret his move. It was not the rank, although he liked it, as much as the sense that at last he was doing more for what he deemed a noble cause. He had willingly volunteered to preserve the Union, but he had come to see the ultimate goal as freedom for the enslaved and their equality before the law. He felt that if he could help the ex-slaves to prove themselves as free and equal, he would be doing a great service.

On August 9, Towne officially became regimental quartermaster. Thorn had finally signed the order on July 31 and sent it to Washington for formal approval. Theoretically, the appointment freed Towne from command of Company F, but he had done so well that he continued to assist in morning drills and in fact became a kind of roving drill instructor to work with other companies in his regiment or other regiments in the camp.[13]

Towne managed to enjoy some leisure. On August 4, he applied for and received a twenty-four-hour pass to go into Philadelphia in the afternoon. He could not forebear to be so close to the city of such historic significance and not see more of it. He caught the afternoon train and reached the city shortly thereafter. He did more sight-seeing and sought a supplier of officers apparel and accessories. There he purchased a sword for the dear price of $15, a belt for $4.30, and a sash for $7. With these treasures, he once again spent the night at the United States Hotel.[14]

Sometime in September the regiment would be sent to the front, so there was much to do in the matter of requisitions, but Towne felt he had things well organized. He posted his July reports and applied for a ten-day furlough so that he might return home for a visit with family and friends while he was stationed relatively close to Susquehanna County. The leave was approved on August 15. He left camp that evening, stayed all night at the United States Hotel, and departed Philadelphia on the 7:15 morning train northward. The train moved slowly along the Delaware and Lackawana's scenic route to Montrose Junction, where he got off. He rented a rig and drove into Montrose, arriving at 9:00 in the evening. Early the next morning he began the familiar trip up the winding road to Forest Lake Centre. It was midmorning by the time he turned into his parents' yard. He sat for a moment gazing over the scene, familiar yet curiously strange. It was so serene on this warm sunny day with a cool breeze blowing gently across the hills. Below him in the pasture Towne's cattle grazed placidly, and in the orchard fruits were ripening or had already been picked. He had been gone for two years, but nothing had changed except himself.[15]

Fortunately, he did not have long to reflect on the anomaly for the watchful eyes of the women had seen him. Out of the house burst Lydia, followed by Phinis and his mother, each a bit slower than the one ahead, but no less eager to greet him. Then, around the corner of the house from the shed came John Towne. Myron felt a sense of shock as he realized his father had closed the blacksmith shop in honor of his son's visit home. Their greeting was a formal handshake and polite expressions of pleasure at seeing each other and inquiries about health, but the soldier realized more fully that father and son were incapable of expressing any deeper feelings to the other. Rachel, Phinis, and Lydia more than compensated.

From that time until his departure, Towne enjoyed a round of visiting with his family and with the Warner relatives in their various homes, feasting, as he termed it, in comparison to the army fare, on all sorts of special treats. One day he drove up to Friendsville to call on Captain Morris, who had received a medical discharge in April, well before Towne left the 143rd. They talked about those who had died on the battlefield or lay wounded in hospitals, some perhaps not to recover. On Saturday, Towne accompanied his father to the Republican township caucus. Those present acclaimed the younger Towne as a local hero. His father was duly chosen justice of the peace again.[16]

Sunday naturally meant that all of Towne's family went to church, where friends and neighbors greeted him warmly. He participated in Sunday School and then took his old familiar place as song leader while his father delivered a discourse on God's support of the Union's noble cause. He prayed long and earnestly for the President, Congress, General Grant, and all of the soldiers. Since John was not alone in having a son in service, the congregation responded with emphatic amens to his close.[17] Myron Towne enjoyed himself, although he felt a little strange, as though this scene belonged in a bygone era.

The high point of the visit home was the trip to Montrose to have family pictures taken. John and Rachel Towne were dressed

John Towne

Rachel Towne

in their Sunday best, and the nature of their attire indicated that they belonged to the prosperous middle class. They might live in a rural community, but they did not look like farmers. They appeared more like a small businessman and his wife. Photography had come a long way since that day in September 1856 when the Townes had sat for daguerreotypes. A new process had appeared soon afterwards which produced the tintype or the more popular card picture. The Civil War cemented the popularity of the card process. The pictures that could be attached to stiff cardboard backing and framed or actually mailed as postcards became the rage. As a loved one left for service, families either took the soldier to a gallery for his picture or begged him when he reached a spot where he could find a photographer to send pictures. In everyone's mind was the thought that the loved one might not return; a picture would be the only thing the family had to memorialize the dead.

Lieutenant Towne's picture at Montrose

Thus, Towne's parents took him to George N. Cobb's gallery. Myron also desired pictures of his family to keep them more clearly in mind. His only regret was that Phinis refused to accompany them, for it was post day. Lydia too was absent, for school was in summer session. Resplendent in his new officer's uniform,

Myron sat for his picture. After they left the photographer's, Towne went to a dentist, who checked the officer's teeth and cleaned them. Towne was impressed with this new evidence of progress which added to the amenities of life. Towne's taste for niceties was growing, though doubtless he did not perceive it.[18]

Tuesday was Towne's last day at home so his parents and sister entertained with a sort of open house. They invited relatives, friends, and neighbors to come by and greet Lieutenant Towne and enjoy cookies and coffee or tea, which his mother and sister, assisted by Lydia, prepared. They worked all morning, but somehow managed to be dressed in good clothes and seem relaxed by the time guests began to arrive. After the last guest departed, the family sat, talked quietly, and then went to bed for Myron would leave early the next morning for Montrose to take the train back to Philadelphia.[19]

It was an all-day trip; he arrived in the city at 7:00 p.m. Once more he sought lodging in the now familiar hotel and caught the early train to Camp William Penn. It had been a pleasurable interlude in the turmoil of war, but now it was time to do his work, "as usual," as he phrased it. He worked hard to complete his August returns, took his turn as Officer of the Day, and volunteered to assist in drilling new recruits, who arrived in large numbers as September approached. So large was the camp population becoming that when Towne went to church on August 28, he found such a crowd that he could not get inside the chapel.[20]

Chapter Ten

From Petersburg to Appomattox

ORDERS FOR THE TROOPS IN DRILL CAMP to go to the front arrived at Camp William Penn in mid-September. Although Towne had been making preparations since his return from Susquehanna County, there were many last-minute details to handle. He must inventory all stores charged to his regiment and go to Philadelphia to arrange transportation and requisition food for the journey. Still, without a commissary sergeant or even a clerk-assistant, he appealed to Major Bates to detail a quartermaster sergeant to work with Towne. Bates responded by ordering Sergeant Allen W. Catterdon to act as Towne's assistant in the Quartermaster's Department.[1] This was a temporary expedient, but it worked for some time.

On September 15, General William Birney came to the camp for a ceremony that marked the end of drill camp and signified that the regiments leaving for the front were no longer recruits but regular soldiers. He presented each regiment with a flag and he made a speech deemed suitable for the occasion in which he stressed the importance of the colors and the obligation to keep them out of enemy hands. Probably all of that meant little to soldiers who were born slaves, but they listened attentively with the rest and joined in the customary three cheers for the general as he concluded and their lower officers gave the signal. Then as they paraded in formal review, he took their salutes, complimented their officers on the men's good performance, and departed.[2] As it transpired, this was not the last encounter these regiments had with Birney. After reaching Petersburg, they were placed in Birney's division and found him a true friend of the colored soldier.

The next three days were devoted to breaking camp, and at 9:00 a.m., September 20, 1864, Towne stood by the train to Philadelphia checking each man of the Forty-Fifth as he boarded to ensure he had his proper supplies. Then Towne and other officers boarded the train. At Philadelphia they directed their charges onto a train for Baltimore. In his more recent trips on personal missions, Towne had ridden on regular passenger trains and had observed with approval how much progress had been made in a short time: trains were faster, the tracks were smoother, and even the cars and engines were larger. He had forgotten how poor the troop trains were in comparison. Apparently, the commercial lines allocated the oldest cars and poorest engines to the military to transport large numbers of soldiers. This time the train made frequent stops due to equipment failures or to take sidings to allow passenger trains or freights to have the main line. They did not reach Baltimore until the following morning.[3]

At Baltimore, Towne and the other regimental quartermasters learned that the transports assigned to carry the troops to City Point would not sail until nine that night, thereby giving the men and officers alike an entire day in the city. Officers conferred and decided that they could, as Towne was quick to point out, trust their men to keep out of trouble. Indeed, Towne felt a sense of relief that he was not responsible for some of the men from his old unit; they would have gotten into all sorts of mischief. On the other hand, Negroes had so long been intimidated that they knew even if free, they would be blamed for anything amiss that might happen. Furthermore, since most of them were from rural areas, as in the case of perhaps two-thirds of his men, they would be even more nervous about a city. Hence, he cautioned his group, the companies he had trained, to do some sightseeing in the business district during daylight hours and to report to the dock area as the sun began to set. He promised he would be there to assist them in lining up to board the boats and handle any problems. Other officers did the same and began to leave on their own errands.

Towne had been through Baltimore on previous occasions, but had seen little of the city beyond the railroad line, so he set off to explore. First, he decided to locate a photographer's studio. That was not difficult, for photographers gravitated to places where soldiers were likely to be found in large numbers such as cities that were major points of departure. He discovered that Catterdon and two other young noncommissioned officers had kept Towne in sight. He was their superior so they apparently rationalized that they should be near enough to run his errands or whatever he might ask. In truth, he guessed they did not quite trust themselves in this big, strange city. With his characteristic compassion and understanding of the ways of youth, he stopped and invited them to join him if they so desired. They definitely did and when they learned his destination was a picture gallery, they expressed eagerness for a chance to have their pictures made to send to family members and friends.

Towne and his assistants located a gallery that looked promising. It operated as Israel and Company. The photographer welcomed them, posed each one carefully, and then offered a group picture for a small, additional fee.[4] Towne, to whom the others deferred because of his rank and age, agreed. In today's army such fraternization between an officer and his noncommissioned assistants would be considered improper, but the Civil War army was less rank-conscious.

By dusk, officers began to assemble their men for boarding at the appointed time. As he observed the *Rebecca Benton,* the ship assigned to his troops, Towne thought it did not look impressive

Towne's Baltimore photograph

in comparison with the steamer he had taken in July to Washington, D.C. This again called attention to the disparity between accommodations now being provided for individual travelers, in uniform or not, and what was made available to the military.

After boarding and getting his men settled, Towne restated his first opinion of the ship. "A poor boat," he characterized the transport.[5] The officers grumbled among themselves; they wondered if this leaky tub which appeared worse than the average troop transport was an indication of the attitude of Washington authorities toward the colored troops. In any case, the *Rebecca Benton* remained afloat (although sometimes it seemed about to capsize) until it reached Newport News. The trip took all night and the next day. Finally, the ship's crew cast anchor and the men spent the night on board, even though they desired to be off the ship. The following morning the boat started up the James. The broad, smooth river made that portion of the trip more pleasant.

At 4:00 p.m. the ship reached City Point. The regimental commanders hurried to headquarters to report the arrival of their units, while company officers supervised the unloading of the men and their gear. Towne seemed to be needed everywhere at the same time to check all regimental property against his inventories. The men had consumed their rations and had nothing in the way of food; therefore, he had to draw more food while at City Point. The entire trip had taken longer than Towne's directives had indicated in relation to rations he was to issue, and the men were hungry. It was Towne's experience that hungry soldiers were less than good material, and to report to the front and have no food was a bad introduction to the battle zone.[6]

With the return of the top regimental officers, Towne, being a staff member, quickly learned that headquarters seemed to have forgotten that these units had been ordered to report for duty. Headquarters had made no provisions for the units; no one seemed to know to which corps they were to be attached or which segment of the line where they were to be sent, much less the elementary matter of rations. Towne managed to get enough food for his regiment largely through his old connections in City Point. He signed orders as though he had full authority to do so, and no one challenged him. The men built fires, cooked, ate, and went to sleep on their ponchos and blankets.

By morning someone in the provost marshal's office directed the new arrivals to the Tenth Corps, but as they started for that portion of the trenches, they were recalled and told instead to report to Benjamin Butler's command. His corps occupied an area known as the Bermuda Hundred north of the James River.[7] Towne and his fellow officers, much less their men, did not know that Butler was a less-than-astute general. When Grant first became commander of all the armies of the United States, he wanted to replace both Butler and Franz Sigel. From reviewing their records, Grant concluded that they were both simply incompetent. Washington immediately vetoed Grant's demand. Both generals were untouchable; Sigel because he was a German-American and the considerable number of German immigrants in key states in the North would regard such a move as ethnically motivated, and Butler because he was the darling of leading Republicans in Congress. They lauded Butler as suitably tough toward rebels, although in retrospect it seems that Butler's toughness was more the result of sheer want of good manners than political considerations. As Grant had feared, both men had failed in their execution of the parts assigned to them in Grant's strategy by which he had hoped to smash Lee's army in a three-pronged thrust and end the war in the late summer of 1864.

As a result, Grant was forced to continue the protracted siege of Petersburg. The new arrivals were little aware of such matters; the men of the Forty-Fifth were more interested in the fact that Colonel Ulysses Doubleday had joined them. They were drawn up in review to greet him and he made a speech which endeared him to everyone. He treated his troops as if he saw no difference in their appearance and had complete confidence in their ability, courage, and willingness. They responded with spontaneous cheering. He added to their delight by telling them that they would be a part of General Birney's division. They felt that they had two friends in the higher echelons. They knew they had more than one lesser officer whom they could trust, and they soon learned that Doubleday would straighten out any problem with an officer who was less than good. One company had a captain who was simply not wholly competent to do the job assigned to him. He created a ridiculous situation in which he promoted and demoted corporals and sergeants in such number that, as Doubleday said, every member of the company had held one or both noncommissioned ranks. Doubleday ordered the captain to change his tactics.[8]

Meanwhile, the Forty-Fifth was about to have its first taste of battle. Grant had decided to bypass Butler by ordering him to detach Birney's division to join General O. C. Ord's corps to attack Fort Harrison, a fortification at the far end of Lee's line. To take it would force Lee's trenches inward and menace still more his already weak supply lines. As Towne checked on all the details, he congratulated himself that he had not held back and accepted any ordnance doled out. When he requisitioned ordnance for his regiment, he had insisted on new Springfield rifles. He checked some at random, firing them to see if they performed properly before he accepted them. As he issued marching rations, he added words of confidence and encouragement to each man. Then he followed with his supply wagons.[9]

Towne feared the slaughter that he felt would follow any assault on a fortified position. Birney's division would have to advance across an open field under the fire of the big guns and the muskets of the garrison which occupied the fort. In an almost unbelievable fashion, the men advanced at doublequick, nimbly sidestepping shells, and leaped into the ditch which protected the fort on the front. That freed them from the danger of the big guns, for they were under the cannon. The men scaled the ramparts and jumped down shooting and bayoneting defenders, who turned out to be few in number and easily demoralized. Grant's spies had told him correctly that this was a weak point despite its facade of strength.

Once the defenders surrendered in disbelief that Federal troops, especially Negro regiments, could carry out such a daring assault, Birney's men decided to celebrate in their own way. After rounding up prisoners, they raised the United States flag and joyously sang "Rally 'Round the Flag."[10] Birney's division was soon relieved of garrison duty and returned to the trenches, but they had proved to themselves and to any doubters that they could fight as well as the race which so long had held the Negroes in subjugation. Grant undoubtedly took note and marked this unit as one which was above average. In early October, Grant sent the brigade, now commanded by Doubleday, to make several probes of Lee's line in search of a weak spot. Two probes produced what Towne termed respectively a "sharp fight" and a "right smart fight."[11] Neither made significant gains, but each resulted in a few casualties and some prisoners. The latter led to a sharp exchange between Grant and Lee, when Grant learned that members of the U.S. Colored Troops were being used by Confederates to strengthen the very fortifications which they had just attacked. Grant wrote to Lee citing such treatment as violation of the military code.

Several exchanges took place between the commanders. Lee first attempted to use the incident as an opening wedge in a plea for prisoner exchange. This was something Grant did not desire, for he knew of the Confederates' desperation for men. Every returned prisoner was immediately put into Lee's trenches. Federals could not play that game, because those held in the infamous Confederate prisons like Andersonville and Libby were so malnourished and diseased that they could not be rehabilitated in most cases. Instead of agreeing to that unappealing proposition, Grant asked Lee to guarantee that prisoners from the colored units would be included in the exchange. Lee, in effect, said no, because anyone who was the property of a Confederate citizen would be returned to the owner. Since southern laws permitted no testimony of colored persons against a white person, any person who wanted a slave could claim a captured soldier as a fugitive, the property of the claimant. Therefore, Grant reiterated that all United States troops must receive the same treatment.

Lee continued to lecture Grant about the merits of slavery and the sacredness of the right of property. Grant refused to budge. He closed the exchange with the statement, "My duty is to protect all persons received into the Army of the United States regardless of color or nationality."[12] Towne and others, in uniform and not, applauded Grant's firmness and became more convinced of the righteousness of the Union cause.

Grant exerted his influence to see that soldiers cast their ballots in the national election. In the day before absentee voting existed, the only way to do this seemed to be to allow the men to vote by regiments and their commanders to dispatch the ballots to the soldiers' home precincts by way of Washington, D.C. Two complications immediately surfaced. One was simple and Grant was able to overcome it; the other was insurmountable.

The first was that those holding desk jobs in the War Department feared the men of the Army of the Potomac would vote for their onetime commander, General McClellan, and not Lincoln. Grant pointed to the fact that there had been too many commanders since McClellan to make any difference by 1864. In any case, Grant had confidence in the men at the front: their loyalty was to victory not the pasteboard peace advocated by the Democrats in the campaign.[13]

The second difficulty was that the election cut out most of the colored soldiers. Except for five New England states, most northern states did not provide for Negro votes. Hence, most free Negroes had no voting precinct and obviously those from slave states, whether ex-slaves or freemen, had no vote. If they were escapees from states in rebellion, there was no place to send the ballots. Therefore, few members of the U.S. Colored Troops voted in 1864. Towne and other firm supporters of equal rights understood, but vowed to do what they could to remedy the situation nationwide once the Union had been restored.

One small step in the direction of the actual elimination of slavery came on November 1, 1864, when Maryland's constitution prohibiting slavery went into effect. This was especially meaningful to members of the Forty-Fifth, many of whom came from that state. General Birney, mindful of that fact and of the hope the action offered to all of his troops, issued a special order congratulating "the brave men" of his command, "who were once slaves." His heart was "filled with joy," as he contemplated the day when all slaves would be freed by the "justice and gratitude of the American people." That there were certain implications here that later generations would deplore, does not detract from the sincerity of his sentiments. Doubleday added similar statements to his order of the day directing that appropriate ceremonies be held to commemorate this "grand and cheering act of justice."[14]

With Lincoln safely reelected, Grant was free to reshuffle commands and effectively eliminate Butler and his scrambling of orders. Birney's division went to the Twenty-Fifth Corps composed entirely of Colored Troops, except for the artillerymen and cavalry attached to it. The commander, General Godfrey Weitzel, proved another officer who treated his men with fairness irrespective of race.

For the remainder of 1864, Birney's division went into winter quarters and rotated duty in the trenches or on the picket line. Winter quarters meant tents behind the lines and out of artillery range. For a regimental quartermaster the onslaught of winter brought the need for heavier clothing for the troops, which required procuring the usual requisitions, garnering of signatures from company commanders, and completing endless forms. Towne spent hours at his field desk in his tent entering the proper numbers in the respective columns and writing over and over the reasons for the orders to which he responded, "To clothe and equip the Company."[15] Paperwork and trips back and forth to City Point permitted Towne little time for himself. Entries in his diary became chiefly notes to remind himself of reports due or similar things. One cold, wet day made him realize the need to make his tent tighter against rain and wind squalls characteristic of the central Virginia coast in winter. After completing that task, he relaxed by writing more fully in his diary and writing a letter to his family.[16] In February, Grant ordered Birney's division to leave the Bermuda Hundred and march across the James to join the Army of the Potomac in the main trenches before Petersburg.

Accompanying the orders came the announcement that Doubleday had been promoted to brigadier general and Major Theodore Glazier named commander of the Forty-Fifth Regiment. Since he had been acting commander since Doubleday became commander of the brigade, it made little difference, but the men cheered spontaneously. Towne spent the remainder of the day and all of the following preparing for the march. He located and checked weapons, supervised their loading, and assigned drivers and directed them into the line of march. Rain began as the troops started, but they reached the new position without incident and settled into trenches.

During most of March nothing changed; the men of the Forty-Fifth and companion regiments were still in the trenches before Petersburg, although at a point closer to that city. On the twenty-eighth, word went to the trenches to the effect that under cover of darkness they were to withdraw by units, leaving only pickets, sharpshooters, and artillerymen on duty, for an important announcement. Even the officers felt mystified, although most assumed the long-awaited attack was at last to begin. Much to everyone's amazement the officer of the day read the official order from General Birney saying that President Lincoln and General Grant would arrive the following morning to review the troops. Towne learned later that the President had come to City Point to confer with the General and decided while there to visit certain troops. The men of the Forth-Fifth were so excited by the prospect of seeing their two chief heroes that some of the company commanders worried that the men might fail to do the proper things in a formal review, but Towne had confidence. He had already observed Grant's relaxed manner; if the President lived up to his reputation for informality, the soldiers would feel at ease. This proved correct. Towne had only a brief glimpse of the distinguished visitors and no basis for judgements. The President and the General rode by the review line, complimented Birney's command, and went on to review other units.

Grant ordered the long-awaited assault to begin. At the word "Charge!" the men raced forward, their muskets blazing. At first they faced sharp fire from the defenders, but Birney's men did not falter. They stormed the first line of trenches and leaped into the second. They had no time to look at what was happening on either side of their segment, but they had the impression that all along the intricate lines of trenches the same thing was taking place. The attack had succeeded; resistance had crumpled. There was only a token force of Confederates remaining in the trenches. Lee's main army had fled in the night. No longer did the men in blue feel bitterness or desire for vengeance. They did not kill the defenders; they called, "Drop your arms, hands up," and similar messages and the Confederates replied promptly and even jovially, "You got me, Yank," and surrendered. The victors did the usual things like gather ammunition and muskets, haul artillery guns from their mountings, and round up prisoners.[17]

The men, cautiously at first, fearful of entrapment, moved into the deserted camps behind the trenches. Once the Federals were sure that the enemy had moved elsewhere, the scene took on a circus atmosphere. Soldiers began to go over the camps taking whatever they saw and wanted. It was a mad scramble for souvenirs. Mindful of numerous stern lectures against looting, some of Towne's men looked at him hesitantly. A few summed up the thought of the many that it was not really looting, for "Johnny" had left it behind, so he likely did not want it. Towne smiled at the ingenious reasoning and agreed with the logic as he gave his assent to a little scavenging. He confessed to himself that he could hardly do less since he was busily going through books and papers himself. This particular camp had been occupied by a North Carolina regiment so Towne located an officer's tent with his desk. There Towne selected two books, *Regulations of the Army of the Confederate States, 1864*, and *Manual of Instructions for Volunteers and Militia of the Confederate States, 1862.* He dropped them in his knapsack for later study. He hoped to ascertain if the rebels had discovered any new approaches to military organization and instruction or had they merely, as he suspected, reissued United States army manuals with new title pages.

Towne spotted a copy of the *Richmond Examiner* for Friday, March 24, 1865, which he also pocketed. He picked up some Confederate money and stamps and the company's muster roll. At a glance, it showed a large number of soldiers marked absent without explanation, suggesting that desertion was rife. Finally, he located the principal object of his search, the quartermaster's invoice of stores. Towne confiscated that for the insight it would provide into the state of Lee's supplies. With these discoveries in his safekeeping, Towne located his men with the warning that they must bring their treasures with them, get the wagons, and be ready to move behind their division as it marched into the city. Grant had already ordered Birney's division with Doubleday's brigade in the lead to go into Petersburg. This was a magnificent gesture on Grant's part, Towne concluded, for there was really nothing in the city worth anything to the Union Army. Nonetheless, to select an all-colored division to take the city so long under siege not only displayed Grant's determination that southerners must recognize the new order, but also marked his desire to let the men of the colored troops, segregated though they might be, know that they were a vital part of the Army, respected and appreciated.

The abandonment of the trenches by Lee's men might appear to indicate that the assault had failed, but that was not true. Grant's objective from the beginning of rebel entrenchment had been to force Lee out of the trenches and into the open field where Grant's vast superiority in manpower would be decisive. Underlying Lee's move was the fact that his supply sources had been closed because Phil Sheridan and his cavalry swept the Shenandoah Valley bare and Sherman cut the railroads from the Deep South. Consequently, Petersburg no longer had any value to Lee, and he could not remain the trenches as his supplies ran out. Now Grant had to catch Lee before he could get away.

While Grant worked out his strategy the troops rested and Towne studied the materials he had taken from the abandoned North Carolina camp. He consulted first what he regarded as his chief find, the inventory of stores. At his first glance he raised his eyebrows in disbelief. The invoice was dated September 19, 1864; it had been filled out and signed, but not filed with headquarters. It was marked "original copy to be forwarded," so it was not a case of keeping a duplicate record as Towne himself did. Furthermore, forms for each of the interceding months were with this September statement, but no attempt had been made to begin work on them much less complete them. Was this a case of simple dereliction of duty on the part of this officer or had disorganization become so great that as early as September a quartermaster had regarded it as useless to send reports? Towne obviously could not answer his own query, but he guessed that the Confederate government, always a fragile thing, was crumbling like the poor paper on which the report forms had been printed.

When Towne turned to his purloined copy of the *Richmond Enquirer,* he found more food for thought. The flimsy single sheet, printed on both sides and folded in half, aroused his contempt. He had never doubted the excellence of the southerner as a soldier or the sincerity of his support of his cause, mistaken as Towne regarded it. However, he had little respect for the political leaders of the rebellion. After reading the paper coming out of the Confederate capital and obviously reflecting the views of the government, Towne concluded they were deliberately misleading their own people and subjecting them to privation and destruction in a callous disregard for truth.

A major story in the paper heralded the inevitability of war between the United States and France. "Thinking men of the North were well aware of the need to recognize" Maximilian's regime, but the "Black Republican administration" persisted in its "futility and insanity." All the war news given appeared in glowing generalities, telling southerners how well everything was with their side. "Our losses from all causes have been almost nothing ... that of our enemy ... severe in men and guns, enormous in government property, and utterly incalculable in the routes of transportation." At that Towne laughed as he thought of how smoothly he had traveled on railroads and steamboats from Virginia to northern Pennsylvania in the past year, while Union armies had virtually destroyed all railroads in the Confederacy and the major rivers were likewise in Federal hands. The column listing slaves "taken by enemy armies" or "enticed" out of their owners' possession, who were being held for their owners to repossess, filled Towne with rage. Some of "his boys"—as he fondly called members of his regiment whom he had helped to train—might be in such a situation. Here was where Towne had no mercy; again he tended to blame a small group of big slave owners, the "slave-ocracy," for having defied all reason in their determination to preserve the wicked institution.[18] He failed to credit the role played by the great mass of nonslaveholders who supported slavery as determinedly as any slave owner.

The pursuit of Lee had to begin quickly or he might escape to the Blue Ridge Mountains, where he and other fleeing Confederates could continue guerrilla fighting for months or years. Grant reasoned that Lee would try to follow either the Richmond and Danville Railroad or the Southside Railroad, which crossed the first line at Burkeville and went on to Lynchberg. Therefore, Grant ordered Ord's command to Burkeville and Meade's to Lynchberg.

Lee's immediate goal was Farmville on the Appomattox River, where he believed he would find supplies awaiting him that had been despatched to Appomattox Station on the Southside Railroad. With Union forces close behind him, Lee ordered the last troops who crossed the Appomattox River to destroy the bridges. Ord too recognized the importance of the bridges, so he directed Birney's division to swing around the rest of the corps and beat the Confederates to the river. Despite fast, forced marching, they reached it as the Rebel rear detachment started to cut the wagon bridge, the last one remaining. A sharp fight ensued, but the arrival of Doubleday's brigade, including the Forty-Fifth, turned the tide in favor of the Federals, who held the bridge. Lee halted to turn and support his rear but saw Meade's army arriving from a different direction and realized he was about to be caught in a trap, so he abandoned his beleaguered rear guard and raced for Appomattox Station.[19]

Birney ordered a brief rest for his tired, hungry troops. Towne and other regimental quartermasters quickly handed out rations: coffee, dried beef, and crackers. The men made fires to heat coffee in which they soaked crackers and then used more crackers to encase slices of beef in a kind of sandwich. Then they were ready for another march. While quartermasters reloaded wagons and pulled to the side to follow the marchers, a courier arrived and handed General Birney an order. Brigadier General R. H. Jackson would replace Birney as commander of the division. There was no explanation for this change. At any other time it might have damaged the morale of the men in the division who admired him greatly, but now it made little difference. The war, they felt certain, was almost ended. Temporarily the division was assigned to R. S. Foster's command.[20]

Meanwhile, Grant sent Sheridan and his fast cavalry around the line of march to reach Appomattox Station and capture the supplies in boxcars there. Lee received word of Sheridan's success and realized there was no hope left. His hungry, ragged men were deserting in droves; many simply tossed aside their muskets and headed for their homes. Grant suggested in a note to Lee that it was time for the latter to surrender. Lee attempted to negotiate on the false premise that he might win at the bargaining table what he had failed to achieve on the battlefield, but Grant countered that there would be no conditions attached to surrender. With no avenue of escape left, Lee capitulated. He asked to meet with Grant, who told Lee to select the place and time.

While waiting for Lee's reply, Grant prepared for all eventualities. Should Lee reject the terms or some hothead on either side ignore the flag of truce and start shooting, Grant intended to be so strong that Lee could not escape again. Therefore, he directed Meade and Ord to continue to move around Appomattox Station and take up positions near the village known as Appomattox Courthouse. Lee had chosen the home of Wilmer McLean at Appomattox Courthouse as the meeting place. Grant further ordered that a wagon train loaded with entrenching tools be at McLean's farm. The wagon train, he directed, was to come from the division of colored troops attached since February to Ord's corps. This, once more, represented Grant's notice of this division as an especially capable unit, well trained, and very determined.

What Grant did not know was that repeated long marches and recent hard fighting had left the equipage in bad condition. As

Foster took command, he viewed wagons and draft animals and made angry, disparaging remarks in which he implied that this was proof of want of care on the part of colored soldiers and their white officers. One has the feeling that Foster did not want to command this unit. To make things worse there was no divisional quartermaster, except an acting official, Lieutenant Dilwyn V. Purington, who gave Foster an even worse report on the "unserviceable" wagons and teams. Purington offered a solution. He could cull the best equipment and take it to Appomattox. The rest he would abandon on the Lynchburg road.

Headquarters would have none of this, and sent a new directive to Foster. Purington must immediately return all unserviceable wagons and animals to Burkeville while a regimental quartermaster took the train ordered by the commanding general to Appomattox. At this point, Doubleday, as brigade commander, seems to have argued that the quartermaster of his former regiment, Lieutenant Myron S. Towne, of the Forty-Fifth, was the one who could handle wagons, animals, and men to the maximum advantage. Therefore, the order read, "Lt. Myron S. Towne, quartermaster of the Forty-Fifth regiment," would command the wagon train to Appomattox, "by order of General Grant." That did not mean that Grant had personally selected Towne, but that Grant's aides had accepted General Doubleday's endorsement.[21]

For years thereafter, Towne delighted in recounting the surrender as he saw it. He marched his train at a fast pace and arrived early in the morning on April 9 at the McLean farm. He directed his wagoners to pull into the space which officers already on duty there designated. Towne had his wagons grouped around an apple tree so that the draft animals had shade and also space to graze. Some of the men scaled the tree, which afforded a view of the dooryard of the house some distance from their position. Towne remained on his horse, which also served as a vantage point. The wagon train was in position just in time for the men to witness the arrival of Lee and the Union officer who had conducted the Confederate general through Meade's lines. Lee wore a new uniform which displayed so much glittering gold braid and buttons that they dazzled in the bright Virginia sun, a jewelled sword, and a fancy silken sash. Towne felt that Lee's attire was almost repellent in its elegance. How could Lee be so arrayed when his men were in rags?[22]

Lee swept into the house, and apparently nothing else happened inside, because the guards returned to their stations by the door and the gate. Soon, a group of horsemen rode into view, causing the men in the tree almost to lose hold of the branches to which they clung as they tried to see General Grant and his escort. As usual, Grant rode his big horse at an easy lope that covered a lot of ground in a short time. His staff leaned forward urging their mounts to go faster in an effort to keep up. Grant wore his customary private's uniform with his lieutenant general's shoulder straps. His boots and trouser legs bore spots of Virginia clay. To Towne this clearly said that Grant felt there were more important things to do that morning than to send back to his quarters for his dress uniform and a fancy sword. Later, Towne liked to tell an audience, "Grant was the real gentleman, not the Virginia aristocrat." There spoke prejudiced judgment, but in a way the contrast Towne had observed was what the Civil War signified.

Observers outside the McLean house did not have long to wait until Lee came out, climbed on his horse, and rode away. Then, a Union officer appeared on the porch and read a brief statement to the effect that Lee had surrendered the Army of Northern Virginia. The troops drawn up along the road went wild as they cheered and hugged each other, and some shot their muskets into the air and a few artillery canon boomed. Towne's men had a different idea. One man grabbed an ax from a wagon and began to chop on the trunk of the apple tree; several other men joined him and soon felled the tree. Then, they chipped little pieces from the bark and tucked them into knapsacks or pockets. Many infantrymen nearby joined in picking up bits already chipped off the trunk or branches. Some men used their big knives to whittle a piece of tree to a size to fit into an envelope to carry or mail home. Towne smiled, but shook his head; the tree had nothing to do with the surrender yet it had been chopped down just the same.[23] With his love of fruit trees, Towne regretted the loss of this pretty tree. Its sacrifice seemed pointless.

Towne assumed he was to take his wagons back to the main wagon train, but by the time he got his excited teamsters calmed and ready to begin the trip, Purington appeared. He brought an order from Foster that as soon as Grant's aides released the siege train, Purington would take charge. Towne was to pick up the unserviceable wagons and animals and take them to Petersburg by "easy stages." Towne smiled pleasantly and agreed that he would be glad to do that provided he could take more men from the Forty-Fifth with him. Purington was more than agreeable; one guesses that he was as bothered by the men as he was by the worn out nags.

Towne rode quickly back to where the bad equipage was parked. As soon as the infantry who followed him arrived, he put details to work at different tasks. Some took scythes and rakes from one wagon and went into the grassy fields along the road to cut forage. Another group got hammers and nails and made elementary repairs on some of the worst wagons. Teamsters unharnessed the drooping teams and let them graze and drink from a nearby creek. Towne walked around giving tired animals a rub and pat here and there. Then, the men tethered the animals and made themselves comfortable around a campfire, where coffee was soon boiling to make even field rations palatable to any veteran.

By dawn, Towne had his force on the move. With plenty of rest and food, and the wagon loads lighter and more evenly balanced, the animals made better time. Forty-eight hours after the main wagon train reached Petersburg, Towne and his supposedly unserviceable equipment reported.[24] Purington was amazed and admitted it. He asked how Towne had brought in fairly good equipment in place of the derelicts left on the road. Towne explained that the wagons needed more work, but were reparable. As for both men and animals, he let them travel at their own pace. He never knew whether Purington learned a lesson from the incident.

On one point all of the officers of the Second Division agreed: the men had shown coolness under fire and "commendable spirit." If Foster had been initially rather condescending toward the nonwhite soldier, he had changed his view. He admitted that he was surprised by the absence of stragglers and the cheerfulness with which the men endured long and rapid marches. They understood the "importance of our movements" and did their "utmost to insure our success." Another officer put it more bluntly: "It should forever put to rest any doubt about the ability of colored troops"; they had proved themselves "to be a body of men upon whom the government may safely rely."[25] Grant had undoubtedly long before come to this opinion. Now, he was about to use these troops in a project which should be the final chapter in the War of the Rebellion.

Chapter Eleven

The Texas Border

One day after Lee's surrender, General Ord ordered the division of colored troops, of which the Forty-Fifth was a part, to return to the Twenty-Fifth Corps, then occupying Petersburg. It was to that point that Towne brought the supposedly unserviceable wagons and draft animals. When he arrived at the main wagon train, he found that the men who had preceded him suffered a letdown from the rejoicing on the day of surrender. For one thing, heavy rain had begun the day they started the march to Petersburg. Slogging through mud when there was a war to be won was one thing, but to do so now that the war was over made little sense. Thoughts of going home filled the minds of those who had homes and families; for others there were plans for getting established as freemen. The men felt almost intuitively that they must act quickly while the former master race was quelled in the South and people of the North remembered the fine showing made by Negro soldiers.

Word of the assassination of President Lincoln added a dimension of shock and grief to the picture. The prompt decision to name their camp, between Richmond and Petersburg, Camp Lincoln pleased the men; however, they desired to quit it soon.[1]

Meanwhile, Grant was still supreme military commander in a situation which was not precisely war or peace. Lee had surrendered the main army of the Confederacy, but certain other small detachments had not technically laid down their arms and taken an oath not to resume the fight. The officials of the self-proclaimed Confederate States of America were in flight, but that did not mean that the states which had by legislative action declared their severance from the United States were now back in the Union or even in good standing. Some troops seemed to be needed in the former rebellious states. To complicate the picture still more was the presence of French troops in Mexico, sent by Napoleon III to establish a puppet regime there as either a step to annexation or as a French dependency.

The United States government had long accepted President Monroe's statement of 1823 as a rule to follow in dealing with the western hemisphere. Consequently, Secretary of State William Seward kept reminding Napoleon he must withdraw French troops from Mexico. If this happened, Maximilian and his claims to be emperor would collapse quickly, for Mexicans were in revolt against the foreigners. While the Civil War continued Napoleon could ignore American protests. Now, Seward argued, with the war ended the United States should back its notes with a force of veterans stationed on the border. Grant felt even more strongly that the rebellion would remain "unfinished business" until Maximilian, who had certainly been encouraged by the Confederacy, was overthrown. Grant, therefore, agreed to place fifty thousand troops from the victorious eastern armies on the Rio Grande. He chose General Philip Sheridan to command the force and the Twenty-Fifth Corps commanded by Weitzel to make up more than half of the total.[2]

Today's historians generally view the decision as linked to racist sentiments. In 1865 racial prejudice was not considered the axiomatic answer to all matters pertaining to the Negro race, but it clearly existed in certain quarters in the Union army as well as elsewhere in the free North. Certain classic examples can be found in reports made by high ranking officers to their superiors. For example, Major General George L. Hartsuff reported in mid-May that the "citizens of Petersburg" complained that colored soldiers participated "in the exciting of the colored people to acts of outrage against the persons and property of white citizens." Ord, under whom the Second Division had served in the last campaign which captured Petersburg and drove Lee to surrender, branded the Twenty-fifth Corps "undisciplined" and said it "offended the white community." He offered the standard charge that the members of the colored troops had been guilty of several "atrocious rapes." Then, he turned his wrath on their officers, by claiming that the colored troops were products of a "want of discipline and good officers."[3]

There is no doubt that these reports correctly detailed the attitude of southern white people, but that some Union officers, who should have defended their soldiers, sided with their recent enemies and accepted all charges as true clearly smacked of racism. However, other officers staunchly defended all United States troops regardless of color or race. Officers of the Twenty-Fifth reacted angrily. Among themselves they said that Ord was jealous of the accomplishments of the Second Division, which outshone his own men in the Petersburg to Appomattox campaign, so he tried to find some way to destroy the fine image of these men. Towne was one of those especially angered. He would gladly testify, if ever required to do so, that the soldiers of his regiment were as good as any in the army.

Weitzel wrote to Grant, strongly defending his troops: "The behavior of my entire corps during the last month has been most excellent," he declared. Weitzel insisted that Ord endorse this evaluation, which Ord did, although somewhat weakly. Grant added his own comment to Weitzel's, "For guard duty and picket duty, on the march and in assault, I consider the negro troops surpassed by no soldiers in the world, and equalled by very few."[4] Hence, it seems that prejudice did not dictate Grant's action in designating the Twenty-Fifth Corps for border duty. He even added a few finishing touches of his own. Most of the men of this corps came from the Chesapeake states or the Middle West; therefore, they would encounter neither friend nor foe in Texas. He thought they would mainly encounter Mexicans, who had never known Negroes as slaves and, therefore would have no preconceived notions of racial inferiority.[5]

Grant had missed one essential point: these men were as eager to go home as any others in the army; they longed to participate in the grand march down Pennsylvania Avenue planned for the latter part of May. Perhaps the Negro soldiers desired it more because this seemed the first opportunity for recognition by the white majority. Furthermore, while their achievements were fresh in everyone's mind was the time to gain such things as good schooling, the vote, and similar aspects of legal equality. They sensed that the delay occasioned by service on the border for an undetermined length of time might be a fatal blow to their goals. When the order was read to the men of the different regiments of the corps, there were cries of anguish and threats of mutiny. Towne and other officers who had established good relations with the men had to work hard to quiet discontent. Indeed, many of the officers were equally distressed. Towne kept silent, but he tended to accept the assignment as an opportunity to experience new and exciting scenes and to glimpse life in another country with a far different culture. He was a youth at the time of the Mexican War; a war which his elders in northeastern Pennsylvania tended to oppose, but a war which nonetheless fascinated him. He enjoyed reading about Texas and the area annexed to the west of Texas and teaching about it in his upper level classes. Now, he would be able to live in Texas for a time and no doubt would be able to cross into Mexico now and then. In a curious way, he looked forward to this as a bonanza.

While the unit awaited departure, the new division commander, R. H. Jackson, revived the long held goal of educating the illiterate or enhancing the level of poorly educated soldiers. He termed it a "duty we owe the race which has just been delivered from ignorance and thralldom." In the previous fall, when the troops went into winter quarters, Birney, then commander of the division, had directed regimental commanders to establish schools to teach reading and writing. In May, Jackson added spelling and arithmetic and required all men to attend classes for one hour each morning and another in the afternoon. He appointed T. J. Johnson, chaplain, to serve as chief education officer and to requisition books and writing materials through the quartermasters of the various regiments. Towne had done what he could as time permitted to teach the men working under him things of a practical nature, such as words and figures needed in the men's work. He tried to answer any question the men asked or to point out unusual things at hand as though it was a casual observation. He had discovered that the men were eager to learn and quick to ask questions if he gave an opening, so he gladly did just that.

A good example of how Towne used practical situations to teach was the way he helped the men to understand their bank accounts. Washington authorities in the Bureau of Colored Troops sought to teach thrift by providing a special bank at which the colored soldiers could deposit part of their pay each month. Officers entered the amount on the muster role and permitted each man to see his record of deposits.[6] When a soldier did not understand or had trouble accounting for differences in totals from one month to the next, Towne tried to use that as a way to teach simple arithmetic.

Jackson evinced a concern about cleanliness and sanitation now that time permitted such niceties. He prohibited bathing and washing of clothes in the little brook that flowed by the camp, and ordered tubs to be used for laundry purposes; each regiment had

One of Towne's assistants

designated hours for washing. On three mornings a week non-commissioned officers took the men of their respective companies to the river to bathe.[7] In this way, the brook would be preserved for drinking and cooking water.

Towne and other quartermasters spent hours preparing for the trip to the border. They had to work with the Department of Ocean and Lake Transportation. It assembled a fleet of fifty-seven steamers and fitted them with bunks for 25,000 men and stalls for 2,139 horses and mules. Based on an estimated twelve-day voyage, the transport service outfitted each vessel with 947 tons of coal and 50,000 gallons of water for each day at sea. Each regiment had to provide its own food, ammunition, weapons, wagons, ambulances, and draft animals through regular channels.[8] That part was familiar, but the length of time and distance from the supply base added a new dimension, as did the conclusion of the war. What was the source of supply? Having become dependent on the proximity to a great supply base which moved southward with the troops ever since the fall of 1863, it was hard for quartermasters like Towne to comprehend what the situation would be on the Texas border. As soon as most of the troops left Virginia, City Point would close. Hence, it would be necessary to order from Washington or possibly New Orleans or Mobile. Such details had not been clarified. There was only the twelve-day estimate to guide regimental quartermasters in their ordering.

Prior to sailing, each man was required to mail home all personal effects, souvenirs, and so forth, for which the quartermasters also had to provide packaging and handle the details of mailing once the men furnished names and addresses. While engaged in that task, Towne sent a sizable package to Phinis with the request that she store it at the family home until he returned.

On May 21 the corps broke camp and marched to City Point to board ships. Jackson's division was assigned to the first thirteen vessels to leave. The Forty-Fifth's vessel was the *Cassandra.* Towne later wondered if the name had not been appropriate for the ill-fated venture. All the fair prophecies for a short stay, an area supposedly more hospitable to colored soldiers, and the accomplishment of an important foreign policy mission capped by a triumphant return proved in retrospect as false as those of the cursed prophetess of mythology. At first all seemed well; the leading contingent steamed down the James to Fort Monroe, where the ships anchored to await the arrival of the others in the fleet. While there the officers left the ships and went to Norfolk to receive their pay, which as usual had long been in arrears. Although that was good, the delay which permitted the visit to the paymaster was not. The advance unit arrived at Hampton Roads on May 26, but the entire flotilla did not assemble until five days later.[9] That meant the same number of days had to be added to the estimated twelve. Five days of rations and drinking water were consumed before the voyage actually commenced. Likewise, sanguine opinions about certain perishable items lasting twelve days now seemed less hopeful.

The delay further exacerbated the problem of sanitation, which the Ocean and Lake Transportation service had apparently ignored. As the fleet rounded the Florida Peninsula, many of the men became seasick. Towne had a good stomach and would have enjoyed the voyage except for his duties and his concerns for the health of the men in his regiment and the chance that they would be without food well before they reached their destination. He was not alone in that unease. On June 10 the fleet docked in Mobile Bay to take on more coal and water for the engines. While the crew loaded these essentials, quartermasters were authorized to go ashore and requisition supplies as needed and available. Towne added mosquito netting to his original list, a bit of foresight for which he later congratulated himself after arriving in Texas.[10] As the voyage resumed, everyone felt encouraged, for the distance now seemed relatively short.

Two days later the fleet anchored off the Texas coast. But before the men could go ashore a violent storm produced seven feet of water that covered the bar. To escape capsizing, the ships headed for Southwest Pass. Before returning to Brazos Santiago when the storm subsided, it was necessary to load more fuel. Therefore, the men of Jackson's division did not go ashore until June 18 and 19.[11] That meant that virtually all rations had been consumed.

Immediately after landing, the officers, especially the quartermasters, faced more trouble. No one from the east coast had been able to anticipate the scorching heat of the southern Texas coast in midsummer. The officers ordered the men to pitch tents immediately to provide some protection, but soon discovered that the canvas seemed to absorb the sun's rays and trap the heat inside the tents so that anyone trying to sleep in them at night was cooked or smothered, depending on how the victims described their plight. Another storm struck two weeks after the first; the wind toppled the tents and rain drenched the men.[12]

Meanwhile, Towne, after a quick exploration of surroundings, found "not a bush or pole at hand" that could be used to fasten down tents or provide protection for horses and mules or storage for supplies. He explained to Washington that the difficulties of making camp in Texas were the reasons for ordering nineteen feet of board and forty-seven feet of scantling to frame a pavilion to protect animals and supplies from heat and rain. In another report on "supplies expended in the public service," Towne described using a barrel of lime to disinfect the sinks.[13] Although vexing and time consuming, his responses to Washington's complaints only represented a minute aspect of the real problem.

The root of the trouble seemed to be that once the unit left the east coast, authorities apparently forgot all about it. Before embarking, the quartermasters were told that supplies which took up a lot space and were not perishable, particularly all canned foods, must be shipped separately. These items the quartermasters duly ordered and marked for their respective regiments with the understanding that such materials would be shipped on freighters and go ahead of the troop transports and would therefore be waiting when the unit arrived. However, nothing awaited them and frantic pleas to Washington received no response.[14]

All food was scarce, but fresh fruits and vegetables simply did not exist. Half the men were sick with fevers and what the surgeons quickly diagnosed as scurvy. Towne had never seen the disease before, but he knew that it had a definite cause, namely, the want of citrus fruits. The lemons and limes of the Caribbean, which had long been used to prevent scurvy among seamen aboard sailing vessels were as yet largely unknown on the Continent, but onions, vinegar, and tomatoes—canned or dried—served the purpose. All during his service in the army in the quartermaster department, Towne had regularly issued vinegar and onions as part of the rations every few days. After supplies became better he put tomatoes on his requisitions frequently. Such items he and the other quartermasters had ordered for the ship that was to carry canned goods to Texas.[15] The quartermasters and surgeons pooled their resources and produced little, so they determined to attempt to buy such items in the Mexican market across the border, but their agents were turned back as enemy spies by Maximilian's border guards.[16]

Weitzel tried to solve the problem. He ordered the regimental commanders to detail men who were well enough for light work to plant gardens. They could work before 9:00 a.m. and after 4:00 p.m. in rotation. Those not working in the garden were to fish. He also decreed swimming for cleanliness with the hope that might prevent the spread of disease. Swimming could afford exercise and pleasure.[17] Most of the men were good at gardening and they had fished, although many from the interior regions thought of fishing as it was done in small rivers or creeks. Even those from the Chesapeake coast quickly discerned differences in trying to fish on the Gulf coast. However, swimming posed a greater challenge. Towne who liked to swim, although he had no claim to having done much of it and certainly not in large waters, but he only paddled close to the shore line. Few of his men followed his example.

Whether any of these efforts would have alleviated the misery of the troops cannot be determined, because Washington finally acknowledged the existence of the men on the border. That, however, only meant that the authorities discovered that the Twenty-Fifth Corps was not where it was supposed to be to do what it had been dispatched to accomplish: guard the border. It did not mean Brazos Santiago on the coast. United States forces were to be stationed all along the Rio Grande from Brownsville to Roma. The troops must move at once.[18]

In later years, Towne described the march up the Rio Grande as the worst experience he suffered in the army. The land was so different from that of the east coast, the mountains of northeastern Pennsylvania where he lived, or the Middle West where he later moved, that he saw it in his mind's eye as an imaginary planet in the far reaches of the solar system. Bordering the river was a semi-arid region that the natives called the chaparrals. It was covered with scrub forests of thornbush and thickets of mesquite, huisache, juniper, cactus, and yucca, all so prickly that the slightest encounter lacerated human or animal flesh. Dense vines hung from the trees and caught horses' harness and soldiers' gear, and wrapped around them as though holding them prisoners. Supposedly, natural paths ran through the chaparrals, but only natives knew where. When the Yankees tried to follow what seemed to be a path, it disappeared into another thorn thicket.[19]

General Doubleday placed Towne in charge of the brigade train in the march up the Rio Grande.[20] Original orders had limited the number of draft animals that could be taken to Texas; therefore, he had less than half the number he would have used for a brigade train in the Chesapeake area. Consequently, he could not load his wagons as heavily as he needed to do except by moving the teams very slowly and unloading the wagons in the worst places, then dragging the loads by hand to reload the wagons when they reached smoother terrain once more. In the worst thickets, teams could not be driven but had to be led by men walking on each side to hold back thornbushes or untangle vines caught in harnesses or wagon wheels. He had a good crew of teamsters, but he could not ride along the train to direct and encourage the men. He had to lead his horse to a relatively good spot to tie it so he could help unload wagons, push the wagons out

General Ulysses Doubleday

of holes, and soothe frightened mules and horses cut by thorns and prickly leaves.

As other officers associated with him later testified, Towne did more than his share of the heavy labor. He had made it his policy to demonstrate to his men what was needed by working with them as occasion demanded. In addition, many of the men were weakened by malnutrition and diseases until they had less strength than normal. Because the officers could get a few extra items from across the border from the sutler, Towne felt obligated to do all he could to spare his men until his pleas to Washington for food brought relief.

Lieutenant Myron Smith Towne at Edinburgh, Texas

Overexertion worsened Towne's bothersome varicose veins and precipitated another ailment, hemorrhoids. During the march, the latter condition became so painful that he began to exhibit noticeable signs of suffering despite efforts to continue as usual. When friends questioned him, he admitted to the problem, and once he reached Edinburgh, which had been designated as brigade headquarters, he consulted the assistant surgeon of the Forty-Fifth, Rufus Hamilton. The doctor diagnosed hemorrhoids and told Towne that he had a companion in misery, Lieutenant Joseph W. Pierce. Hamilton admitted treatment of the condition was uncertain under the best of circumstances and more difficult during arduous military service. He offered Towne the same advice he had already given Pierce, which was to bathe frequently in cold water and avoid lifting heavy loads. Later, Pierce told Towne that the baths offered only temporary relief.[21] As for the lifting, Towne dismissed that as impractical, particularly in view of his new position.

Once the brigade settled into the four posts assigned to it, Doubleday received a discharge by special order, and Brevet Brigadier General L. F. Haskell became brigade commander. One of his first acts was to appoint Towne brigade quartermaster on September 21, 1865.[22] The position carried the rank of captain, but Haskell told Towne that while the commander would gladly recommend Towne for promotion, the War Department, now that the war had ended, had suspended all field promotions. However, the rank, likely of brevet captain, would come with Towne's discharge.

The brigade occupied four posts—Santa Maria, Ronco Blanco, Sasquavas, and Edinburgh—extending over a seventy-mile stretch. Now there was at least a dirt road in relatively open country along the riverbank so that Towne could ride his horse to lead a few wagons and teamsters to deliver supplies from the headquarters' supply pavilion. While making a delivery, he would receive a requisition for the next delivery. Nonetheless, to cover the territory required many hours in the saddle, which prevented any improvement in the hemorrhoidal condition.[23]

Towne was thankful for one thing: in mid-August crates of canned goods and fresh fruits and vegetables such as apples and tomatoes began to arrive, and within two weeks scurvy and other diseases caused by inadequate nutrition disappeared.[24] However, Towne continued to feel angry and resentful that the authorities in Washington had been so negligent in the first place. Why had not the food shipments been made as promised? He could understand a breakdown of supplies in the midst of fierce fighting, but in this case there was no excuse.

With the recovery of health, the soldiers experienced boredom and a new wave of discontent. Weitzel issued orders directing company commanders to keep their men "contented and happy." He listed education to make the men "as fine a body of soldiers as there is in the army" as the goal.[25] This meant more classes, something dear to Towne's heart. His regret was that he lacked the time to act as a teacher now, but he determined to do as much as possible to educate the teamsters he took with him, and he rotated them so that as many men as possible had an opportunity to work in supply. They liked it not only because Towne was firm but fair and treated them with kindness and consideration, but because of the opportunity to get out of camp, travel, and see a few interesting sights. Towne enjoyed that aspect himself, and he talked with the men detailed to assist him about what they saw as they traveled. He called upon his memory to provide background to Spanish culture and Mexican history.

Because he dared not take his men and equipage across the border, he would send them sometimes in a rather remote stretch of territory along the proper route on the American side, while he slipped across on a rickety bridge to the Mexican side to explore a little village that seemed to him to have been lost in time. He had learned that the Mexican border guards were very accommodating once a coin mysteriously appeared in a gloved hand and then dropped with a clink at the guard's feet. Smiling gaily, the guard would wave the man in blue across after picking up the coin and pocketing it.

Towne would then ride the dusty road through the village, making observations, perhaps not altogether valid, but useful to himself. Once he saw a tired-looking man propped against the side of a hut. Seemingly the man slept, although one could not be sure because of the wide, shaggy-brimmed hat pulled over his face. At another hut a woman squatted in the open doorway as she pounded corn into an earthen bowl. [26] Towne marveled at such a

A home near border seen by Towne

primitive culture persisting in the midnineteenth century, an age which seemed to him to be veritably bursting with new and better ways of life. He, like his contemporaries, tended to regard such cultures as "backward," although, unlike many of the day, he was not contemptuous, nor did he seek opportunities for exploitation. Rather, his feelings were those of pity and the desire to uplift backward peoples and bring them the blessings of modernization. True, he did not see the role of the United States as an active one, but merely supportive as in this effort to force Maximilian out of power and in order for Mexicans to govern themselves. Once the foreign oppressors were gone, Benito Juarez would come to power, establish a democratic government with education and opportunity for the peons to own their land. He would accomplish the last by taking the vast holdings of the Roman Catholic Church and the aristocrats. Then, progress would come to the land south of the border. One must not forget that Towne and his generation were not necessarily chauvinistic or hypocritical, but only naive.

One of Towne's chief adventures while he served on the border was the opportunity to go into Brownsville on occasional leaves.

These excursions proved memorable. The population he discovered numbered two thousand five hundred, all but five hundred of whom were Mexican. A polyglot mix of North Americans, Spanish, and French made up the remainder. Many of the French were deserters from the troops supporting Maximilian or adventurers no longer seeing prospects for enrichment since the days of

Typical street scene in Brownsville

Maximilian were numbered. These Europeans hoped to stay in Texas. Consequently, the small city had an enticing cosmopolitan atmosphere.

Brownsville looked to Towne like an enlarged version of the villages he occasionally visited on his trips up and down the river. On a market day he saw peasants carrying firewood on their heads, pulling casks of water, going home with their purchases, or coming in from the country with items to sell in the market. The main street seemed to run from the market. One-room, one-story, frame shops, some with facades to simulate an upper story, lined the street. All had porches, where most business transactions took place. Dominating the street was a large Catholic church of massive brick and stone construction. Towne could not detect any

Brownsville as seen across the Rio Grande

Transporting a barrel of water

particular architectural style, but the structure was impressive in a rough sort of way.[27]

Two shops particularly attracted Towne's attention and that of his fellow officers, who also made brief visits to the city when off duty. These were the pawnshop and the photographer's gallery. One day in the pawnshop Towne saw a base viol. It fascinated him as he felt its smooth surface of shiny wood and timidly drew the bow across the strings. The sound struck his keen ear as pleasing. He departed that day, but he searched for a book for a beginner learning to play such an instrument and found one for the violin. He thought that the base viol was in essence a big violin or what country folk called a fiddle. Although, he had never played one for the dancing that occasionally took place in his home area, he was familiar with them and had even used a fiddler to assist him in conducting a singing school. He bought the book. Then he returned to the pawnshop, not sure whether he hoped the instrument was gone or still available. It was there, and after suitable haggling, he made the purchase. He spent some time mastering a few basic aspects so that he was able to "chord," as the term was, the tunes of familiar hymns or folk songs.[28] He smiled as he thought of the fun of showing off his oversized toy when he reached home.

Returning home was the thought on everyone's mind by October of 1865. The number of soldiers on the border slowly diminished as personnel received special discharges for a variety of reasons. Surely that signified a general order would arrive soon. With such thoughts in mind, men who could get leave to go into Brownsville frequented the picture galleries to have portraits made as a visual reminder of their time on the border. The officers who had been thrown into close comradeship desired to exchange pictures with their friends. Of an even greater importance to Towne was the opportunity to buy pictures of places of interest that the photographer offered for sale. Towne bought a collection of street scenes and even some pictures that represented types of citizens of the town and its hinterland. He also purchased an ornate album into which he put his pictures and then placed it with his base viol and other items ready to ship home.[29]

Washington indicated that preparations should commence to break camp and be in readiness for the final order to march to the coast to await steamers that would carry the troops back to the east. As post quartermaster, Towne had to complete an inventory of all supplies that had been issued to him, showing place of origin, current condition, or disposition if no longer in existence. Frequently this meant holding boards of survey in which he and his assistants explained under oath why an accounting could not be made precisely. Those then on the board, duly ruled that there had been no want of care or attention on the part of the quartermaster and his assistants. It seemed foolish, but such were the requirements of the military bureaucracy.[30]

In addition, Towne had to spend hours in the saddle going from post to post to collect materials and get requisitions for clothing and equipment needed for the trip. By the time the troops would reach Philadelphia, winter would have set in; hence, greatcoats must be ordered to keep the men warm. He acquired a second horse so that one could rest while he rode the other; this is an example of his thoughtfulness toward animals, but it provided no respite for the rider. The hemorrhoids had worsened so that sitting at his desk was uncomfortable, but riding in the saddle was sheer torture. In desperation, he appealed to Colonel Edelmiro Meyer for assistance. Towne proposed to Meyer, who now commanded the Forty-Fifth, that Captain Josiah Paul's hernia was so bad that he was unfit to march or drill. Perhaps Paul could assist with some of the quartermaster's work. The colonel not only agreed but detailed Paul to work under Towne. An odd situation perhaps, but protocol no longer seemed to matter. Paul readily agreed, and he and Towne took turns doing paperwork or riding the rounds. As more materials were turned over to the quartermaster from the different posts and regiments in the brigade, Towne and Paul traveled by a boat that now plied up and down the river.[31]

On October 24, orders from the War Department officially listed the Twenty-Fifth Corps as "to be discharged." Severance would actually occur at Philadelphia, although discharge papers

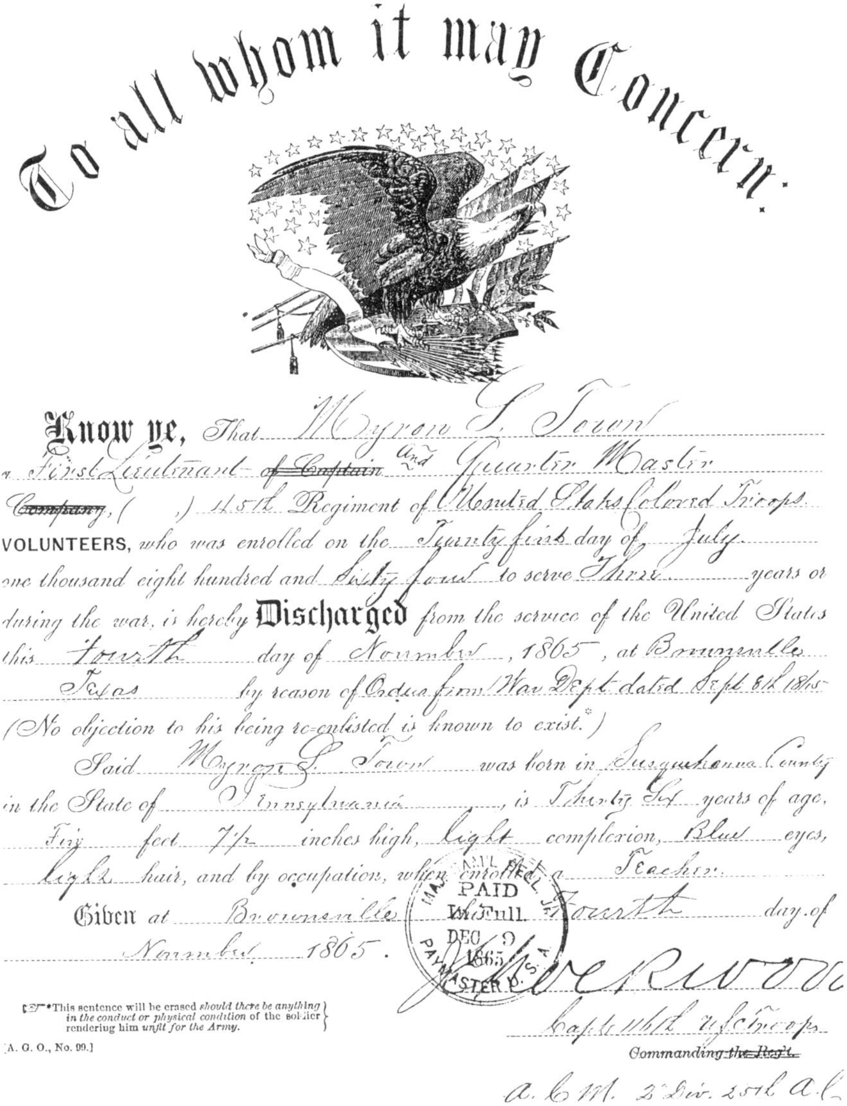

To all whom it may Concern.

Know ye, That Myron S. Towne
a First Lieutenant ~~of Captain~~ and Quarter Master
~~Company~~, ( ) 45th Regiment of United States Colored Troops
VOLUNTEERS, who was enrolled on the Twenty first day of July
one thousand eight hundred and Sixty four to serve Three years or
during the war, is hereby Discharged from the service of the United States
this Fourth day of November, 1865, at Brownsville
Texas by reason of Order from War Dept dated Sept 8th 1865
(No objection to his being re-enlisted is known to exist.*)
Said Myron S. Towne was born in Susquehanna County
in the State of Pennsylvania, is Thirty Six years of age,
Five feet 7½ inches high, light complexion, Blue eyes,
light hair, and by occupation, when enrolled a Teacher.
Given at Brownsville this Fourth day of
November 1865.

PAID In Full DEC 9 1865 PAYMASTER U.S.A.

[illegible]
Capt 116th U.S.C. Troops
~~Commanding the Regt.~~
A.C.M. 2d Div. 25th A.C.

*This sentence will be erased should there be anything in the conduct or physical condition of the soldier rendering him unfit for the Army.

[A. G. O., No. 99.]

Towne's discharge

arrived November 5; hence, the official place of discharge was Texas and the date that of November 5, 1865. Once more Towne turned to the Transportation Department to obtain accommodations for the brigade. In addition to steamers for the trip through the Gulf and up the Atlantic coast, he asked for a riverboat to carry supplies from the posts to the point of embarkation. That eliminated the need for a wagon train.[32]

Mexican guides now went with the troops as they marched to the Gulf coast. The November weather was sunny and pleasant, and the men sang and joked as they marched. Towne and Paul supervised the placement of the last box and parcel onto the supply boat and then climbed aboard. They could say that they needed to watch over their supplies, but in truth no one cared.

Once at the dock where the two vessels assigned to the brigade were anchored, Towne directed the loading of men and supplies. Haskell recalled the seasickness which plagued the men on the outbound voyage, so he ordered Hamilton to travel on the *Essex* and the assistant surgeon, Henry A. Morris, to travel on the other vessel, the *Thomas J. Sparks.* It so happened that the *Essex* was the first loaded, and it pulled out to permit the *Sparks* to come closer and take on the remaining men and gear. Because Towne was in charge of all loading, he traveled on the second steamer. By the time the *Sparks* sailed, the *Essex* was well out to sea. The weather was fair when they sailed, but as they lost sight of land, the sky turned dark and ominous. The sailors scanned the sky, checked the wind velocity, and shook their heads dolefully. They muttered about tropical storms called hurricanes that struck with little warning.

Rumors swept through the regiments on board. Some men went from nervousness to downright terror. The captain of the vessel ordered all passengers to go below. He altered the course in an attempt to make a run for Padre Island. The ship reached land just as the storm struck, but its intensity was so great that wind and waves slammed the ship onto the rocks and sand dunes and pounded it until it keeled over at an alarming angle.

Officers and men huddled in the vessel's hole were relatively safe, but many were seasick and scared irrational. Morris, fearful that some men had sought shelter in a hiding place on the deck, went up himself and tried to make his way along the nearly perpendicular deck to search for any sick, lost soul. Unhappily, the good doctor lost his footing, was swept overboard, and drowned in the turbulent sea.

By morning the storm subsided. Islanders rowed out to the steamer, took off passengers and crew, and then unloaded supplies still stoutly boxed and carried them to safety. They dispatched messengers to the mainland to telegraph New Orleans, where the ships were to rendezvous. There two ships divided their loads with a third so that one could go back and take the survivors of the shipwreck on board.[33] This was the last misfortune to face the troops sent to the border. From there, things went relatively well.

While in New Orleans, Towne set up a temporary office and received more equipment that had not been turned over to him in Texas. He drew and issued food and other supplies for the long voyage around Florida and up the Atlantic to Philadelphia. By the end of November the transports were again at sea. Towne sat at his desk completing his audits for the month, undoubtedly with a sense of satisfaction, for this would be his last major monthly report. He added to his sense of well-being as he wrote across the top in the line marked "location" the phrase "en route to Philadelphia."[34]

The flotilla made good time up the coast once it rounded the Florida Keys; it turned into Delaware Bay and edged into the city's port during the first week in December. Orders called for a quick march to Camp Cadwalader, just outside the city, where the men received pay and formal dismissal. Towne said good-bye to his comrades and the men of his company who had served so faithfully under him in the Quartermaster's Department. Then he turned to tasks he had to perform before he could leave for his home. On December 8, he made the rounds at Schuylkill Arsenal to check in a variety of items such as the regimental flags from his brigade and to get signatures from the proper official for each article to include with his final report. Not until the tenth was he able to draw his pay and receive official severance from the army.[35] Military service had consumed nearly four years of his life.

Actually, he was not entirely free from military red tape even after his return to Forest Lake. In January 1867 Towne received a communique from the Office of the Quartermaster General challenging his overissue of grain for horses and mules under his jurisdiction during the months of October 1864 to March 1865. In view of the fact that he had followed a directive from no less than the commander of all the armies, Ulysses S. Grant, to the affect that such adjustments were to be made when only short forage was available, Towne felt annoyed. His reports for the months in question had carried a notation of the reason and cited the general order. In fact, Towne had made doubly sure the Washington office could understand by attaching a special authorization from General Ord to whose corps the Forty-Fifth was attached for the months of February and March. Why the matter had come up at all at this late date, Towne never knew. Presumably his repetition of the reason satisfied whoever had dredged the matter out of old files, for Towne heard no more of the matter.[36] Except for repeated applications for pensions or pension increases many years later, Towne could say his military experiences were behind him. However, they lived in his vivid memory and assisted him in the process of educating his son, Frank, of Towne's elderly years.

Chapter Twelve

Starting a New Life

TOWNE'S HOMECOMING AT THE BEGINNING OF 1866 was anticlimactic. Other veterans had returned almost a year before with grand celebrations on the Fourth of July, which roughly coincided with their severance from the military. By the time Towne arrived, he felt that people were looking at him with a kind of "Where have you been all this time?" attitude. True, his family expressed unbounded pleasure to see him, worried because he had lost weight and appeared tired, and tried to get him quickly back into the familiar routine. Their intentions were good and he appreciated their efforts, but that, in a sense, was his problem—he did not want to go back to his old life. Time in the military had been filled with travel to places he would never have seen had he remained a rural schoolteacher, farmer, or sawmill operator in Susquehanna County. When his military service ended, he felt adrift without a real place in the world. It was not that he desired more of the military routine, but he was bored by the monotony of life in this almost forgotten corner of Pennsylvania.

As Towne sorted through his options, he rejected most of those that appealed to many of his comrades from the service. For one thing, his age posed a dilemma. By the time he was mustered out of the army, he was thirty-six, too old he felt to go to Montrose or some other nearby town and start as a junior clerk-bookkeeper in some establishment. He could easily do that with his experience in the Quartermaster's Department, but he felt that at his age he must succeed quickly. Success meant climbing the socioeconomic ladder; that is, rising to a level somewhat higher than what his parents had reached. That was Towne's goal.

Traditionally in America, land was the main source of wealth, which produced status. However, by midnineteenth century as industrialization advanced, goods and services became more important. There was a continuous increase in the items turned out by factories and mines that were brought to a nationwide market created by the railroads. This momentous change was already underway, but it leaped forward under the impetus of war. Towne had seen it while in the service, but he felt its impact still more after his return from his six-months' "exile" in Texas. He was not alone.

To the victorious North all things seemed possible, even divinely foreordained, in the years following the end of fighting. An array of new, desirable goods appeared at affordable prices; the more that was produced and sold, the more prices declined until all but a fringe of working-class poor could enjoy these wondrous creations. Something called the standard of living began to change the meaning of success. To be somebody in one's community was to command most, or at least a considerable portion, of the amenities of life now available.

Towne was well aware of this change in the quality of life, and he knew he wanted to partake of these comforts. He had viewed them even in the midst of war on his trips to Washington and visits to Philadelphia. Now these comforts appeared in Susquehanna County. No longer was the county isolated by the Endless Mountains. Railroads linked it to the outside world. In the spring of 1866 Towne arranged to take Phinis to Binghamton, across the state line in New York. They caught the early morning train northward. They spent much of the day walking in downtown Binghamton, visiting a few shops and seeing the sights in the growing city. He took her to a picture gallery, where he insisted that the photographer pose her so that her dress with its billowing skirt and sleeves, intricate tucking, and lace trim would show to the best advantage.[1] This was his sister's first opportunity to ride on a train, look about a city, and have her portrait made. She

Phinis Towne Deuel

reveled in the day, the unexpected outing, and the chance to be alone with her beloved brother. He not only enjoyed being able to do something special for her, but he also relished the opportunity to get away from the humdrum nature of rural life. However, small as the day might seem in the larger context of life in the era following the war, it symbolized much about the new age. So much had changed since John and Rachel Towne's marriage forty years before. Despite Myron Towne's introspective nature, he missed the vital aspect of the day's outing. Binghamton was more than a pleasant city to visit. It was on the point of becoming a major railroad and industrial center. Along with its economic growth would come educational and cultural enhancement.

With Towne's experience and his ease in working with soldiers, he could have become a personnel manager or some similar middle level executive in a big bank or business. This would have brought real wealth and a share in the new life-style of the upper middle class in eastern cities. Or perhaps more to his own taste, he could have read law in the office of some lawyer with strong Republican political ties who would have liked Towne's political credentials. After passing the bar exams, Towne could have become a partner in an established firm or start his own law office. The result would have been the same, a generous slice of the newstyle economic pie. For all his reading of the city press and his realization of how life was changing, he could not break the ties that bound him to the past.

Towne was not alone in seeking to escape the confines of a community that seemed to offer little opportunity for the new style of living. John Towne closed his blacksmith shop and hired a man to take care of his farm so he could devote his time to the work of the church. He could go occasionally to Montrose on business and buy a few niceties for his wife or granddaughter, but even he was not quite satisfied, although at first he tried to pretend otherwise.

Feeling secretly rather proud of his son's musical talent and the interesting instrument he brought home from his travels to "foreign" lands, the elder Towne had his son bring the bass viol to a Sunday School picnic, where Myron Towne sang several solos, accompanied by the instrument. His audience was quite impressed. The presiding elder, who was present for the occasion, and the church steward both insisted that Myron Towne bring the instrument to church each Sunday and strum it as accompaniment to congregational singing.[2] While pleased that his rudimentary skill was considered good by the musically untutored, Myron Towne felt it was another reason to build a new life. He had no desire to spend the rest of his years as a rustic dilettante.

For generations the West was seen as the location of greater opportunities for success seekers. It was no longer necessary to move into the virtually unknown wilderness, as Jehiel Warner had done, or to go where there was a family connection, in the manner of John Towne. Advertising agencies touted the wonders of partially settled areas with improved farmlands where the first work of clearing, plowing, fencing, and building had been completed. Land companies and small loan operators, sometimes one and the same, tried to entice newcomers from the East to buy on credit, the seller taking a mortgage usually for two to four years' duration at 10 percent interest paid annually.

Towne scorned the Great Plains; what he had seen of Texas had soured him on any experience with dry, treeless, flat country. He sought something similar to northeastern Pennsylvania except with better soil, hills instead of mountains, and greater accessibility. He sought that in the central Midwest. To explore possibilities, he wrote for brochures of various land companies that inserted advertisements in the Binghamton or Montrose papers.

Towne was not alone in his desire to move; persons he had known from his time at Harford University, now no longer in operation, had moved to Illinois, Iowa, or Missouri. Inquiries to those for whom he had addresses extolled the merits of their new communities. Perhaps that was to be expected, for who would want to admit to a mistake of judgment in such a crucial matter. But, at least, there seemed to be opportunity out West.

The prevailing restlessness affected the elderly as well as the young or middle aged. In 1869 Eli Warner informed the family that he, his wife, and their two surviving children, now grown,

Phinis and Jerub, would move shortly to Otter Creek Township in Carroll County, Illinois. There he had purchased land which Jerub would farm, while Eli would operate a small loan business with the proceeds from the sale of his holdings in Susquehanna County.[3]

As Eli's letters arrived praising northwestern Illinois and its great potential, John Towne began to talk about following the same course as that of his brother-in-law. He did not want to farm in that area. Rather, his plan was to sell his holdings in Pennsylvania and move to a small town in the Middle West where he too would engage in the small loan business. Money was in great demand "out West," and that demand offered a bonanza to enterprisers. Eli and his family had transferred their membership to the Methodist Episcopal Church in Lanark and described it as having an attractive building and friendly, devout members. That decided matters for John and Rachel Towne. She expressed her desire for a house in Lanark that would be within walking distance of the "meeting house," as she always referred to the church building. John agreed with her judgment and merely added the idea of a large house with enough land for an orchard and garden.

Meanwhile, Myron Towne had completed his arrangements. He would go to a small town in northeastern Missouri, called Kirksville, the county seat of Adair County. It was roughly thirty miles south of the Iowa border and seventy miles west of the Mississippi River. A brochure from the Adair County Immigrant Aid Society described the county as intersected by a ridge covered by a "great primeval forest" composed of oak, hickory, walnut, and maple. The Chariton River drained the area and it was fed by numerous creeks. Towne quickly visualized a sawmill on the river or a tributary. He would cut timber and process it into railroad ties or, better yet, into lumber for the furniture factories of Chicago or St. Louis. Kirksville had two railroads, one of which, the north-south line, led by way of junctions with other railroads to big city markets. An east-west road, actually in the process of being built, would also lead to Chicago and, when completed, to Kansas City and Omaha on the Missouri River.[4]

With his destination determined, Towne began to sell his land. In April 1869 he conveyed the major portion of his farm to William C. Tilden, and in March of the following year, he sold Tilden the house, its outbuildings, and the land on which they were located.[5] He gave a list of those persons owing him money to his father to collect. That was a task John Towne was glad to undertake and which he would do well by virtue of his office as justice of the peace as well as his natural persistency. Then, Myron Towne told his family farewell and departed for the West.

Once he reached Kirksville, he began to view his new surroundings. He saw that Kirksville, like most Middle West towns, was built around a town square, where the main shops were located. He learned that three land companies did business in the downtown area, so he obtained listings of property for sale from each. According to his plan, he thought he should buy land to the west of the city. However, his immediate goal was to find a dwelling place. He had also determined prior to leaving his homeland that he did not want to live on a farm. Once in Kirksville, Towne decided he would buy only a small place with enough land for a barn to house the wagon and team he would need for timber cutting and for an orchard and garden, such as the site his father was trying to locate in Lanark. Later, as he prospered, he could sell this place at a profit and buy a better dwelling.

Therefore, Towne purchased a small frame house on a one-and-a-quarter-acre plot across the railroad tracks just west of the downtown area. It was not as good as the structure he had sold to Tilden in the spring, but it would do for the time being. The seller had already moved to Kansas so Towne was able to take possession immediately[6] and send word to the family to ship his possessions to him.

Back at the land offices again, Towne found available some of the timbered land he sought. He purchased forty acres about two miles west of Kirksville.[7] This tract was close to Big Creek, the stream which Towne assumed, from a study of the atlas, to be a good location for a sawmill. After riding through the area and viewing the waterway he was less certain. Not only was the creek smaller than the Wyalusing, where he had located his sawmill in Susquehanna County, and less swift, but its overflow was far more uncertain. Towne was to learn something that his geography books had perhaps told him, but which he had not visualized clearly: the unpredictable nature of rainfall in the Transmississippi region. In a year of heavy rains the creeks that fed the Chariton would overflow, and a mill could not function in high waters. When the rains did not come, the creeks dried to muddy ditches. He would need to dig sloughs and drainage ditches to operate a sawmill profitably. But that was self-defeating because the initial expenses were too high, so Towne settled for cutting timber, hauling it to a mill, and shipping it to St. Louis or Chicago.

Despite his preoccupation with making a new start in life, Towne made acquaintances in town and participated in his new church home. There were enough Methodists in Kirksville to constitute a station church with a resident minister and a building in the process of construction. He participated in the cornerstone laying in the summer of 1871 and the dedicatory service on January 21, 1872.[8]

News from home was strangely disquieting. At first, all seemed well. John Towne reported to his son in May of 1870 that in the two months since Myron departed his father had collected fifty dollars on the accounts. Not long thereafter the younger Towne received another sixty dollars. Some of the "vagabond accounts" his father rated "worthless," but he offered other debtors the option of paying just what they owed without interest.

That, John Towne guessed, would induce more payments when crops were marketed in the autumn.[9]

All of the larger family rejoiced over Frank Warner's ordination by the Wyoming Conference and his assignment to the

The Reverend Frank Warner

charge at Nicholson, Pennsylvania. Frank was not only a cousin, but a member of Towne's church in Forest Lake Centre. He had also been a student in the school where Myron Towne taught at least one term after Justus Franklin, as Frank Warner then was called, had been old enough to attend. Now Frank was an ordained elder with a station church instead of just a circuit rider. The Methodist Episcopal Church had become more sophisticated also in the post-war era.[10]

The disturbing part was that "little" Lydia had, at fifteen, suddenly decided that she was a woman in love. The object of her affections was Erastus Henry Burdick, the son of Barnett Burdick, who had moved to Putnam County, Missouri, in 1868. The son had remained behind to work long enough to make sufficient money to buy land. Beginning in New Jersey, he worked his way westward. When he reached Susquehanna County, he learned that John Towne needed a hired hand so Burdick went to the place where he was directed and offered his services. Towne hired him and was pleased with the young man's work until he discovered that Lydia had become too friendly with Burdick. Although properly reared according to the standards of the day, she had unfortunately little opportunity to meet or socialize with young people outside her numerous second and third cousins. Burdick was almost the first young man she had encountered. When he announced that he would leave at the end of the harvest to head farther west, she was disconsolate, until he asked her to accompany him. Then, he said, they must be married and leave at once.

When Lydia announced this decision to her unsuspecting mother and grandparents they were absolutely horrified. Phinis resorted to earnest, motherly advice: about waiting until Burdick was settled, and then he could return to visit Lydia; then they might not have anything in common by then and have no desire to marry. Lydia could get more education at one of the many normal schools now appearing nearby. No doubt Phinis thought of other inducements, but to no avail. John Towne resorted to a stern lecture of short duration. Lydia was under the age for a woman to marry without parental consent and Phinis would not give her consent. Towne himself absolutely forbade his granddaughter to marry.

Lydia seems to have threatened to elope, and probably to have nothing more to do with her family, if she could not marry with

Lydia Deuel Burdick in her marriage dress

their blessing. The threat appears to have worked. Phinis told her brother in letters, as painful for her to write as they were for him to read, that she and her parents had agreed to the marriage. They gave Lydia a nice, though simple, wedding in October 1871. She had a new gown, a rose corsage, a handsome locket, and a wedding picture to display this finery.[11] After the wedding, Lydia and her groom boarded a train for Iowa where someone, likely her new father-in-law, met them to take them in a wagon across the state line into Missouri to a town in eastern Putnam County called Martinstown. There she would be about twenty-five miles from her uncle Myron. Despite his promises to visit her as soon as possible, he was not able to do so.

John Towne suffered greatly from the defiance of his beloved granddaughter, whom he had indulged far more than either of his own children. No doubt his pride had been dealt a blow, also. In any case, he determined to leave Pennsylvania quickly. In the fall of 1871, he sold his land to Ambrose Spencer for $5,565, retaining the plot where the church was located, which he deeded to the Fairdale Circuit. The sum was too great for Spencer to pay all at once so Towne continued to hold title and to occupy the house while Spencer made payments on the purchase price, plus interest.[12] With the coming of spring, Spencer began to farm the land. As he made more payments, he became anxious for the Towne family to vacate the house, and the family agreed.

John Towne had completed the purchase of a house and grounds at the edge of Lanark, but he did not want to move until work had been done on the house under his nephew's supervision. Therefore, the Towne family accepted Asa Warner's invitation to move to the homestead while they prepared for the migration to the West. Phinis continued to operate the post office in what had so long been her father's blacksmith shop and now was the precinct polling place. On April 24, 1873, she sent her resignation to Washington with her last report.[13] Then she departed in the wake of her parents, who had left earlier in the month. Instead of going directly to Lanark, Phinis detoured into Iowa where Henry Burdick met her to take her to Martinstown so that she could stay for a time with her daughter and meet her infant granddaughter, for on August 28, 1872, Lydia had given birth to a baby whom she named Mary Eliza.[14] Due to the fact that Lydia was barely sixteen and had only been married ten months, her family suffered further distress.

With his sister so close, Myron Towne was determined to see her, and after some effort they worked out an arrangement whereby she would ride into Adair County with a neighbor of the Burdicks who was traveling that way to a grist mill on the Chariton River; there Towne would meet her and take her home with him for a few days. She could leave from Kirksville on the train to Iowa, where after several changes, she would proceed to Lanark.

Details are somewhat vague, but one can surmise that Towne's delight in having his sister in the role of his efficient housekeeper once more, if only for a few days, caused him to share with her how dreary and lonesome it was to come home to an empty house each night after a day of timber cutting and have no food ready. He had to get his own supper, try to clean a bit in addition to the outdoor chores of taking care of his team of horses, bringing in water and fuel and similar tasks. In her forthright way, Phinis gave him the conventional advice of the day: he needed a wife.

Since Phinis understood from her own experience, as well as her close relationship with her brother, just how skittish he felt about marriage, she tried to convince him that a properly arranged marriage of convenience was what he needed at his age. Perhaps, she hinted, that where they had both erred twenty years earlier was in marrying for love. What she had just seen of Lydia's situation and the grief it had caused all of Lydia's immediate family had further disillusioned Phinis with romance.

Towne confessed under the influence of Phinis' gentle persuasion that he had increasingly wondered why he was working so hard; what value would his attainments have if he had no immediate family to enjoy it. Besides, he needed a partner and a helpmate to share with him the creation of a new life. By this admission, he placed his future in her hands, and to his secret amazement she behaved like a practiced matchmaker. Perhaps she was easing her own sense of guilt for failing to find the right husband for Lydia. She wanted to find the right mate for her brother.

That was not too difficult. All one had to do was to look to the numerous family connections. When she arrived in Lanark, Phinis consulted Aunt Sally Warner, Uncle Eli's wife. She had been a Cole, and that family had branches extending into all the New

England states, northern Pennsylvania, and upstate New York. It seemed that one of the "cousins," Winthrop Cole, had an unmarried daughter of the age at which spinsterhood began to loom on the horizon. Instead of remaining in a remote area of rural Vermont from which the young men had left largely to go to the West or the cities to seek work in the growing factories, she had herself done both. She was Ellen Theodora Cole, now living in Peru, Indiana, where she worked in a textile mill.[15] She lived in a room rented from a family to whom she had been referred by a mutual acquaintance in Vermont. This seemed better to her family and to Sally Warner than living in a rooming house. She had told Ellen, or Nellie as her family called her, about Myron Towne, and his aunt urged that he write to the young lady.

At that point, Towne recognized that he was in the clutches of determined women who intended that he marry Ellen Cole. For a moment he was tempted to say to his sister "Et tu, Brute," the phrase they used when one got the other into something the victim was not quite ready for. But, he had to admit that he had asked for it. As he thought about the letter, he decided that he might pursue the matter further. He had come to the conclusion, assisted by Phinis during her visit, that he did need a wife. Opportunities for a man his age in a relatively sparsely settled region were limited, and the Towne family had certain standards with which he was in full accord. The Cole family was a solid middle-class one of old colonial stock. More important was the fact that Towne admired the young lady's independence and determination. She had courageously left home to pursue her own goals, her search for success as it were. This was a quality he admired in a woman and saw in his sister. He would like that in a wife. Now that he could think clearly about the failure of his marriage to Sarah Wright, he concluded that one of the problems had been her unwillingness or inability to cut the ties with her father, mother, and siblings and make a life for herself with her husband.

She could have occupied herself profitably with the post office, the church library, or even as a record keeper for his sawmill instead of running home for a life of dependency on others. That may have been only partially accurate, but it conditioned him to approve of Ellen Cole sight unseen.

Towne wrote to the lady, received her polite, formal note in return, which in a guarded way encouraged him to continue the correspondence if he were so minded. In Dickens' words, she was "willing." Proof came in a letter from Reuben Gardner in the fall inviting Towne to call at their home should he be in Peru, Indiana. It sounded as though Towne had been summoned by Mr. Gardner, who evidently felt that he stood in loco parentis to Miss Ellen. The guardian wanted to be sure his ward would not be "betrayed." Conventional mores had developed definite guidelines by the postbellum years.

If Towne had any doubts that he was being committed to matrimony, his mother's firm injunction that he must not dally with this young lady clinched the point. Phinis added her more worldly view that this was likely the best chance he would have to find a suitable partner. Obviously, she had concluded that suitability was more practical than romance. From the perspective of a forty-two years on this earth, Towne agreed. Therefore, he prepared to travel to Indiana after his crops were harvested and he had made the last major cutting of timber prior to the onslaught of winter.

Actually, it was after Christmas that he made the trip. He had alerted both Ellen Cole and Reuben Gardner to his arrival. His first meeting with the young lady became one of his best stories in later years. He may have embellished it to sharpen the punch line, but it basically conformed to fact. Towne related that he stepped off the train at the station in Peru and looked about. The day was chilly, but the sun moderated the temperature so it did not feel as cold as he had expected. Two young ladies occupied a bench on the platform who were trying to look indifferent as they eyed the passengers who descended. Towne approached the ladies, hat in hand, and bowed politely. He asked permission to inquire if the ladies could give him directions to the home of Mr. Rueben Gardner, who was expecting the traveler. The brightening countenance of each told him he had guessed correctly, so an impish streak, which he had long kept under control, took possession. With a roguish twinkle in his eye, he added, "Would one of you ladies be considering matrimony?" One giggled, but the other responded with her own question, "Would you be Mr. Myron Towne, sir?" At his quick, "Miss Ellen Cole?" they both burst out laughing and by so doing throw off the constraints which might otherwise have hampered this hasty courtship.[16]

The couple apparently decided during the next few hours and the following day that they had much in common. As he had assumed from her neat, well-phrased letters, she had clearly made the most of her common school education, just as had the other women of his family. Her manners were refined, and she presented an attractive appearance. She was not pretty, but she had blue eyes and softly curling, light brown hair cut to shoulder length. She was the first woman Towne had met who had cut her hair, but he guessed that she had done so as a safety precaution while working around the spinning and weaving machines. He rather liked it for it gave her a more youthful appearance than her thirty-two years, which she had told him was her age. She was very thin, but her simple skirt and jacket fit to perfection.

After a pleasant day visiting and enjoying a well-prepared meal with Mr. and Mrs. Gardner and the other young woman, who was Ellen's roommate, Towne asked Ellen if she was agreeable to becoming his wife. She frankly confessed that she had already decided if he was tolerable, she would consent to marriage. Again, they apparently had another private joke—he was glad he had convinced her that he was acceptable.

Towne made the necessary arrangements the next morning after breakfast at the hotel where he had spent the night. He obtained the wedding license and the services of a Methodist preacher. The Gardners agreed to host the wedding on the following day; immediately thereafter the couple could leave on a train bound for Missouri. On the morning of December 31, Towne and the Reverend Samuel Wyckoff arrived to find all in readiness at the Gardner home.[17] Ellen, or Nellie, as Towne was trying to remember to call her, was wearing a simple but stylish dress of brown silk, with collar and cuffs of cream colored lace and a bow of pink ribbon fastened at the neckline with ends extending to the waist. The most striking feature of her attire was the long, elaborately carved earrings that reached halfway to her shoulders. They caught Myron's attention because none of the women in his family had pierced ears.

Myron S. Towne

Ellen T. Cole Towne, 1873

Following their arrival in Kirksville, they dressed in their wedding finery and went to Morris' Studio on the north side of the square for photographs. Morris posed them in what had already become the proper arrangement for a wedding picture, with the man seated and the wife standing slightly to the side behind the chair. Then he asked to take a separate picture of each. Towne liked Nellie's portrait so well that he ordered an enlargement in a massive ornate gilt frame. She urged him to make his into a picture to hang also, so he did, though he used a smaller oval walnut frame to match those he had chosen for the pictures of his mother, father, sister, and niece.[18]

In the months that followed, Towne grew more and more pleased with his marriage. Nellie kept the house neat and clean; she prepared good meal and she made attractive curtains, cushion covers, and other little decorations. Fresh wallpaper and paint in the spring brightened the rooms. His growing appreciation for Nellie as a person deepened his gratitude to his relatives. Towne knew he would respect her and honor her, but he had not quite expected to find his regard for her growing into conjugal love that differed greatly from the romantic attraction to Sarah. With Nellie he felt comfortable and at ease, and she seemed equally fond of him. They could share opinions and thoughts, and they could joke with each other in a kind way. The future now looked bright, but that very fact motivated Towne to strive harder to make money. He wanted to provide a better life for Nellie.

Shortly before his marriage Towne had purchased two lots at the corner of Franklin and Baldwin Streets, just west of the new campus of the First District Normal School of Missouri. The price was $300, which reflected the rising land values brought by Kirksville's growth now that it was the seat of Missouri's first state-supported normal school.[19] He proposed to build a nice house on the site, one suitable for Nellie and the family she desired. Unfortunately, the lumbering-farming operation had not prospered as

Towne had anticipated and the acreage at the west edge of Kirksville had few possibilities. He had miscalculated the growth of the town; it was expanding rapidly to the east, south, and north; but not to the west. Proximity to the railroad, which he had seen as desirable when he planned his lumbering business, proved a detriment. Already the phrase "wrong side of the tracks" had come to be a reason not to live in certain parts of towns across the Middle West. His scattered holdings in the county were not productive. The poor soil of the Chariton hills made tillage unprofitable. Grazing was a possibility, but he lacked the capital to go into livestock and he would need more land, so that was not an option.

Another problem was that the time Towne spent traveling over his land, cutting timber, and hauling it to the shipping point near his dwelling worsened the hemorrhoids, which flared up anew, just as the doctor Towne had consulted in Montrose before he left for the West had warned.[20] Towne began to look for other enterprises.

Meanwhile, Nellie urged that they start their family. Towne cautioned delay until his prospects were brighter; furthermore, he emphasized that two children would be the absolute limit. He thought in terms of a boy and a girl, which he had come to see as the ideal family, just the way he had experienced it. Nellie argued her age as a reason to throw caution to the winds and go ahead. When she became pregnant in the summer of 1874, she was overjoyed, but her husband felt strangely apprehensive.

Chapter Thirteen

Death

ALTHOUGH TOWNE HAD SEEN DEATH in many ugly forms during his years in the army, he had been able to accept it as something to be expected in war. One had to take that position or he would be unable to perform his duties effectively. Death in civilian life was different, but it was something that had not touched his immediate family except for the deaths of his grandparents, both of whom had lived to great age, and two of his mother's brothers who were certainly not young when they died. However, in the decade after his marriage, five members of his immediate family died, only one of whom could be called elderly.

In May of 1874, a telegram from Phinis informed Towne that Lydia had died. Phinis was on her way to Martinstown and wanted her brother to meet her there for the funeral and burial service. Nellie insisted he go and bring his sister home with him. Phinis could, as she had once before, leave from Kirksville to go back to Lanark.

Towne departed before dawn the following morning, and by late afternoon he had arrived at the farmhouse. There he found Phinis holding Lydia's baby, now twenty-one months old. The child had latched onto her grandmother as if she lacked any other sense of security; little Mary kept her arms locked around Phinis' neck with almost a stranglehold. Phinis explained that Lydia contracted typhoid fever and died in three days despite the fact that everything possible was done for her, but "to no avail."[1] The good news, as Phinis saw it, was that Henry Burdick had told his mother-in-law to take Mary to rear as her own. Henry and his father were planning to move to Kansas to try their luck there, for they were not successful in Putnam County. In such a move Henry could not be burdened by an infant. Towne thought this said much about the character of Burdick, but he was glad for his sister. Having little Mary would greatly relieve Phinis' grief over Lydia.

At Phinis' insistence the Methodist minister who served the Unionville church was brought to the farm to preach the funeral sermon and perform the burial ritual. He laid heavy emphasis on how happy Lydia must be in her new home with her Savior. He warned the grieving relatives not to think of themselves but only of her good. This disturbed Myron. He felt a sense of bitterness from the moment he had received Phinis' sad news. Towne kept thinking to himself that if Lydia had not married Burdick and gone to live on this farm in what Towne tended to regard as a miserable place, she would have been alive and well and able to perform a real service in the world. Or, having married and had this baby, Lydia should have been spared so that she might raise the child herself, as undoubtedly she wanted to do. He could not accept the idea that she had been eager to abandon her child by going to heaven at the age of seventeen.

Towne tried to keep these feelings from showing as he took his sister and her ward to his home in Kirksville. They left with what few items Phinis had been able to find that belonged to either her daughter or granddaughter. Phinis made a touching appeal to her brother to get Lydia's body if the Burdick family sold the farm and moved away. She did not want Lydia left "out there alone." Towne bit his lip under his little beard to keep from arguing the point. If Lydia was in heaven with the Savior, then she was not alone on the Burdick farm. However, he concealed such errant thoughts and agreed that he would bring Lydia's body to Kirksville for burial in the city cemetery located west of the square, not far from Towne's home.

Once in Kirksville, Phinis acted more like her normal, competent self. She and Nellie became firm friends, as if they had known each other since girlhood. Phinis' main complaint while with her brother and sister-in-law was that Mary had no "decent" clothes. This came up forcefully when Towne insisted on taking them to a photographer to have a Mary's picture taken. The calico dress

Mary Burdick, 1874, in her "common" dress

with a bit of rickrack trim was certainly unpretentious, but even Phinis had worn dark calico dresses when she was a child, although they were probably better made. Phinis' worry about suitable attire pointed to the fact that Towne standards had advanced. Myron himself was somewhat more disturbed by Mary's straggly hair, but he urged the photographer to do the best he could. The result showed Mary sitting on a blanket spread over a table. She was wearing scuffed, high shoes and a "common" dress. Her face was marked by a scowl and a pout; all attempts by relatives to induce her to smile had failed.[2]

Letters from Lanark after Phinis reached home described a round of sewing to make Mary a stylish wardrobe. John Towne proudly handed his wife and daughter money to buy materials, and Phinis and Rachel created outfits no doubt the envy of others in the Lanark Methodist Church. Rachel Towne and her daughter dressed well, but not in any way ultrastylish or fancy; however, for the baby it was different.

Towne could not devote more than casual interest in these details even though he enjoyed letters from his family, for he was too concerned about his wife's condition. To his unpracticed eye, Nellie appeared less well than most mothers-to-be. In the fall she developed a severe cold that left her with a persistent cough. The doctor to whom Towne took her gave her some cough syrup and promised the cough would soon cease. When it became worse, the doctor said the cough would end after the baby was born. Towne found that illogical, but he had to admit he was not a physician.

Nellie had a difficult delivery, and the baby boy was so "puny" that the doctor prepared the new parents for its quick demise. But with both father and mother, as soon as she was able to be up, taking turns holding it and wrapping it in warm blankets to keep in some heat, the strangely cold little boy survived for a time. Towne appeared determined to will his son to live, while Nellie prayed almost steadily as she rocked the baby. The doctor offered little hope, but they kept trying to keep a spark of life in the frail infant.

Nellie wanted to name the baby Winthrop after her father, but to preface the name with something else, and they settled on

Frederick. Seven weeks after his birth Frederick Winthrop Towne died on April 20, 1875.[3] Towne bought a lot in the city cemetery and contacted the Methodist minister, James M. Parker, to provide a simple graveside service. Towne gave the preacher a poem which the grieving father wished to be read at the funeral, that summed up what he and Nellie felt:

> 'Tis a little grave, but oh! have care!
> For world-wide hopes are buried there;
> And you, perhaps, in coming years,
> May see, like us, through blinding tears,
> How much of light, how much of joy,
> Is buried with an only boy.[4]

Perhaps Parker felt a qualm about giving clerical sanction to the thought expressed by the author of this verse. It was not proper for parents to mourn in quite this vein. Hence, he added a short homily in which he stressed the happiness that the parents felt that their son was already in the arms of the Savior without having to go through life's trials and temptations to reach the happy home.

Towne listened without conviction and with a growing hardness of heart. He wanted to guide his son through life's vicissitudes and share with his son the joys and sorrows that must inevitably come. Furthermore, if God gave parents like Myron and Nellie Towne a child they badly wanted, why would he then snatch it away from them? This suggested a capricious divinity, not the kind of loving Father ministers and church literature had come to portray. Towne could believe in that view of the deity, but he could not reconcile it with a God who took babies out of their mothers' arms. Nellie was inconsolable and kept reiterating the thought that she could not leave baby Frederick out there alone, thus echoing Phinis' sentiments about Lydia. Mothers did not rejoice that a daughter or son in young adulthood or infancy had gone to eternal bliss.

Towne's family problems may have distracted him from seeing the significance of a major development under way in the economy of Adair County. In the 1870s the counties of northeastern Missouri from Randolph County to the Iowa border were about to experience a mining boom. Towne missed the significance, although he caught a glimpse of it. From his acreage at the west edge of Kirksville he concentrated on the building of the railroad from Quincy, Illinois, westward, because he saw in it the chance to sell railroad ties, which he cut from his timber lands and hauled to the sawmills around Kirksville. Other enterprising citizens engaged in the same task, but reacted quicker to the discovery of coal.

In 1873, construction crews laying the tracks west of Kirksville struck coal as they dug and hauled dirt to lower the grade of some of the fairly steep Chariton Hills. Landowners west of Kirksville like Solomon F. Stahl watched the rail lines slowly moving westward in the hope of enticing railroad officials to designate a spot on their land as a stop in exchange for the right-of-way. A village would form around the stop and the landowner could sell town lots at a profit. This happened and Stahl became a stop on the O. K., as the road was popularly termed, but Solomon Stahl also grasped the importance of the discovery of coal on his land. He recruited would-be miners for his new town, sank a mine shaft, and began to haul coal to the surface by the end of the decade. Once the mine was running, he sold it to a Pennsylvania firm, moved to Kirksville, and went into banking. He made more money as he progressed in that business.[5]

Other big landowners followed the same route, but they also virtually deforested the Chariton Hills to use the timber for mine props. Examples of local exploiters of the coal discovery were John L. Porter, Samuel M. Pickler, Valentine Miller, and C. J. Baxter. They quickly sold the mining rights to outside companies, but they stripped the land of timber and went into retail sale of that product, becoming small lumber barons, not coal barons.[6]

Somewhat later, after Towne sold his acreage at the edge of town, coal turned up there. Years later, Towne's son would speculate that had his father stayed in Kirksville he would have owned a coal mine. Towne also had small holdings in the wooded hills, and there was coal in the Big Creek area. He lacked the large tracts of some of the big operators, but had he stayed a little longer, he could have used his propensity for borrowing to raise capital to buy more land before values began to rise. Or had he waited, he could have sold his holdings at a much greater advantage, built on his town lots, and done like Stahl, by going into banking or some other business. He might have opened a hotel in Kirksville. Instead, he snatched the first opportunity to leave Kirksville after baby Frederick's death. His motive was his concern for his wife. He followed an idea popular in the post-Civil War era among the middle class that a change of scene would work wonders for physical health and mental outlook. Nellie's grief destroyed her appetite; she lost weight that she did not have to lose, and she had frequent colds accompanied by coughing. It concerned Towne greatly that he lacked the means to afford her comforts and even some luxuries. He must hasten to achieve a better income.

Towne made the rounds of Kirksville land offices and in the autumn of 1875 he found something to his liking. There was a hotel for sale or trade in Unionville, the county seat of Putnam County, northwest of Adair County.

By consulting the Missouri atlas and a prospectus issued by Unionville promoters, he learned that a railroad was being built through Putnam County which would link Unionville with the main line of the Hannibal and St. Joseph railroad at Brookfield and go northwest to connect with the Burlington line across southern Iowa. Unionville, the only town of any size in the county, was founded more than a decade after Kirksville; it was quite a bit smaller, but Towne considered both to be advantageous. It had the elements to become a major trade center. Towne was too close to the milieu out of which such expectations developed to see the weakness. On the strength of just such nebulous advantages, every town or village in the Middle West harbored delusions about becoming a great metropolis. In the era of rapid growth that followed the war, even sensible people were beguiled.

Towne's realtor opened negotiations with Clement Johnson for the purchase of the hotel. Johnson had asked $3,500 but he accepted Towne's offer of $700 and twenty-two acres of land in the Chariton Hills for which he had paid $372 less than five years earlier. Towne could feel that he had done rather well.[7]

Upon his arrival in Unionville, he felt pleased by what he saw. True, the town square was surrounded by empty lots dotted by a few one-story shops, like those he had seen on the Texas border. The Empire House, as the hotel was styled, was one of the more pretentious structures. It boasted two-and-a-half stories and had a veranda running along two sides. Behind it was a large barn with ample room for expansion. A little ceremony took place in the hotel after his arrival to mark the change of proprietors. A few townspeople came to meet the new owner and welcome him to town. He found things very much as described by the seller. The innkeeper and his wife had their living quarters, but they could take their meals with the guests in the dining room. They could also use the hotel parlor to entertain personal guests as well as the guests of the house. There were hired girls to do the cleaning, cooking, and laundry work under his wife's direction. Nellie's outlook brightened considerably, as she dressed in better fashion and acted as a kind of gracious hostess and mistress of the establishment.[8]

Towne also liked his new role. As he had anticipated, it called for the skills of purchasing, distributing, and record keeping that he had developed in the army. The work was far lighter than farm-

UNI AND BUSINESS DIRECTORY. UNI 639

Unsold Wm, physician.
Untenaner J E, hotel and saloon.

UNION VALLEY,

A postoffice and settlement of 12 persons, in Nodaway county, 15 miles southwest of Maryville, the county seat and trading point; it has a daily mail. Joseph T. Van Ausdall, postmaster.

BUSINESS DIRECTORY.

Campbell B W, physician.
Milam Rev S H (Methodist, South.)
Parrish Joseph V, blacksmith.
Van Ausdall J T, Wagon Maker.
Wood F, dentist.

UNIONVILLE,

An incorporated town of 1,000 inhabitants, is the county seat of Putnam county; it is on the B. & S. W. Ry, 10 miles south of the Iowa line, and 235 northwest of St. Louis; it was settled in 1853, and is beautifully situated in a highly productive farming region, abounding in coal and hardwood timber; among the interests of the place are a steam flouring mill, woolen mill, bank, 1 monthly and two weekly newspapers, 3 churches, 2 good hotels, the City and the Empire; a line of stages run to Milan semi-weekly, distance 24 miles; grain, hay, hogs, lumber and hoop stock are shipped; express, American; telegraph, Western Union; mail, daily. W. T. O'Bryan, postmaster.

BUSINESS DIRECTORY.

American Express Co, James Turner, agt.
Baird John M, blacksmith.
Barnett George W, attorney at law.
Berry A C, physician.
Berry Thomas, Lawyer, Real Estate Agent, and Propr Real Estate Register.
Boynton Samuel W, physician.
Brawford Z T, County Clerk.
Brown Thomas, blacksmith.
Bruer Wm T, Propr Putnam County Ledger.
City Hotel, John M Eareckson, propr, w s Public Square. (*See adv.*)
Comstock James M, collector and treasurer.
Conger Lucien W, Cashier Putnam County Bank, s s Public Square.

CITY HOTEL,

UNIONVILLE, MISSOURI,

J. M. EARECKSON, Proprietor.

This House has been entirely renovated and newly furnished, and is now open for the reception of guests. The best accommodations in the city.

Headquarters for Commercial Travelers. Good Sample Rooms.

STOP AT THE

EMPIRE HOUSE,

N. E. Cor. Square, Unionville, Mo.,

M. S. TOWNE, Proprietor.

Free Bus from all Trains. Headquarters and good Sample Rooms for Commercial Travelers.

GOOD LIVERY AND FEED STABLE IN CONNECTION WITH THE HOUSE.

Unionville City Directory, with an advertisement for the Empire House, Towne's hotel ing or lumbering. He could dress in better garments and keep clean. There were intervals of free time in which he could read or write letters. He soon began to plan improvements. He bought a coach large enough to seat several passengers which would be pulled by a team of four horses. It made regular runs to the railroad station to carry guests to and from the hotel. Atop the bus there was a sign which read "Empire House" on one side and "M. S. Towne Proprietor" on the other. Towne also added a livery stable with horses and buggies for hire to take care of salesmen making the rounds of country stores and nearby hamlets.[9]

These additions required a greater outlay of capital than Towne could command on the heels of the move from Kirksville and the purchase of the hotel. Therefore, he borrowed $300 from a small loan operator in Iowa, using the hotel as collateral. When this was not enough, he applied to Hugh Marshall, who was in the lending business in Unionville as the prelude to opening a bank, for a $150 chattel loan on the hotel's contents.[10]

To facilitate his ability to borrow, Towne wrote to ex-Congressman Galusha Grow to request a reference. From 1851 to 1863, Grow had represented the district in which Susquehanna County was located, and he served as Speaker of the House for the last two of those years. He obliged Towne with a letter terming Towne a "very worthy man of good habits and ... integrity of character." Grow noted that Towne had been "a reliable working Republican from the first formation of the party to the time of leaving Susquehanna County." The former Congressman, now a railroad executive, told Towne in a cover letter, "It will afford me pleasure at all times to do anything in my power to aid you."[11] Whether Towne used this generous offer and laudatory endorsement is not clear.

Meanwhile, Towne learned that the people with whom he dealt in the hotel business could be strange and sometimes dishonest. Carnival and fly-by-night promoters of patent medicines came the hotel first and then tried to defraud its proprietor. Towne's first experience taught him that lesson. Soon after he took over the hotel, two men came to town and took a room. These men claimed to be advance agents for a company that would present a "gigantic" minstrel show. They hawked tickets around the square and sold a large number because people of the town were starved for entertainment. On the morning of the performance the two men skipped town. No performers appeared and the ticketholders discovered they had been duped. Towne found that the men had departed without paying for their lodgings and had even taken the sheets from their bed.[12]

When a medicine man arrived, Towne refused to let him have a room until the man signed a chattel mortgage on his trunk, which contained his costume and the books and medicines he planned to sell. Towne kept the trunk in his office and permitted the man to only take what he needed for a performance. Finally, when the man realized he was not doing well in Putnam County and prepared to leave, Towne held the trunk and its contents until the medicine man could pay for the room. Privately, Towne wondered what he would do with the junk, but he gambled that the man would try to redeem his belongings. True enough, the money arrived in the mail, including enough to pay for shipping the trunk to the man's new address.[13]

On February 27, 1877, Nellie gave birth to a healthy daughter. Nellie had an easy delivery and was so happy with the baby that the mother's health seemed better than it had ever been since she and Towne were married. She desired to name the baby Fanny after her mother, so Towne readily agreed.[14] In his less demonstrative way he was equally delighted with the baby daughter. Both parents were eager for a picture of this beautiful, almost miraculous child, as they perceived little Fanny to be. Nellie dressed the infant in a dainty dress and bundled her in blankets, and Myron and Nellie carried their daughter to the photographer

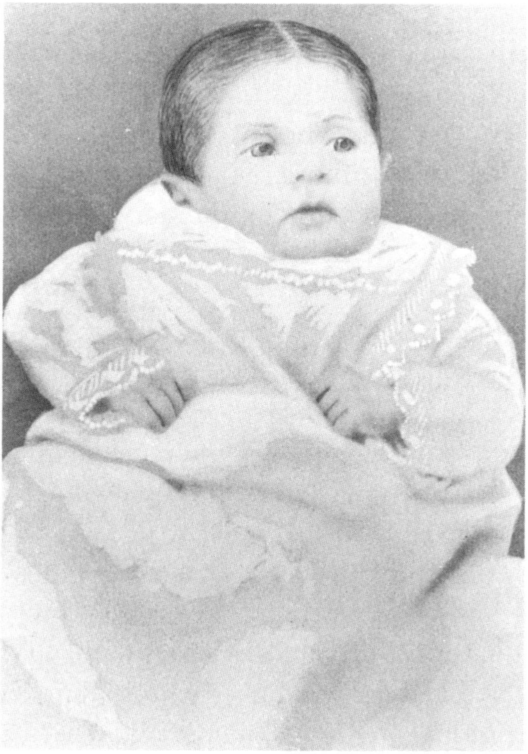

Fanny Towne, infant daughter of Myron and Ellen Towne

whose studio was a few doors west of the Empire House. The photographer worked to focus his camera in such a way that the child, although lying on her blanket appeared, to be sitting upright. Fanny cooperated by opening her blue eyes wide so that she looked as precocious as her doting parents believed her to be.[15]

On the last day of March word came from Lanark that Towne's father had died. Towne prepared to leave immediately, and Nellie desired to accompany him and take baby Fanny with them. Towne felt uneasy but he did want his mother to meet Nellie and he agreed that they could not leave Fanny. Since spring had arrived, the weather should be favorable, and Nellie, took extra pillows and blankets to keep the baby comfortable and protected from drafts. The trip a was longer one than a look at the map would suggest. There were several changes from one rail line to another with long waits at each point. Despite all of the parents' precautions, Fanny became sick at one of the stops. She vomited repeatedly and refused to take more milk. When they reached Lanark, she was hardly responsive to any stimuli. The doctor whom the family hastily summoned prescribed medicines which seemed to have little effect.[16]

Towne left Fanny in the care of her mother and grandmother. He and Phinis went to the undertaker's place and viewed the body of their father. As he looked upon his father's face in the coffin, Towne told his daughter-in-law many years later, he felt "no regrets."[17] What Towne meant by this enigmatic phrase escaped her. She interpreted it to mean that he so disliked his father that he was not sorry his father was dead. That seems unlikely. True, their relationship had often been an uneasy one, but there was no enmity. On the contrary, there was a confused and thwarted love. John Towne never understood his son, but John had desired the best possible for Myron. John had pushed too hard and aroused a kind of stubborn refusal in his son to follow the father's stern admonitions. As he grew older, Myron Towne had come to the conclusion that he and his father were both creatures of their own personalities. They could not escape what that did to them. Hence, Myron felt "no regrets" for that was the way things had happened, and no blame could be attached either to John Towne for the way he had handled his son or to Myron Towne for failing to follow his father's directives.

Instead of dwelling on the past, Towne felt he and his sister must do what they could to prepare a nice funeral and settle their father's business. Towne assumed the task of writing the obituary. He gave his summation of his father: "Deceased was a man of more than ordinary ability, of firm and decided character." After detailing the usual facts of John Smith Towne's life, Myron Towne described the "positions of trust," such as school director and justice of the peace, which he held for "more than twenty years." The eulogist devoted several lines to the deceased's relationship to the Methodist Episcopal Church, where he had been class leader, singer, "fervent spirit," and "main anchor" of the church in Forest Lake Centre. "His home was the rallying point of the brethren when the church was in its infancy and the home of the itinerant minister always." Towne concluded with the statement that John Towne enjoyed life in his "beautiful home in Lanark," but "he was willing to go when the Master called and he died triumphant." Towne made a copy for the minister to read at the service, another for the Carroll County newspaper, and a third to send back to the folks in Susquehanna County to put in a paper there.[18]

Phinis explained to her brother the nature of their father's will. John Towne had bequeathed the house, its furnishings, and a thousand dollars to his wife. At her death, this property would go to Phinis with the stipulation that John Deuel, or any other husband she might take in the future, should not acquire any interest in or control of this property, nor could any money from the estate be used to pay the debts of John Deuel. The remainder of the estate would be shared equally by John Towne's daughter and son. The will named Rachel Towne and Phinis N. Deuel as joint executors.[19] Phinis explained to her brother that she would continue to operate her father's lending business, which was doing quite well.[20] Therefore, she assured him, each would have a nice share in the estate.

The funeral in the Lanark Methodist Church was impressive, but Myron Towne could not concentrate on it. His mind was too preoccupied with anxiety over his baby daughter. Fanny was worse, and the doctor offered little hope. On April 5, she died in her mother's arms. This meant another trip to the cemetery, this time to place the tiny coffin of Fanny in the Towne lot beside her grandfather. Bereft of their second child, Myron and Nellie Towne returned to Unionville.[21]

From the time of Fanny's death, Nellie's always frail health deteriorated to the point that she stayed largely in her room. Towne took her to Kirksville in the hope that the physicians there were more knowledgeable. They consulted what he termed a "counsel of M.D.'s," who agreed that Nellie suffered from "consumption." The only cure, they believed, was to leave the damp climate of the eastern zone of the Middle West for the arid or semiarid climate of the high plains or mountains. They suggested Colorado as the preferred location. However, the doctors told Towne that they doubted Nellie could survive the trip to the West. Meanwhile, they prescribed daily doses of cod liver oil taken with small sips of whiskey. The intent was to stimulate her appetite and encourage her will to live, which the doctors found singularly weak.[22]

Towne suspected that Nellie had decided that death would free her husband from being "burdened" with a sickly wife and permit her to go to their babies in heaven, for she accepted the evangelical view of death, but he refused to accept that decision. He insisted on going through the daily dosings with cod liver oil and whiskey, despite the fact that both the taste of the concotion and the idea of taking alcohol were repugnant to his temperate wife. More to the point, he made desperate efforts to sell the properties he had accumulated in Putnam County to secure the money to take her "out West." However, land was not moving as fast as he had anticipated so he could only sell at a loss. In fact, the only offer he had received by 1879 was to trade the hotel and livery stable for a farm.[23] That obviously did not solve his need for cash. The last hope was the money from his father's estate.

Towne's mother and sister were completely sympathetic to his need, but they too faced hurdles. More than a year before John Towne's death, Ambrose Spencer sold the Towne farm in

Susquehanna County to Abel H. Patrick before completing all of the necessary payments on the property. Patrick tended to be slow about sending the payments with the annual interest. Foreclosure, the only weapon at the hand of the holder of a deed of trust or, as in this case, the original warranty deed, was self-defeating. The family in Illinois would merely have a farm in Pennsylvania to try to sell at a distance or rent without being able to supervise the operation of the tenant. Hence, Rachel and Phinis did what John Towne had done since he sold the land, namely, give the purchaser time to make the payments even though somewhat late. In 1878 the executors had hoped to complete settlement of the estate in the April term of court in Carroll County, but they were unable to do so. Rachel Towne enlisted the help of her nephew, Asa Warner,[24] who had become the backbone of the family. He still lived on the Warner homestead, where he operated what farmland was left to the big house and served as the local preacher for the Forest Lake Centre Methodist Episcopal Church and the administrator of its library, the outgrowth of the library begun by his grandfather.

As his need worsened, Myron Towne wrote to Asa himself. The bitterness he felt became more evident as he pushed his pen across the sheets of Empire House stationery. He noted that he had "done the best" in Unionville of any place he had lived since adulthood only to have "fortune turn against us." The hotel had brought a good return on his investment and the livery stable showed an even greater profit. Now, to save his dear wife's life he must sell these moneymakers and go to Colorado, where many invalids competed for housing and where jobs that he could fill would be scarce.[25] He would have to spend too much of his capital to get his wife into comfortable surroundings and pay for her medical care to be able to open a hotel there. True, that would be a profitable enterprise, but one with high initial cost and overhead.

Not until September 1879 did Patrick make the final payment on Towne's father's property.[26] When Towne received his share of the estate it was too late to save Nellie, if the move to Colorado could have done that. While Towne desperately sought buyers for his enterprises and waited for the settlement of his father's estate, Nellie made her own decision. She would not go to Colorado; she preferred to die where she was, where she and Myron had enjoyed brief happiness together. He was fifty years old, too old to try to begin a new life in a strange and unappealing region. Her obsession against leaving little Frederick resurfaced, so she asked of her husband one favor, a small one compared to what he had offered. After her death she wished Myron to take her body to Kirksville to be buried in the plot he owned so that she could lie beside her firstborn.[27] She had earlier accepted the notion that Fanny was safe, buried near her grandfather. Towne rejected the implications, but he would never let his wife know that. So he readily promised her this request, and she dropped asleep contentedly, as he sat beside her. He knew that she would awaken all too soon racked by violent spasms of coughing.

In preparation for the sad trip, Towne wrote to his sister to learn if she wished to sign a form allowing him to open Lydia's grave and take her to Kirksville for burial. Phinis would not need to worry any further about the whereabouts of the Burdick family, who had indeed left Putnam County. This was what Phinis had desired from the time of Lydia's death, so she immediately sent him the necessary papers, along with one for which he had not asked. She wanted him to accept the payment she enclosed and in return deed her a half interest in the cemetery lot in Kirksville.[28] Towne assured his sister that was not necessary, but he understood her feeling. Indeed, he suspected that in the back of her mind was the thought that she might someday wished to be buried beside her daughter. That was, he guessed, unlikely to happen, but Phinis desired to keep the option viable.

On Monday evening, September 6, 1880, Nellie who had been only semiconscious for several days, breathed her last. Towne arranged a special kind of funeral for the next evening. Instead of a service in the Methodist Episcopal Church that he and Nellie had attended church before her health precluded it, he decreed a private service in the hotel parlor at 7:00 p.m. He ordered invitations from the local printer, who set the type and printed the number of copies Towne desired. In addition to the simple statement of Nellie's full name, Ellen Theodora Towne, and dates of birth and death and the locale of each, the invitation stated: "Her remains will be taken to Kirksville for burial."[29] No clergyman was to officiate. There is no record of anyone's writing a eulogy or of who may have read one. Towne could be very loquacious at times, but at others he could be singularly reticent.

Towne made it clear to his sister that he had sent two of his draymen to Martinstown to disinter Lydia and bring her coffin to the Empire House, where it was cleaned. Then on the morning of the eighth, the Empire Livery Stable dray took the two coffins to the railroad station, where Towne joined them to travel to his first home in Missouri, with the bodies of his wife and niece in the baggage coach. Before returning to Unionville the following day, Towne purchased monuments for each of the graves in the lot that he and his sister now owned jointly. He told her that he had chosen "nice monuments" for each.[30]

Nellie's death seems to have marked the climax of Towne's relationship with organized religion, even though he never relinquished his membership in the Methodist Church. When he remarried three years after Nellie's death, he selected a woman who was herself a baptized Methodist and who transferred her letter to the Unionville Church after their marriage. He would also rear their older son, Frank, as a Methodist. At least, he saw that Frank went to Sunday School as a boy and appeared pleased that Frank married a Methodist and became a firm supporter of the denomination. On occasion, Towne participated in some special church activity and he contributed to it from time to time, but he ceased largely to attend its services, and he certainly was no longer a church worker as he had been during his years in Pennsylvania.

What the root of the matter was, Towne never articulated. The timing suggests that it had to do with the deaths of his niece, his two babies, and his wife. The fifth death to hit the Towne family in that six-year period, that of John Towne, did not enter into the picture for, as the son had written, his father had lived a relatively long life, had done many things, and "died triumphant." Therefore, Myron Towne accepted easily the popular idea of death as a joyful homecoming. But he could not reconcile that view with the deaths of young women eager to rear children or be of assistance to their husband. Worse yet were the deaths of babies less than two months old. Perhaps Towne could and eventually did work out his own acceptance, but the efforts of the clergymen and devout church members, even the women of his immediate family, struck him as hypocritical on the part of clergy and pathetic in the case of the women, whom he saw as unduly influenced by the preacher.

Chapter Fourteen

A New Family

IN THE SEVEN YEARS or more since Towne had come to Unionville, he had established a routine that made it relatively easy to operate the Empire House. The only change caused by the death of Nellie was that he had to devote part of his time to the supervision of cleaning and meal preparation in addition to his regular duties.

Each morning and afternoon when the two daily trains came, Towne was in the office to take payment and keys from departing guests before the hack took them to the depot. When the bus returned with new arrivals, he welcomed them, had them sign the big register, and issued keys. He took pains to call traveling salesmen's attention to the availability of horses and buggies from the livery stable which they could rent to take them on their rounds. Many of these patrons came back for repeated sojourns. One of them was Harry Trigg of Centerville, Iowa.[1]

Trigg was a big, bluff, breezy sort, almost the prototype of the new breed of drummer, or traveling salesman, produced by railroads, improved rural roads, and large-scale manufacturing. Intense competition in the national market of the postbellum era had forced both business combination and intense efforts to sell the products that factories turned out in undreamed-of quantities. Many young men sought the jobs to drum up business in remote areas. Certain characteristics either were required to get the jobs or were developed by them, for they were paid on commission, based on how much they could sell. Small town hotels and livery stables served the salesmen and profited indirectly from the sales.

Sometimes, as Towne was to learn, salesmen peddled other wares than their regular line. Harry Trigg had begun his trips into Missouri shortly after Nellie's death, while Towne still wore the customary black mourning band on the left sleeve of his jacket. Naturally, Trigg inquired and learned that his host was recently widowed. Assuming that remarriage was likely, Trigg evidently decided on his own brand of matchmaking.

Trigg had a maiden aunt, the youngest sister of his mother, Susan Stewart Trigg. This lady, Elizabeth Stewart, had lived with the Trigg family since 1860, when her father died, leaving her an orphan at the age of twelve. Her mother had died when Elizabeth was two. She became an unpaid hired girl in the Trigg household for more than twenty years. It appeared that Susan Trigg "enjoyed ill health," and yet had produced six children in rapid succession; hence her unmarried sister was welcomed as the family drudge, or so it sounded to Towne.[2] He found himself feeling a little sorry for this woman. Finally, as Trigg rambled on the subject on several visits, Towne realized that the Triggs now wanted to get rid of the unmarried aunt, no longer needed since the youngest Trigg was now a schoolgirl. Therefore, Trigg was trying to find a husband to take "Aunt Lib," as he called her, off their hands.

In truth, Towne had been reflecting on his situation. While he unquestionably missed Nellie, loneliness was not his major concern. He had to admit that operating a hotel without a female partner was difficult. Perhaps he was beguiled by a curious delusion. His marriage with Ellen Cole, although clearly one of convenience, had worked out well. Hence, he seemed to think another contrived union would be equally good. In his old age, he was fond of quipping that widowers should be shut up somewhere until they recovered from the delusion that they could recapture the happiness they had enjoyed with the departed spouse by marrying someone the male fancied was like his dead wife. He implied that he had succumbed to the fantasy himself. On other occasions, he described his circumstances more harshly: he needed a housekeeper.[3]

Whatever his combination of motives, Towne decided to learn more about Miss Elizabeth Stewart. He utilized Harry Trigg's tale about how sorry "Aunt Lib" felt about "poor Captain Towne" who had lost his wife and little babies as an excuse to write a polite note thanking her for her kind expression of concern and hinting that he would like to meet her, should he ever happen to be in Centerville. In a few days a reply arrived. It was brief, but it told him much about the lady. She had very limited education and little acquaintance with or access to niceties for she wrote with a pencil on a cheap tablet. Her grammar and spelling were uncertain from the number of erasures, and her handwriting was childish, totally unlike the neat, graceful script of the women of his family. Nonetheless, the substance of her missive was clear. She would be pleased to meet Captain Towne. To his surprise, the next day's post brought an invitation from "Mrs. J. T. Trigg" requesting that Mr. Towne call at the Trigg home on the second Sunday following the date of her note. Her son Harry would meet the train and escort the guest to the house. The Triggs were in a hurry.

Having entered this exchange with matrimonial intent, Towne accepted the arrangements and duly met Elizabeth Stewart on that Sunday afternoon in the early spring of 1883. When he and Trigg reached the house, Harry introduced the two women who greeted them. After looking him over briefly Mrs. Trigg disappeared with her son, and Towne and the maiden sister-aunt settled down in the parlor to get acquainted. He asked a few polite questions, trying to put her at ease. She did not hesitate to respond: She proceeded to tell him her life history. As she did so, he made various judgments. She was a talker, he mentally categorized, who probably craved a sympathetic listener. She wanted it understood that she suffered from a cruel fate which had deprived her of her mother. After her sister married, her father put her in charge of the household including her two older brothers, or so she said, so that she stayed home most of the time. Thus she apparently explained her lack of schooling. Her father had operated a store in Bentonsport, Iowa, but when he died the husband of an older sister sold the store and gave each younger child two dollars as his or her share while he went to Memphis, Missouri and opened a bank. Miss Stewart had no doubt she had been cheated. As she recounted the wrongs done to her, her eyes would fill with tears or fairly snap in anger.

Towne decided that Elizabeth Stewart looked her thirty-five years; her thin, dark hair, pulled into a little knot on top of her head, displayed streaks of gray. Her face was round, with pudgy cheeks and a full lower lip that almost simulated a pout. She was short, under five feet, he judged. Her complexion was dark and sallow. Her eyes were almost black and very expressive, as he noted during her recital. Her hands were square with blunt fingers and stubby nails; when she rather uncertainly offered him her hand, he noted how rough and work-hardened it was. He could not help feeling sorry for her. When he departed, the Triggs, who had joined the lady to see him off, urged him to come again. He countered by requesting permission to write to her again.[4]

Several exchanges followed, and by June, Towne wrote to ask if she would be willing to marry him despite the age difference, since he was fifty-four, nineteen years her senior. Obviously, she considered him her only chance as well as a good catch, and she accepted the proposal without question. They set June 14 as the day and the Centerville Methodist preacher as the officiant. On the previous day, Towne procured the license in Centerville, so that everything was ready for the ceremony in the Trigg parlor. Elizabeth wore a much nicer dress than the very plain one she wore when he previously saw her. To his compliment, she naively admitted her married niece had lent it to her; apparently she had nothing suitable. She had also tried to curl her sparse hair enough to form a fluffy bang across her forehead, which he told her he liked so she continued to do it in that fashion for special occasions. As soon as the ceremony was completed, the Rev. I. P. Teter, the bride, and the groom signed the marriage certificate. Then the newlyweds departed for Unionville.[5]

Towne noticed that his new wife signed her name Elizabeth Towne, using no maiden name or initial, and she continued to use that as her legal signature throughout her life; but when they got off the train at Unionville, she answered the questions of the reporter covering the "locals" for the *Unionville Republican* with a different version. While Towne supervised unloading the small trunk that seemed to contain most of her possessions, she told the reporter that she was the new Mrs. M. S. Towne and that she was the former Lizzie Stewart. The paper duly recorded that "On last Thursday Mayor Towne returned from Centerville with a life companion. He was married to Miss Lizzie Stewart that day."[6]

Towne could not decide what to call his wife. She informed him very firmly that she disliked the name Elizabeth and had never been called by it. She had always been called Lizzie until the last Trigg child was named Elizabeth and called Lizzie. Then the family started calling the relative living with them Libby or Lib. Towne and his family had never cared for nicknames and he felt almost hostile toward "Lib;" it sounded like the name of a horse or mule, more likely the latter, he thought. To substitute such a term for even Lizzie, because Mr. and Mrs. Trigg wanted to use it for a child, added a further indignity. In the end he settled the matter by addressing her directly, sometimes with the title "wife" or after it became appropriate, "mama." In later years, she claimed when she was miffed at him, that he only addressed her as "Say you."[7]

Later in the summer of their first year of marriage, Towne took his wife to Lanark to meet his family. She was quite impressed with the large, well-furnished house with its spacious grounds. She appeared to feel that she must ingratiate herself with these more affluent relatives-in-law by offering services not appropriate to a guest. After a well-prepared supper which Phinis served, Libby, as she had asked her husband's family to call her, insisted that she would do the dishes. She likely reasoned that Phinis must be tired from so much cooking, she should go with her mother, granddaughter, and brother to the living room while the guest washed the dishes.

His wife's attitude grated on Towne's nerves, but he excused her on the ground that she had lived so long in the position of the "poor relation" that obsequiousness had become second nature. She had learned that she must be constantly useful or her sister-in-law and husband would not keep her. However, Towne knew his sister well. Phinis preferred to do things herself so that things would be done her way. Her mother naturally understood so she tried to discourage her new daughter-in-law. Therefore, with her husband and mother-in-law each firmly taking her by the arm, they managed to get the newcomer into the living room. Phinis hastily closed the door and went to work. In short order, she joined them and they enjoyed a pleasant evening of conversation in which the Townes introduced absent family members, mainly Warners, to Elizabeth. It came to an end when Rachel Towne announced that she was ready for bed.

At that moment the new member, still longing to be useful, created a classic contretemps. She offered to brush "Mother Towne's" hair. Phinis hastily retreated behind her mother's chair as she gave her brother a look of incredulity accompanied by the "how-could-you" stare she had used when they were children and he was caught in some peccadillo. He decided retreat was in order and edged toward the doorway into the hall. While Rachel Towne

Rachel Towne, age seventy-six. Note the cap was fixed to show hair that did not exist.

thoughtfully considered the offer, her daughter-in-law added the blandishment that she had brushed her sister's hair nightly because the latter affirmed that she slept better as a result. The older woman smiled and thanked Libby for her thoughtfulness. Then, indicating that she still had the fabled eyes in the back of her head possessed by all good mothers, she directed her son to bring the brush from the dresser in her bedroom. Knowing that she had caught him trying to escape, Myron dutifully got the brush, a soft baby brush, and handed it to her. She passed it to her daughter-in-law as she removed her ruffled cap revealing a totally bald head. The look of horror on Elizabeth's face was so comical that Phinis and Myron fled, closing the door noiselessly as they heard their mother explaining that the soft brush did make her scalp feel good because it stimulated the circulation.

Myron and Phinis laughed until the tears ran down their cheeks. Whether the episode taught Elizabeth Towne anything or not is problematic, but the story was one of Towne's favorites to repeat to his son and later daughter-in-law when his wife was not present. However, with somewhat less ornamentation, Elizabeth even told the story on herself.[8]

On the day before they left, Towne proposed to take all the women folk to the photographer for pictures. The eldest and youngest were most agreeable; the two women of uncertain age declined firmly. Whether Towne had meant this to be a wedding picture is not clear; if so it was not made, and indeed there was no wedding picture of Towne and his third wife. At seventy-six, Rachel Towne still took a good picture. Of course, her great-granddaughter, Mary, was the star. Her fancy ruffled taffeta dress, elaborate hair ribbon at the top of her head, and a locket that really was too much for a child to wear made her almost over-dressed.[9] The day when Phinis had to apologize for Mary's calico dress was long gone.

As Towne and his wife prepared to return to Unionville, his mother went to a drawer of the sideboard in the dining room and took out a small flannel case stitched in sections to hold silver pieces. From it she took the coin silver spoons John Towne had presented to his wife on their fiftieth wedding anniversary, not long before his death. These spoons, which had become popular after the Civil War, symbolized luxury for the newly affluent. They were clearly luxuries because they were well-nigh useless and therefore were only good for show. They were so malleable that they could only be displayed on spoon racks designed for that purpose. John Towne had been uncertain about how to have them engraved. He wanted his wife's initials, but should he use R. W. T. or R. T.? After some debate with himself, he decided to have six

Mary Burdick, age ten

engraved each way. Now his wife proposed to do the same thing; that is, she would divide the spoons between her daughter and daughter-in-law so that each had three of the R. W. T. and three of the R. T. spoons. Myron and his wife were to take their spoons when they left.[10]

Back in Unionville, Towne and his wife settled into a routine. Things appeared to be going well as both the hotel and livery stable showed increasing profits. However, once more malign fate struck. On the night of December 12 the Townes had retired for the night, but for some reason Towne felt wakeful. He made a final check through the hotel before going into his apartment. A patent medicine man had checked in that afternoon smelling of liquor and had not appeared for supper. Fearing the man was on a binge,

Towne checked on the man's room and was reassured by loud snores and darkness. The guest's kerosene lamp was out and he was sleeping off his inebriation. Nonetheless, Towne was awake when he heard someone running down the stairs shouting, "Fire!" Towne jumped out of bed and into his trousers and boots and grabbed a coat as he dashed out. He paused only long enough to tell his wife to stay there until he sent a crew to get everything out of their apartment, the parlor, and the office.

The man who took care of the livery stable and lived over it was running toward the hotel, shouting for neighbors to come quickly. A hasty check indicated that all guests were downstairs including the drunk "doctor," who had been virtually dragged out by other guests. Towne directed the evacuation of the contents of the public rooms and his apartment, while the livery manager took charge of the efforts to put out the fire. A line of men pumped water from the well and passed buckets to those on ladders trying to douse the flames. The fire was spreading fast, so Towne ordered efforts to be concentrated on saving the barn, with its valuable horses and vehicles, and the contents of the hotel which had been placed at a safe distance.

Once, as embers fell in a widening circle from the collapse of the roof and upper story, Towne looked around to find his wife and saw that she sat stoically on the big chest that held all of his school and military records, pictures, and other treasures. She had wrapped herself in a quilt, tied a scarf over her head, and appeared to be keeping a watchful eye on their possessions placed nearby, including the wardrobe that contained their clothing and the big secretary from his office that contained his books.

The hotel was a total loss, but the contents had been largely saved as well as the livery stable. The Unionville paper poked fun at Towne for saving his "plug hat" without realizing that it simply happened to be in the wardrobe along with other garments. Towne, in a letter to the editor, called attention to the fact that no lives had been lost nor had any guest or firefighter suffered serious injury. However, the financial loss was devastating.

Towne valued the hotel and its contents at six thousand dollars, but carried only two thousand dollars in insurance. He desired to rebuild, but the insurance would not provide sufficient funds.[11] He dreamed of a building large enough to accommodate more guests and some public functions. Then he realized he lacked the money and Unionville could not support such a facility. That was Towne's perennial problem: he had the mind of a successful entrepreneur in a region where venture capital was lacking and chances for success were not good.

On the day after the fire, Towne and his wife moved their salvaged belongings into a small house east of the square, where they lived for six years. On August 25, 1884, eight months afterward, a baby boy was born. The doctor pronounced the boy to be a perfect infant despite the mother's lament that his ears stuck out too prominently. She continued to fret about that, refusing to accept assurances the doctor and nurse offered that the baby would soon grow out of the small defect, if it were that.[12] Towne had hired a woman to act as a nanny for the baby for the first few months of its life. He had been haunted by thoughts of the fate of his firstborn and seemed to feel this step might be the difference between survival and early death. Immediately after she had bathed the newborn and wrapped him in soft, white blankets, she brought him to the father, who held the child, studied his features carefully, and decided that the child was a true member of the Warner-Towne family. As the doctor scribbled on a notepad details for the local paper, he asked about the name. The new mother began to talk about John, saying it was the name of both grandparents so it would be appropriate. Towne cut in with his own announcement, "I wish to call him Frank Warner, after my cousin, an ordained elder of the Methodist Episcopal Church."[13]

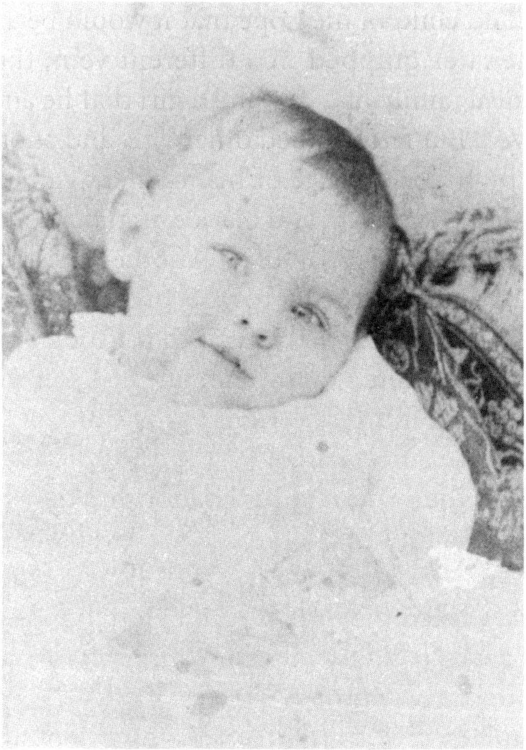

Frank Warner Towne as a baby of four months; his ears do no appear overly prominent.

That decision symbolized the relationship that quickly developed between father and son. Frank resembled Towne in that the boy was blue eyed, sandy haired, and fair skinned. More important, he was serious minded and studious. Under Towne's tutelage his son learned to read well before he entered the first grade, and he became an avid reader. By the time he was in the upper grades, he had read with understanding most of the books in his father's library.

When Frank was four, a second boy arrived. Towne had tried to dissuade his wife from a second pregnancy due to their ages. He was nearing sixty and she was past forty. It was dangerous for her and his chances of survival until a second child reached maturity were not good. She insisted and he reluctantly consented to attempt a second child in the hope that it would be a girl. He still fancied, as he later quipped in a different vein, that he might recreate the ideal family of a boy and a girl that he and Nellie had almost achieved. But fate decided otherwise, and another boy was born. The baby was the image of his mother, with a round face, dark complexion, black hair, and black eyes that soon appeared to be what people termed pop-eyed. The mother insisted on naming the child Myron Stewart.[14] Towne protested strongly. He approved of Stewart, but he begged that it be combined with another name. He pointed to the anomaly of a son with the same initials as the father and yet no right to the suffix of "Junior." She was adamant, so he surrendered.

That became the pattern of his relationship to his second son; Towne soon washed his hands of any responsibility for the boy's upbringing. This stemmed partly from temperamental differences. Efforts to teach the boy to read before he was old enough for school proved fruitless. Indeed, young Myron did not even learn the alphabet or number system. He was slow in school. Teachers complained of inattentiveness, carelessness, inability to follow directions, and plain laziness. He misbehaved and acted silly at times. Theories about learning difficulties were in their infancy and had not yet reached Unionville. Myron's mother blamed the teachers, his older brother, and his father. She assumed everyone else was at fault except herself and her darling. Towne largely ignored his younger son beyond superficial amenities in their home, and Frank followed his father's lead, only perhaps a bit stronger. Four years' age difference and lack of any commonality of interests meant that there was little companionship between the brothers.

Without really intending it, Towne increasingly shut his wife out of his innermost life and thoughts. He shared these with his older son. If she had needs or interests that he might have tried to understand, he made no attempt. That unquestionably made her more and more possessive of her "baby." While appearing quite proper and praiseworthy, the Towne family was curiously divided. Elizabeth Towne alternated between an air of martyrdom marked by complaints about not knowing what properties her husband planned to buy, sell, or mortgage and an abrasive manner in which she set him or anyone else, especially business associates, "right" about any and all matters. She asked Towne for money rather frequently, which he always gave her without question; although he suspected, and sometimes Frank told him in a worried manner, that she either gave money to Myron to waste or was covering up the fact that Myron had taken money out of her purse or dresser drawer. Towne told Frank not to worry about it; Towne would talk to "mama" and Myron and stop the practice. Seemingly, Towne did not; he dreaded the tears and recriminations that would ensue.[15]

Towne wanted his wife to dress somewhat better to reflect the position which he held or wanted to hold in the community, but Elizabeth did not seem interested in clothes. One good outfit for church, the Ladies' Aid Society, or Relief Corps meetings seemed her limit. Otherwise, she wore old things until they were threadbare or common house dresses. When they were first married Towne also tried to educate her better. She read some of his newer fiction, occasionally and dutifully studied the special pages of *The St. Louis Republic* that now arrived in Unionville by train only a day late. Metropolitan dailies by the 1890s had added all sorts of features, including patterns for garments for adults and children. Elizabeth Towne dressed her sons in the latest styles for both Sunday and school attire. Her boys wore knickers, short jackets, blouses with wide collars, and large bow ties.[16] That pleased the father greatly, but some other things disturbed him.

Elizabeth Towne never mastered spelling or neat, legible handwriting. Worse was her pronunciation. She would pick up a "new" word that had caught her attention and promptly add it to her vocabulary without consulting a dictionary or gazetteer. Towne tried at first to give her assistance by using the word again in his response and pronouncing it correctly. She ignored him and continued to say it her way. In addition, her Middle Western twang endurable, at first, became more disturbing when he heard Frank using the same idioms. One day, he stopped the boy as they walked together to reprove him. "Son," the father said to the boy who was talking about the hogs, "it is not 'hawg,' your mama says 'hawg,' but the word is 'hahg.' Remember that, and that goes for other words such as fog."[17] Frank Towne never forgot the lesson and his pronunciation always smacked of the East in which he never lived. One wonders what other lesson he also acquired in the little homily.

The Towne family in 1892: M. S. Towne seated, Frank W. Towne standing by his father, Myron Stewart Towne seated by his mother, Elizabeth Towne.

Chapter Fifteen

Life on the Dairy Farm

IN 1890 TOWNE SOLD THE LIVERY STABLE and moved to a farm at the edge of Unionville. Despite his recognition of differences rising from the dramatic change of the last decades, he still viewed land as a road to success. He had been purchasing various plots of land south of town from the time he moved to Putnam County. By 1890 he owned more than 250 acres. Almost 200 of these acres were contiguous; 60 acres were in two plots, 40 and 20 acres respectively, to the south and east of the main farm. There was a two-story frame house on the northwest corner of that land, and situated almost precisely one mile from the square in Unionville. Garfield Street formed the northern boundary of the farm. Therefore, the house was inside the Unionville school district.[1] This permitted Towne's sons to attend the grade school and high school there. Towne had attended a one-room rural school and taught for years in such schools in Pennsylvania, but his sons must have better. Middle-class standards now called for improved educational facilities, and Towne aspired for a little more than the average.

Before moving, Towne had directed a carpenter for a great deal of remodeling. His goal was to have as many comforts and amenities of urban living as possible. He exercised his ingenuity together with features he recalled from the houses of northeastern Pennsylvania. He built a connecting link between the dwelling and certain outbuildings. He enclosed the back porch, thereby making it possible to step from the kitchen onto the porch and then into a toolhouse on one side and coal- and woodshed on the other. Through the toolshed one turned into a passageway that ended in the outhouse. The passageway was neatly covered so that no one needed to brave cold, rain, snow, or wind to go to the outhouse. He made more improvements in the kitchen. Across one end, he built a long, wooden frame with a top big enough to hold a large washbasin, with a long counter on each side. At one end of the sink there was a small pump which could direct water into a bucket. From there, the water went into a big boiler attached to the range where it was heated by the fire. When laundry or dishes were to be done one held the bucket under the spigot of the boiler and drew out the hot water. The water was then carried back to the basin lined with zinc in the middle of the long counter. Once the laundry or dishes was done, the stopper was removed from the basin and the water went down a pipe into a space under the kitchen where an underground pipe carried it well beyond the house. Towne also built storage cabinets under the sink for pots, pans, skillets, and other utensils.[2]

To continue his climb up the economic ladder Towne decided to begin farming. In view of his age, frequent bouts with hemorrhoids, and increasing lameness from varicose veins, a shift to farming seems odd. However, Towne did not intend to engage in tillage; rather he proposed to operate a dairy. Although Unionville had not grown as fast as its promoters had anticipated, it had ceased to be a rural village. People no longer kept a cow, but the grocery stores still offered only canned milk. Most households relied on a relative or friend in the country to bring milk, butter, or other dairy products to town weekly or at least from time to time. Towne saw a need for a dairy that could make daily deliveries to each household that bought the service. Another factor in Towne's decision was his recognition that without the hotel, the livery stable was less profitable. Once more, Towne faced the need to maximize his income and accumulate an estate. He had started a new family at an age when most men were ready to retire. Now, he must guard against the possibility that he might die before his sons were self-supporting. He also felt obligated to leave his wife in comfort. He thought the new venture had real possibilities. He was qualified to handle such an operation because he and his father had both raised cattle in Susquehanna County. He christened his operation the Fairview Dairy.

For his cattle Towne chose Holsteins. He kept careful records that convinced him he had made the right decision, for the big black and white cows gave more milk with a lower fat content that the more popular Jersey breed of his neighbors. He scorned Jersey milk as being of two layers, thick cream on top of "chalk and water," or "blue milk," as he termed it. He enjoyed looking out at the handsome Holsteins grazing on his rolling pasture.[3]

However, Towne imposed an additional burden on himself from the beginning of life on the farm. He desired to be a gentleman farmer, who supervised and managed rather than perform the physical labor. He engaged a full-time hired hand and made him responsible for driving the cattle to pasture each morning, bringing them back to the big barn, and seeing that each went to her milking stall each evening. Towne and his sons, as they grew older, might assist in the milking, but the hired man did all the cleanup and carrying of the milk pails to the cooling area. He also had to keep the machinery in good repair, taking it to the field as needed and returning and cleaning it after usage. Towne purchased the latest in mechanical items such as the sulky plow, planter, cultivator, and hay rake, and he insisted they be housed in the machine shed and not allowed to remain in the field for weeks after being used, as too many farmers seemed to do.[4]

To relieve his wife of drudgery, Towne engaged a live-in hired girl, who did the heaviest housework such as washing and cleaning in addition to the work of preparing the milk each morning for delivery and washing and airing the big milk cans after they were returned empty. She was also in charge of making butter and cottage cheese from unsold milk. At times of extra work such as canning, he hired a few part-time girls. Towne did not interfere in what he considered his wife's domain, but he frequently wished that she could handle it better. She was sadly disorganized and would stop the girl before a task was completed and take her to something else which could have waited. Worse yet, in Towne's eyes, his wife would stop in the middle of dish washing, let the water grow cold, while she called to the girl in the midst of some major task, "Let's go to the barn and see the new calf."[5] While it was customary to treat hired help as if they were adjunct family members, Towne felt, perhaps because of his military training, that there was a line of demarcation. He did insist that hired help eat in the kitchen rather than in the dining room and that they complete their duties as soon as they had eaten. His wife, he felt, appeared to see no distinction or refused to practice it. The younger son, as he grew older, followed his mother's example, while the elder son like his father was polite, but even more distant. The dairy farm did not bond the divided family.

One task Towne refused to delegate to anyone was the planting and tending of fruit plants, bushes, or trees. He arranged a careful progression of fruit from strawberries, through raspberries, blackberries, cherries, peaches, pears, plums, grapes, and apples. At picking time he urged his sons into service. The older boy not only enjoyed the time with his father, but acquired a similar love of fruit, not only to eat it fresh in season and canned in the winter, but to watch it grow and develop.[6] The younger son liked to shimmy up a tree and show off a bit before he went to the serious task of picking. In fact, he wanted to eat as he picked and then he was eager to get out of further work once his stomach was full.

Soon after the Towne family moved to the farm, the last member of the family arrived. One evening in March, Towne went to the barn after supper to check on the new calves. It was a cold evening with a strong wind. As he swung his lantern onto the hook so that it lighted the main area, he heard a piteous mewing. There was a kitten somewhere in the barn that had strayed from its mother, he concluded; he must locate it. Towne had a deep regard for all living creatures. He grew up in the household of a blacksmith who treated horses with real respect. In the army Towne was noted for his ability to handle horses and mules. Cats were something to be cared for as well. They had been part of his boyhood; his mother and sister always had a house cat besides the barn cats. He followed the sound and discovered a kitten whom none of the barn cats seemed willing to claim. He refused to leave it there to starve or be trampled by a cow, so he tucked it inside his jacket and carried it to the house.

Once inside the kitchen, Towne set the kitten onto the floor and called his wife and Frank to come. The kitten did not walk well; its tiny legs were unsteady, but it tried to get to the eager six-year old kneeling on the floor. Meanwhile, Mama got milk and poured it into a pan to heat on the stove, while Towne went to the cellar to get a small but sturdy wooden box. His wife warmed soft rags at the back of the stove. Deciding the milk had reached the right temperature, she poured it onto a saucer. The kitten had not yet learned to lap milk, so Mama dipped her finger into the milk and let the kitten lick her finger. Frank thought this was exciting, so he took over while his mother placed the cloths in the box to make a warm bed. Towne examined the foundling and pronounced it a female and a perfect maltese. Her coat was a smoky blue-gray with only one small tuft of white under her chin. He thereupon christened her Mali. Since Towne pronounced the name with his eastern broad "a" it sounded like Mahly so most hearers translated it into Molly, while his wife called the cat "Mawly."[7]

However her name was pronounced, Mali became a full-fledged member of the family. She tolerated no other cats or dogs in her territory. She would upon occasion go to a sunny spot outside the back porch while her friend and rescuer visited the barn lot. One day, while sunning herself, she spied a neighbor's dog who had entered the yard; someone had forgotten to close the gate. The dog's owner had cautioned Towne not to let his cat out because, the owner threatened, his dog would kill her. Mali had her own ideas on the subject. After warning the dog with a series of spits and hisses, she leaped onto his back, dug in all claws of her front and back legs except for one front paw, which she raked across the face of the dog, shredding nose and eyelids. Shrieks of anguish from the dog had no effect on her until the dog tore through the gate. Then, she jumped from his back and marched triumphant into her own yard. Towne, who had rushed to Mali's defense, so he thought, closed and hooked the big gate. He laughed as she walked ahead of him to the house, the hair on her neck gradually losing its stiffness and her tail declining in size.[8]

Mali decided that her nights belonged to Frank. When bedtime arrived, she ran upstairs ahead of him and leaped onto his bed, where she curled on his feet and stayed all night. When he was in the second grade he developed measles. His mother had read in the *St. Louis Republic* how to treat communicable diseases. She decreed that Frank should stay upstairs and she would bring food up to him. She washed and scalded all dishes and silver he used. She even covered her dress with a big, coverall apron and hung it upstairs to prevent any chance of germs reaching little Myron, then three. When little Myron developed the measles, she was desolate. She could not understand how her baby caught the disease when she had been so careful. Towne smiled and asked if Mali did not spend most of her day with her young master Frank.

Elizabeth responded that the boy, whom she would not allow to have any reading materials and had to stay in a darkened room to guard his eyes, quickly became bored once he no longer was feverish or sick, so of course he played with Mali on his bed. Towne questioned further, "But didn't Mali come downstairs for her meals? Didn't Myron get down on the floor to play with her? There, Mama, is your carrier."[9] He added the then popular thought that now Myron would not need to miss any school because of the disease, which he would otherwise have contracted, as Frank had, from schoolmates once an epidemic began.

Shortly before Christmas of 1891, Phinis notified her brother of their mother's death.[10] Towne and his wife and older son had visited Lanark at least twice in the summer, and on the last occasion, Rachel had seemed quite well despite increasing difficulty in walking due to arthritis. Therefore, despite her age, her death shocked her son. He quickly prepared to make the trip and his wife decided to accompany him, but they hired the woman who had cared for both boys when they were born and still sometimes looked after three-year old Myron to stay with them. In this way Frank would not need to miss school and the baby would be spared the danger of sickness from the long and tiring trip in possibly severe weather.

Once in Lanark, Phinis detailed the funeral plans and they visited until Mary arrived for supper. She had graduated from high school the previous May and now worked in a local store. She apparently spent her money on clothes for she still was a fashion plate, so her uncle thought. Mary did not resemble any of the Towne or Warner family he decided. She was tall, big boned, and had a broad face. Her hair was curled and ratted to form fluffy bangs and side puffs, and Towne decided even after she removed her modish little hat that she had escaped having thin hair like her great-grandmother, grandmother, and mother. On the side, he warned Phinis to be prepared for another youthful marriage.[11]

Mary Burdick at the time of Rachel Towne's death, 1891

Towne's speculation proved correct; at the age of twenty Phinis' granddaughter married. However, Mary's choice of a husband shocked Phinis and disconcerted Towne even more. On December 28, 1892, the young lady married John F. Schmucher, the son of German immigrants of the Brethren persuasion who had come to Lanark in the 1870s. Mary Burdick became the first member of the Towne family in ten generations on Phinis' direct line of descent to marry a second generation American and one whose ancestry did not go back to the British colonists of the seventeenth century. Myron shook his head sadly, not entirely out of snobbery but because he regarded the cultural and value system of this particular immigrant group as very different. Towne had no desire to force these folk to give up their "old-country" ways, even though he deplored their efforts not to abandon any German culture. He recognized that the vast number of immigrants increasing each year was another aspect of the changes sweeping over the nation. In some respect, he regarded this as good, but not for his sister's granddaughter and ward. The melting pot had not functioned sufficiently long for John Schmucher and many other Germans. German pietists seemed determined to impose their beliefs on old stock Americans. Mary went to the Church of the Brethren with his family.

Phinis Deuel in 1898, when she was about seventy, seated on the right; others are Mary Burdick Schmucker, her husband, John Schmucker, and their first two sons.

Subsequent events confirmed Towne's foreboding. Schmucher was a blacksmith. John Towne prospered as he practiced that trade, but that was early in the century. Now in a mechanized economy, Towne doubted that Mary's husband could make a decent living. Towne did not scorn the means by which his father had succeeded; however, subsequent generations must do better. For John Towne's great-granddaughter to slide back into the strata from which he had risen would have pained and angered him. As Myron Towne grew older he displayed some of the same characteristics. Worse yet seemed the German proclivity for large families; by 1904, Mary had borne six children, five of whom were boys. John's meager income did not support such a family. They lived with Phinis in the home she had inherited when her mother died and Phinis' money paid most of the expenses. She had retired from the small loan business and performed much of the cooking, cleaning, and child care. Towne regarded it as a sad way for Phinis to spend her last years.[12]

But all of this lay in the future. In 1891 mourners filled the Lanark Methodist Episcopal Church for Rachel Towne's funeral. Towne could mourn his mother but, as in the case of his father, feel no terrible loss because he knew she was ready to join her maker. She would have had no desire to become helpless so it was well she could be taken at the age of eighty-four. As the funeral procession formed outside the church to take the casket to the Lanark cemetery to place beside her husband and Myron Towne's infant daughter, the bell began to toll. Myron stood by the first carriage, which would carry the immediate family, counting the slow tolling until it reached eighty-four strokes. Then, as its sound died away in the cold still air, he said softly to himself, "This marks the passing of a noble woman."[13]

Towne recounted the incident in a talk he gave in the Unionville Methodist Episcopal Church on January 27, 1892. The pastor, Samuel Knupp, was serving his first year in the Unionville charge. A graduate of a seminary rather than one who had gone through the traditional pastoral course of study, he tried to offer different types of services for Sunday evening services, already less well attended than had once been the case. He also appeared to be trying to work more of the laity into leadership positions. Either he had learned something of Towne's prior work in the Forest Lake church or he simply saw that Towne was better informed and more scholarly than most of the parishioners. For whatever reason, Knupp asked Towne to give a talk on "Bells" in connection with the installation of a bell in the sixteen-year-old church as part of a renovation project.

Towne delved into his books and carefully researched the history of bells. He cited famous individual bells such as St. Paul's and described the making of bells and the ways of creating different tones. Since he was speaking in a church, Towne devoted more attention to the use of bells in religious ceremonies, from the time of the ancient Egyptians to the present. He described vividly the way priests in the Roman Catholic Church had until eighteenth century, used "bell, book, and candle" in the ritual of excommunication. As the bell tolled, the priest would intone, "Out be thy name taken from the book of life, as this candle is cast from the sight of God into the deepest pit of Hell among fiends and damned creatures among whom everlasting pains endure." After a pause to insure that this sinister picture made its maximum impact, Towne added his own religious philosophy. "In our day of religious light and freedom we are amazed that men should arrogate to themselves the power of the great Creator and final Judge of all, to damn their fellow men."[14]

Towne described the custom of tolling the bell out of respect for the dead. In rural England two hundred years earlier the tolling of the bell would notify the parish of a death. By counting the strokes, one for each year of the deceased's life, a hearer could judge reasonably well who had departed from the community, and Towne noted how the custom had continued in Lanark at his mother's funeral.

Towne could not conclude without a patriotic peroration on the Liberty Bell. Its concept of "liberty and equality for all people" inspired the "soldiers of freedom" to "battle for the right and by their victory smite the chains" from four million slaves and "bid the bond to go free."[15] Towne was determined that people must remember what he and his comrades, especially in the colored regiments, had fought to establish. He had not turned his back on the Fourteenth and Fifteenth Amendments regardless of the position of presidents, Congress, or the courts in the post-Reconstruction era.

Life on the dairy farm proceeded smoothly, but Towne still became restless and longed to travel. He frequently went with his wife and sons to visit her numerous relatives in Centerville, but he desired more than those trips. In fact, as time passed, he let his wife go with the boys while he stayed at home. He longed to go back to his old home. In 1888 the 143rd gathered at Gettysburg to dedicate the regiment's monument in what had now become a national park, but he was not in attendance. However, those who came from Susquehanna County formed an association to meet annually and elected Asa Warner, secretary. He promptly began keeping the roll, complete with addresses and other current information about all members of Company H, and each year he mailed information about the annual meeting. In 1892 the group voted to meet at Gettysburg in September 1893, and Towne notified his cousin that if all went well, he would meet Asa and Stanley there.[16]

When people in Unionville heard that one of their leading citizens planned to go to this historic shrine, they remembered with almost a sense of shock that he had actually participated. Thirty years after the great battle, it had retreated into a national legend, and young people in the Middle West found it almost beyond belief that one of their own townsmen had lived through it.

One of those impressed was none other than John Carroll, general counsel for the Burlington system. He maintained a home in Unionville, a mansion on West Main Street, where he lavishly entertained people from St. Louis, Chicago, or elsewhere. He spent the legislative session in Jefferson City, where he was one of the three railroad lobbyists who in combination disturbed railroad passes without which, it seemed, politics could not function in Missouri. As a consequence, the triumvirate was able to control most legislative action. Reform sentiment was once more on the rise in America, and Towne had long regarded himself as a reformer so he was not thrilled when Carroll stopped him on the street one day and insisted that Towne come with him to his office. There Carroll produced a piece of paper on which he scribbled a few words and handed it to Towne. "As you see, Captain Towne, this pass will be honored not only on any of our roads but all of the eastern lines that you may need to use in traveling to Gettysburg."[17]

At Towne's inquiry as to why he was being given this pass, Carroll answered that the railroad magnates desired to honor the nation's noble heroes. Towne suspected that it was a not too subtle attempt to keep him from exercising his frequent penchant for writing letters to the editor in protest of this or that in the community, state, or nation. Nonetheless, he took the pass and used it. Perhaps he soothed his conscience with the thought that he might as well partake of the largesse of the great corporations along with the politicians. Always a little short of money, Towne was in truth glad to save the cost of transportation.

It was a delightful trip home to his native state, even though he did not get to Susquehanna County. He enjoyed the scenery as his train sped through the beautiful hills and mountains of Pennsylvania. He appreciated the marked improvement in rail service over the twenty-three years since he had left the East. At Gettysburg, he had a good time with his cousins Asa and Stanley Warner and other old comrades in arms who were present. Asa had arranged for pictures of the group to be taken at the monument which depicted the young color bearer of the 143rd shaking his fist at the advancing Rebels as the Union troops retreated.

The group from Company H toured the cemetery and visited souvenir shops, where Towne bought some picture booklets depicting the different monuments and other items now housed on what he had last seen as a field covered with the unsightly

Group from Company H of 143rd Pennsylvania Volunteers at Gettysburg, September 1893, pictured in front of regiment's monument. Towne is seated second from right between Asa Warner, far right, and Stanley Warner, on Towne's right.

debris of war.[18] He explained to his cousins that the souvenirs were for his precocious nine-year-old son. Towne was beginning to sound more like a doting grandfather as he spoke of Frank.

At the next opportunity to visit his early home came, he was forced to forego it. In 1900 Asa Warner arranged a grand family reunion of all the descendants of Jehiel and Phinis Moody Warner to mark the one hundredth anniversary of Warner's arrival in Susquehanna County. There Asa, the one living in the vast Warner house, hosted the reunion. He and his brother Frank, the Methodist minister, planned an ambitious program, which Asa described to his cousin in Missouri. He and Frank had agreed that Cousin Myron should be the featured speaker. They even offered him a topic, "Westward Expansion."[19] Exactly to what they referred Towne was not sure, but he decided to do as speakers from time immemorial had done: shape the topic anyway he chose. He looked forward to the task.

Group of descendants of Jehiel and Phinis Moody Warner at side of Warner homestead at the reunion of 1900

However, he felt he could not spend the money for the trip. By 1900 the lobbyists had been stripped of much of their power or were becoming fearful of using it as reform burgeoned. Frank was already in high school and his father had set his sights on college for his son—nothing less would do for a young man with so much talent. Young Myron was another story, and even more of a responsibility. To meet these obligations, Towne planned a venture which he firmly believed would finally solve his problems. He must study it from all angles and until it became reality, he needed to watch his expenses. That meant no expensive trips. Hence, he researched and wrote his address, but sent it for Frank Warner to read.

In his speech Towne described the movement of population from New England following the Revolution into the Middle Atlantic States and on into the Trans-Appalachian region, then across the Mississippi, and finally to the far West and the Pacific Coast. He lauded the boundless energy of these pioneers and the ideals of liberty and equality for all that they carried with them. Towne then described the way the settlers replaced the wilderness with fields of grain, green pastures, herds of cattle and sheep, houses, fences, and barns. They built churches and schools; cities sprang into being, and government brought law and order. Technology kept pace with the growth of population. Entrepreneurs developed mineral and forest resources and built railroads and networks of wire to carry first signals, then the human voice, and now electricity across the nation. These devices wrought miracles of communication and greater comforts for the common man.[20]

When he completed his essay, Towne felt he had extolled the past, but in reality he had celebrated the present. Without realizing it Towne had become, like his compatriots, present-minded. This was his last great effort in historical research and writing. However, the exercise had served to remind him of the many changes he had witnessed in his seventy years of life.

Chapter Sixteen

Politics and Public Service

PUBLIC SERVICE WAS PART OF THE CREED Myron Towne inherited and practiced in Pennsylvania. He had joined with his father in efforts to win their corner of the state for the Republican Party in 1856, 1860, and 1868. Towne was committed to the party's program of equal rights for all persons regardless of "race, color, or previous condition of servitude." He brought these ideals with him to Missouri. Adding to his Republicanism was his devotion to his old commander, General Grant, whom Towne supported for the presidency in 1868 and 1872.

However, as time passed and the party abandoned efforts to enforce the Civil War amendments, Towne became increasingly disturbed. Only the Democratic Party's nomination of Grover Cleveland three times in succession kept Towne in the Republican fold. He scorned Cleveland as a "draft dodger" who had hired a substitute to go in his place to avoid conscription. Towne proudly stated that he had not waited for a draft, but had volunteered to fight for what he deemed a righteous cause.

For some time Towne tried to concentrate on holding local offices as he and his father had in Susquehanna County. In April 1882 Myron ran for mayor of Unionville, was elected and reelected each year until he moved outside the corporate limits in 1890.[1] Since Unionville was a city of the fourth class, the mayor served as police judge.[2] Most of his cases were simple, but occasionally one offered some challenge or an opportunity for Towne to air one of his concerns.

In one case three young men received summons from the town marshal for racing horses, using the city streets as their racetrack. After hearing the testimony of the marshal and citizens who claimed the actions of the young men had disturbed decent people's slumbers, Towne ruled. He fined the youths and delivered a stern lecture. He closed with an admonition about caring for their horses. On the rutted streets of the town, a horse being urged to great speed might fall and suffer a broken leg. Towne could never accept irresponsible behavior toward animals.[3]

There were ceremonial duties connected with the office of mayor which Towne rather enjoyed. When Union veterans, old settlers, or one of the proliferating fraternal orders decided to hold a reunion in Unionville, the mayor was expected to welcome the group or to give the principal address at the opening meeting. Towne became a popular speaker because he had a strong, clear voice, he enunciated his words distinctly, and he had a fund of stories to illustrate significant points. To look the part, he broke his rule against stiff hats and bought a silk hat, the one "saved" in the hotel fire. His speeches represented the florid oratory of the Gilded Age, but he delivered them well. He used vivid adjectives and standard cliches calculated to bring his hearers to their feet cheering or wiping their eyes. Speaking at an Old Soldiers Reunion on September 18, 1889, he appealed to sentiment as he closed:

> Comrades, we are growing old. Old Father Time is fast sweeping us off; most of the old leaders are gone. By the dark turbid waters of the flowing Hudson, the Old Chieftain is laid to rest. The shores of his tomb are washed by the incoming tide from the deep blue sea; the battling waters are a fitting emblem of the swinging masses of boys in blue that he commanded on so many battlefields.... Soon again the last bugle's blast on to the charge will be heard, not to grapple with a human foe, but with

> the grim monster from whom there is no retreat.... The last long roll will be sounded ... to cross over through the dark valley to the shades of eternity, from which no mortal has ever returned.[4]

By the 1890s Towne grew more disillusioned with the Republican party of his old heroes, Lincoln and Grant. Towne remained fiercely proud of his role in "saving the Union and freeing the slaves," but he disdained the appeal to "vote as he shot." New issues called for new programs, and he felt the Republican party had not kept instep with economic trends.

As a man trying to run his farm like a small business, Towne was dependent upon credit. As prices fell, interest rates did not decline proportionately in rural areas. He did not automatically adopt currency inflation as a solution as did many farmers, but he did favor the organization of farmers to work cooperatively for their interests. He joined the local grange, a unit of the Patrons of Husbandry, and took the position of song leader.[5] That did not entail abandonment of the Republican Party, but it indicated that he was moving farther from its official position.

It appears that the final break with the "Grand Old Party" resulted from a local squabble. Everyone seemed to agree that Towne had been a satisfactory city official, so not long after he moved to the farm, various persons suggested that he run for county judge. In Missouri the county court was made up of three judges who acted jointly as an administrative body with jurisdiction over roads, bridges, and similar matters. Individually, each judge served in the capacity of a justice of the peace. This was the office John Towne had held for many years, and Myron Towne, now that his father was gone and the son could judge his father from a different perspective, rather fancied the idea of following in his parent's footsteps. Consequently, Towne indicated an interest in the office and felt encouraged by the response.

After Towne filed for the office, a whispering campaign to the effect that he was a secret Democrat began. That was too much for Towne's pride to accept. He wrote an angry letter to the editor of the *Unionville Republican* denying the charge, but clearly indicating that such a shift was not impossible. He declared that he was not a "partisan bigot"; he had always scratched the ticket whenever he felt that a candidate was not worthy, and he would continue to do so. Sarcastically he vowed, "I will not sell my birthright for a 'mess of potage' or eat dirt for any office in Putnam County."[6] With that letter Towne clearly destroyed any chance for a place on the Republican ticket. Putnam County's solid Republicanism precluded any hope for election as a Democrat.

Finally, the Democratic repudiation of Cleveland in 1896 and the nomination of William Jennings Bryan on a reformist platform completed the process by which Towne left the Republican Party and affiliated with the Democratic. He did not do it half-heartedly; he became a strong member of that party. He convinced himself that he had not left the old party; it had abandoned him. The party had forsaken its heritage; rather than being the voice of idealism and progress, it spoke for the rich and privileged.[7]

Not only did Towne become a Democrat, he, perhaps without fully intending it, brought his elder son with him. In a curious way Towne enjoyed the kind of distinction that being a Democrat in Unionville conferred. To be a Democrat in such a strongly Republican county as Putnam was to be different and one of a select company. Neal Marshall of the Marshall National Bank was a Democrat and hosted the local caucus at his bank. His son, Hugh, was Frank Towne's age and they were friends. When young Marshall went to Princeton after graduation while Frank began to work on a local newspaper, their friendship continued. In the summer, Marshall would drop into Frank's newspaper office for a chat, or they would meet in the bank where young Marshall worked in summers and where Frank Towne did his banking. Marshall had fallen under the spell of the new President of Princeton, Dr. Woodrow Wilson, so soon Marshall was declaring himself not only a Democrat but a progressive, and a supporter of Wilson for the presidency as he left academic life. From other influences, Frank Towne had also become progressive-minded, and he too supported Wilson as the nominee of the Democratic party, when he left Princeton for politics.[8]

The elder Towne, although he still believed that he was a reformer, was not quite comfortable with the bright young people of the twentieth century who seemed to feel that governmental commissions and agencies staffed by experts could cure all of society's ills. However, he was pleased to see that his son studied issues thoughtfully and exercised wise judgement. Certainly they both agreed on the power of the press to enlighten the masses.

By the beginning of 1910, the break between Theodore Roosevelt and his successor offered hope for the resurgence of the Democratic Party. Bryan, as titular leader of the party, despite his three failures in the presidential sweepstakes, came forward as the one to reply to President William Howard Taft's classic failure to think before he spoke in relation to the Payne-Aldrich Tariff. This tariff was opposed bitterly by insurgent Republicans, and after it passed they begged Taft to veto it. But Taft at Winona, Minnesota, had termed it "the best tariff the Republican Party had enacted."

Bryan, who was already scheduled to speak at the Unionville Chautauqua, told reporters as he boarded a train at Omaha that he would reply to Taft in the Unionville address. Consequently, reporters from a number of metropolitan papers and the major wire services converged on Unionville. [9] Neal Marshall invited the small group of Putnam County Democrats to a watermelon feed in honor of the distinguished guest. A local meat market cooled several melons in one of its big iceboxes and delivered them to the grassy plot behind the Marshall Bank, where the melons were cut and sliced as the Chautauqua officials escorted Bryan from the train. Towne and his son were among the small group of guests. The press had been excluded so Towne dreamed of his son writing a feature story which the big papers would be eager to buy. This would mark the beginning of Frank Towne's career as a big city reporter, editor, and finally, perhaps, publisher.

The fond father may well have been right about his son's talents, but, alas, Bryan proved poor copy. He was too engaged with eating watermelon to utter any words of wisdom. He stuffed huge pieces in his mouth one after the other, letting the juice drip down his fat jowl and onto the napkin he had tied bib fashion around his neck. He spat the seeds onto the ground until his chair was ringed by seeds and rind. The more he ate, the hotter he became; perspiration coursed down his cheeks mixing with the juice on his napkin. Somebody supplied a palm leaf fan, but Bryan was unable to wield it. Both hands were engaged in stuffing melon slices into his mouth. As his face grew more scarlet, Marshall and Chautauqua officials feared their big-name speaker would never get to the platform. Therefore, they urged that it was time to leave for the Chautauqua grounds. Hugh Marshall ushered guests out the side gate onto the street, while his father took Bryan inside the bank to clean up.

As Towne and his son walked to the grounds of the high school where the Chautauqua tent was located, Towne spoke in great disgust, "Bryan eats like a hog."[10] Bryan had lost a friend in Unionville. Nevertheless, Bryan handled himself well once on the platform. He still commanded a dramatic oratorical style and a matchless voice. He castigated Republicans not just for their betrayal of the promise to reduce the import tax, but as proof of the corrupt alliance between the great corporations and the Republican Party. Towne had to admit that he admired Bryan's courage in using such language to an audience composed of far more Republicans than Democrats. They probably did not care what he said; they were happy to have such a person speaking in Unionville, a feeling that Towne also shared. Caring nothing about either, big city reporters scribbled wildly in their notebooks, as they sat on the edge of chairs or benches, ready to race each other to the telegraph station at the depot to file stories with the dateline "Unionville, Missouri, August 24, 1910."[11]

Much as Towne savored contacts with important political personages in a small town in a remote part of the Middle West, he felt greater pride in a few chances that came his way to use his influence against the denial of equal opportunity on the basis of race, poverty, or both. One incident came to his attention around the turn of the century. The background was shrouded in uncertainty and local gossip, but it seemed that a girl of a poor family from an area near town, which was generally termed "the holler," gave birth to a child who appeared to be of mixed blood. No colored people lived in Putnam County at that time, but nine months earlier a circus had been in town to put on a performance. Supposedly some of the roustabouts were Negroes, hired in the South where the circuses wintered. Therefore, the gossips put together these bits of inferential evidence and drew a conclusion. The child was Negroid, fathered by a circus hand, and the girl was a disgrace not only to herself and her family, but to her race.

Towne seemingly did not hear the sorry tale or ignored it if he did. He had no time for idle gossip; however, his interest was aroused by the sequel. When the child reached school age, the mother brought him to the elementary school for enrollment. The uneasy primary teacher ignored the mother and son until she had registered all of the other children, giving each mother or guardian instructions about what supplies the child should have and similar first-day-of-school business. While doing this she managed to summon the school principal, who arrived and took the mother into the hall to inform her the child could not attend the Unionville school; he could only attend a colored school according to the laws of Missouri. However, Unionville, with no colored population, had no such school. To the principal's amazement the woman put up a strenuous, if confused, protest. She seemed to have grasped that an education was a right, not a privilege, and that it provided a means to climb out of "the holler" literally as well as figuratively. When she was ushered out of the school building, still protesting, she told her story to people she saw on the street as she left. She vowed to return. Although Towne was not in town when the brouhaha occurred, he heard about it that afternoon when he did come in to transact some business. Far from seeing it as humorous, his sense of justice was outraged. Inwardly, he vowed to do something quickly.

Ascertaining that the school board would meet as it normally did on the night following the beginning of the fall term, Towne announced at supper that he was going into town on business. To his wife's string of questions about the nature of the business and why it could not wait until the next day, he said nothing beyond the statement that he would return soon. Towne put on his hat, got into the surrey, took the reins from the hired man, and drove down the lane as the hired man opened the big gate. Towne headed Dolly, the elderly mare he always used to pull the surrey, toward town.

At the superintendent's office, where the board met, Towne walked in and announced that he had a complaint to make. The shocked board members and school superintendent uttered conciliatory phrases and assured "Captain Towne" that they were at his pleasure. He questioned the refusal to enroll this boy from the hollow. To the chorus of explanations about the laws of segregation, he asked a simple question: How did they know that the little boy was colored? He dismissed all responses dealing with circus hands as hearsay evidence not admissible in a court of law. When the superintendent fell back on color of skin, kinky hair, and prominent whites of the eyes, Towne asked what degree of curl did the hair need or what color of skin was required to prove the person was colored. This was too much for the men; there was a dead silence. Then, Towne reminded his audience that even in the days of slavery a child's status was legally that of the mother. In this case, the mother was Caucasian; therefore, regardless of superficial appearances the child must be presumed to be of the same race, unless she registered him as Negro. The school authorities did not examine each child enrolled to determine the hair texture, degree of darkness of skin, or similar items of appearance; this child was being subjected to unequal treatment dictated by the lowly status of the mother.

At that point Towne launched into his favorite theme about how he and his comrades had fought for four years to establish freedom and equality for all races and creeds. He quoted from the immortal Gettysburg address about a nation "dedicated to the proposition that all men are created equal." At that point the board members shifted uneasily in their chairs; and they looked to the superintendent to help them sort out this persuasive argument. The superintendent had been attracted by Towne's logic. The superintendent confessed that there was no place on the district's records for race or color because, he admitted lamely, it was simply assumed that all the students were white.

Then, the superintendent offered a compromise. He doubted it would make any great difference to enroll the child, since children from that area seldom attended school regularly or stayed in school lower than two or three years. Sensing that he had won his case, Towne did not push the other aspect, that of the assumptions about people from the hollow, although later he rather wished he had. Instead, he thanked the board members, donned his hat, and left. Shortly thereafter, he shared his triumph with his son. Frank listened intently, obviously impressed by his father's decisive action, although Frank had been brought up to believe in equality.[12]

In later years, Towne liked to say that he had been instrumental in integrating Unionville schools even for a relatively brief time. It would be long beyond his lifetime when the courts would demolish the rule of "separate but equal," much less decree that schools must be integrated. It is true that the Unionville situation did not prevail for long and no precedent was established for the future. Nevertheless, Towne felt that some good did come from the incident.

In the year following the fight to enroll the child in school, the mother and her family moved to Iowa. Not only were schools there open to children of all races, but a new packing plant was being opened in a small city not far from the Missouri border. There the adult members of the family hoped to find jobs and likely did.[13] Towne liked to think that by doing battle for the right of the child to attend school, he had demonstrated to the woman that there was some justice in the world and some opening in the line of demarcation through which she might climb. In Towne's view that was what America, the land of opportunity, was all about.

Chapter Seventeen

The Great Venture

SPECULATION HAD ALWAYS BEEN A PART of the American pattern for climbing the socioeconomic ladder, but in the late nineteenth century economic gambling took on a feverish character; with the coming of the new century the pace quickened. Schemes for expanding old businesses, creating new ones, opening heretofore untapped markets, and combining corporations into giant oligopolies were abundant. It was not only industrial and financial titans of the major cities that joined the race. Small town enterprisers tried to participate, although they had to tailor their schemes to different conditions. Land had to be their source of capital and basis for credit. This was not new, but by the late nineteenth and early twentieth centuries it represented speculation in town lots instead of selling partially cleared land and moving farther west as the pioneers had done.

It was to such a venture that Towne turned in 1900. He had moved to Unionville in 1875 with the thought that the town would grow rapidly to become the major city of north central Missouri and southern Iowa. In the optimism of the new century Towne believed that Unionville was indeed booming. Preliminary census returns indicated that the population had almost doubled since 1890. Coal mining had developed in northern Putnam County. A manufacturing plant, the Monroe Drug Company, maker of Putnam Fadeless Dyes, had gained a wide market. Three newspapers, three banks, new specialty shops, and a department store gave downtown Unionville the illusion of a city.[1] It was time for the corporate limits of the town to expand so it could accommodate more people.

Towne incorporated his scheme into this rosy picture. Since Fairview Dairy adjoined the city on the southern edge, he could make an addition from the northern third of the farm. He could

Warner Street in Fairview Addition

divide it into lots, build houses, and sell them at affordable prices and still make a tidy profit on each. It seemed very simple and certain. Unfortunately, once more Towne had misjudged the situation. Unionville's economy was based on agriculture. Improved methods steadily reduced the number of farmers needed to produce food and fiber for even a growing market. This surplus agricultural population sought jobs in larger places than Unionville.

Lack of nearness to major rail lines precluded the growth of industry. The mining companies working the Mendota mines provided housing as part of the employees' pay. When the coal vein ceased to be profitable, operators and miners would move to a new field.

Nevertheless, Towne committed himself to a venture he saw as both financially profitable and socially progressive. He envisioned the Fairview Addition having deep lots for gardens and lawns with neat houses facing tree-lined streets, all available at prices, young couples could afford. Towne convinced himself that he would be doing something to improve the quality of life in the community and provide assistance to people who needed a little help to move into middle-class status. He sketched the addition and named the two streets that paralleled Garfield Street. He chose Warner for the street south of Garfield and Stewart for the next one. That way he had honored both sons, his mother, and his wife. The cross streets would be simply extensions of existing streets.[2]

Towne engaged a surveyor to make an accurate plat, which he presented to the board of aldermen with a petition for annexation on July 7, 1903. Two days later the aldermen gave their consent.[3] The Fairview Addition was a reality, at least legally. Much had to be done despite the fact that in anticipation he had been clearing the land and cutting out undergrowth from his woodlot to create sufficient space for the streets. He did grading for them so that once the addition received approval, building could begin. Nonetheless, there were costs that had to be met long before sales could start. He had to hire odd-job labor even though he used some of his farm machinery for grading and so forth. In other words, he had to put money into the project in advance and, as usual, he lacked cash to do so.

Consequently, Towne followed the customary procedure; he borrowed two thousand dollars from Prudential Insurance Company, using the projected addition as his collateral. Towne had long been an inveterate borrower. He had sought loans to buy additional properties, improve them, or to pay other debts. After he reached Missouri, he called on relatives in the small loan business as well as local lenders. In December 1874, the wife of his mother's cousin by the name of Samantha C. Warner of Granby, Massachusetts lent Towne two hundred dollars at 10 percent interest for three years. He gave her a deed of trust on his house on its one and a quarter acres at the west edge of Kirksville. When he traded this for land on the edge of Unionville, which became the nucleus of the dairy farm, he repaid the debt to Samantha Warner, only to borrow again and repay in 1881.[4]

Phinis' small loan business, which she had inherited from their father, was doing quite well by that time, so to buy more farmland Towne turned to his sister. She lent him $1,140 in 1882. It was a complicated deal. He mortgaged a house and lot just east of the square which was valued at $750. To make up the difference he turned over to her a note for $393.75 which A. J. Smith and Isaac Garber had given him on another transaction.[5] Towne repaid Phinis promptly, showing that he refused to take advantage of his sister. She was a good businesswoman, so she treated him as if he were not her beloved brother.

Numerous other debts were incurred to other small loan operators, some men and at least one other woman, and then came the big loan from the eastern insurance company to finance the first stage of construction in Fairview. To insure this loan Towne had to mortgage the entire "120 acres more or less," as the deed phrased it. That in turn made it more difficult to sell the Fairview lots with or without buildings on them. Towne was not unique in buying via the mortgage route. Most small purchasers—especially first-time homeowners, the group he targeted—lacked money to buy outright. Hence, they signed a note for the amount and the seller held the deed to the property until the debt, plus interest, had been paid. This created a problem, for

Towne had mortgaged the land himself; that meant he had to add each lot's share of that debt to the second mortgage he would hold on the lot or lots purchased. As a result, the total price was higher than the buyer first thought. That in turn made it more difficult for generally poor persons to keep up the payments. If they defaulted, Towne had no recourse but to foreclose. However, speculators who frequented sheriff's sales to pick up a nice piece of property at a very low price were not attracted by the Fairview lots for they knew there was too much interest involved to be a bargain. Towne was then forced to buy his own houses.[6]

Why did a man past seventy who was making an adequate income as the operator of a dairy elect to gamble on such an inherently flawed venture? The answer lies in Towne's original decision to begin a family when he was past middle age. He was nearing fifty-six when his older son was born and sixty when Myron arrived. In the summer of 1900, when Towne began to plan his Fairview addition, Frank completed his second year of high school. In two more years he would graduate and Myron would be sixteen and also in high school. That in itself was a problem, because if Myron continued doing as poorly as he did in grammar school, Towne feared that his younger son might not graduate. However, Frank definitely—and perhaps Myron, if he could improve his attitude and work harder—must go to college. Towne always desired to be a step ahead of others in status. Now that high school attendance was coming to be the norm in rural America, Towne saw college as the next goal. After all, he reminded his family and close associates, he had attended a college back in Pennsylvania fifty years earlier.

In that summer of 1900, Frank began to work in the printing office of George Stille, publisher of a newspaper, the *Pantagraph.* Young Towne found the printer's trade precisely to his taste. He acquired skill in typesetting; his phenomenal memory and keen eye which quickly spotted an error in spelling, punctuation, or capitalization seemed ideal assets for the role of an editor. Never before had the printed page reached the height of influence and support it had held in the early years of the twentieth century. Schools of journalism developed to educate young men and women in the arts of reporting, editing, and publishing. The University of Missouri had begun to offer courses in journalism. Therefore, Towne aspired to send Frank to Columbia to study, so he could command a much better position than working for one of the three newspapers in Unionville. However, that took more money that Towne felt he could use from dairy profits and still support the other three family members at home. This reasoning led Towne to take what seemed to him at the time a practical solution—sell a considerable portion of the farm as town lots.

By 1902, when Frank graduated and his father had intended the young man to enter the university in the fall, the Fairview project was not yet a reality. Frank smiled as his father apologized and tried to explain that in another year things would be better, so it was only postponement of higher education, not abandonment. Frank assured his parent that Stille had offered a full-time position as printer, reporter, and proofreader-editor. It was a wonderful chance to learn the practical side of the business. He could stay at home and save a major portion of his salary even while providing for his own modest needs. When conditions had not changed in 1903, Towne was again forced to postpone assistance to his son. Frank appeared quite satisfied to continue work at the *Pantagraph*. Somehow, Towne felt a trifle disturbed.

Finally, early in 1904, Towne learned the secret of his son's desire to remain in Unionville: Frank had fallen in love. It seemed that the young lady was Mary McCoy, daughter of Abel McCoy, who lived on West Main Street beyond the railroad station. She would graduate from high school in 1904. Frank had begun to woo her ardently. Taking advantage of the relatively good salary he made, he ordered a dozen red carnations for her from a florist in

Albia, Iowa, to be brought to Unionville on the morning train on Valentine's Day. Frank proudly told his father that none of her friends would get flowers since Unionville had no florist and no one else had Frank's standing with trainmen, with whom he had rapport from meeting trains in his capacity as a reporter doing the "locals."[7]

As other presents followed, such as a beautiful locket for the lady's birthday and a lovely little turquoise and pearl ring when she graduated, Towne's apprehension grew. In early September his fear became reality, for Frank announced that he and Mary planned to marry at once. He had purchased a fine diamond engagement ring which, he assured his father, he had paid for.[8] Towne reiterated the need for higher education to go far in journalism and promised that he would somehow assist Frank to enter the university that fall. Then, after more study, he could consider matrimony. Frank assured his father that was not possible. Mary wanted marriage now; things were not good in her home, Frank explained rather vaguely. Clearly, he feared that the lady he had courted so carefully would marry another if he did not act quickly. He viewed Mary as so wonderful that every young male in their crowd was a potential suitor.

Towne had difficulty grasping such sentiments. In time-honored fashion he concluded that there was something strange about young people anymore. When he and Phinis were in their teens or early twenties, they were not courting or being courted, and so he thought it strange that their children and grandchildren should behave this way. Perhaps Towne reacted against the concepts of early marriage and marriage based on love. When he and his sister had succumbed to Cupid's arrow, their marriages failed. Although neither Lydia's nor Mary Burdick's resulted in divorce or desertion, he regarded both as disasters. However, Towne had always trusted Frank's judgment and discernment. Perhaps this young woman was precisely the right wife for him. At the same time, Towne could recognize her desire to marry the son of a relatively prosperous, well-known citizen because her father, Abel McCoy, was neither.

At this point Frank's imminent marriage merged with Towne's current enterprise. He fancied himself a facilitator for young couples striving to become homeowners, a test of solid middle-class standing. Towne had to provide as much for his favorite son. The large house on the corner of Thirteenth and Washington Streets, which Towne had purchased in 1900 and remodeled for himself and his wife when he retired, had several lots along Washington. On the one next to the corner of Fourteenth Street, he could build a house for his son by using the man working on the Fairview houses. He would put the builder to work quickly, but meanwhile Frank and his bride-to-be should wait until it was finished.

House built as a wedding present for Frank W. and Mary E. Towne

A sort of compromise ensued. The contractor gave November 1 as the date when the house would be ready, and Frank and Mary set the wedding date for October 12. They would spend the intervening three weeks at the farm.[9] Joe Barry, Mary's brother-in-law, was scheduled to bring his wife, Mary's older sister, home to have her second child in October. That would mean six adults, a two-year old boy, and when it arrived, a new infant in a four-room house.[10] Towne conceded that Mary had a right to flee.

After meeting his new daughter-in-law Towne fell under her spell as readily as his son. She was attractive, but her manner was her greatest charm. She won him instantly by asking permission to call him "Daddy Towne." She listened avidly to the stories of his youth, military service, and so forth, and she made perceptive comments. She read widely, a trait that apparently had attracted Frank in their first contacts in the Sunday School class for young people in the Methodist church. Since he was two years ahead of her in high school, they had only peripheral contact there especially in view of his employment after school and on Saturdays during his last two years in school.

By the first Christmas after his son's marriage, Towne was determined to give Mary something rather special to mark his appreciation for her presence in the family. He went to town and searched in the jewelry store for something in the way of china. Handpainted china, often reproductions of well-known prints or paintings, had become quite the rage. It was to the young middle class something akin to the coin silver spoons of the post-war years. Towne knew what he wanted. Charles Dana Gibson's drawings of a beautiful woman had become so popular that they were being reproduced on plates to display in china cabinets or on plate racks and sideboards. Towne saw Mary as a small town example of the Gibson Girl. She seemed to exemplify all of the characteristics, including her pompadoured hair and gray-green eyes with their bright direct gaze or pensive, faraway look. She carried herself so proudly that she seemed almost haughty on occasion, yet she was gracious to everybody, including the elderly, children, and the poor. She represented, he felt, the new woman of the twentieth century, as did Gibson's creation.[11] Hence, Towne determined to buy her a plate of that genre.

He found two plates in the jeweler's shop priced at one dollar each. After debating which was the more attractive, he decided on both. Towne was so elated by his success that he told the jeweler that they were exactly the right gift for his daughter. This was too much for the shopkeeper. As he took the money and handed over the carefully wrapped package he remonstrated, "You don't have a daughter, Captain Towne," thinking no doubt that the old gentleman was growing senile. Towne responded indignantly as he

Mary Towne in the Gibson Girl style shirtwaist and skirt. She is wearing the locket and wide gold bracelet her husband had given her prior to their marriage.

clutched his purchase and stamped out of the store, "Of course I do; she's Frank's wife."[12] In a way, Mary had already taken the place of Fanny or the daughter that Towne had always desired.

Delight with his new daughter by marriage did not solve Towne's inability to sell the Fairview lots at an advantage. He had to incur further indebtedness, by turning to local lenders for smaller amounts: five hundred dollars from the Farmers Bank of Unionville in 1909 and seven hundred dollars from B. H. Bonfoey Loan Brokerage in 1910.[13] Financial worries were coupled with Towne's anxiety about his younger son. At sixteen, Myron had failed most of his high school subjects and stopped attending school. The only thing he seemed capable of doing was driving the milk wagon and making the daily round of deliveries to customers. Towne doubted whether Myron would be able to operate the dairy himself if his father retired or died.

Myron too was enchanted with his new sister-in-law. Like his father, Myron adopted her as a family member. He gave her the pet name "Sis" and confided in her as he never had to anyone else. She in turn decided to make him her cause. She listened to his complaints, reasoned with him, and tried to influence him to "make something of himself." As the first step she urged him to go back to school, and she offered to help him with his studies. He listened and agreed with her, but did not act on her recommendations. He preferred to hang around the pool hall instead of attend classes. [14]

Mali also succumbed to the charms of the new member of her human family. Mary won the confidence of the spoiled, elderly cat by cautious approaches and periods of quietly ignoring Mali. Soon Mali indicated her acceptance by rubbing against the young lady's ankles. In short order Mali decided she approved Frank's choice of a bride. Then Mali apparently pondered in her sharp feline brain how to reward this charming creature. She either determined to make a supreme effort in her old age or else she simply indulged in a last fling. In any case, in the early spring she produced two beautiful kittens identical to their mother. They were perfect maltese with silky fur.

As soon as the kittens were weaned Mali signified no more interest in them except to bring them to Mary when she and Frank made their regular Sunday visit to the farm. Mary had already named the kittens Socrates and Xantippe, names her husband informed her were only partly accurate for both were female. Xantippe, quickly shortened to Tippy, proved more precocious about appearing to follow the directions of humans. Mary and Frank adopted Tippy and she became their pampered "child" for the next thirteen years.

Finally, in 1912 Towne made a decision to solve both of his problems at the same time. There seemed little hope for Myron and none for Fairview. Towne would sell the dairy, land, cattle, machinery—even the surrey would go into the big sale.[15] That would provide funds to invest that would yield enough income together with the Civil War pension to enable Towne and his wife to live comfortably in the house in town. He sold the south forty and its companion twenty acres separately and used the proceeds to buy a small farm for Myron somewhat farther from town.[16] Without his parents' guidance, Towne hoped, Myron would be forced to at least fend for himself. For the last time Towne staked his future on a throw of the dice. Once again the wheel of fortune would deal him a lethal blow.

Chapter Eighteen

Shattered Dreams

DURING THE SUMMER OF 1912 Towne and his wife prepared to sell the farm and move to town once the crops were harvested and the fruit was picked. Meanwhile, Phil, the faithful hired man, largely operated the dairy with some assistance from Myron, who drove the delivery wagon as usual. That anything was amiss easily escaped Towne, who had ceased to pay much attention to what his younger son did. Thus, the blow that was about to come struck him totally unprepared.

In August, Charles M. Cooper, who had purchased three of the lots in the Fairview Addition in the usual fashion of mortgaging the property and paying Towne in small installments, came to the house to see him. Assuming Cooper came to talk about the mortgage, Towne invited him into the room Towne used as an office. Instead of being meek and rather pleading, as was usually the case with delinquent debtors, Cooper charged at Towne demanding restitution for the wrong done his daughter. Towne had no idea what was behind this accusation, and was speechless for a moment. Recovering enough to see the need to take charge of the situation quickly, he ordered Cooper to state his case clearly and briefly. What Cooper told his quasi-landlord left the latter in a state of shock. Cooper's daughter, who was the hired girl engaged to do housework for Towne's wife, was "in the family way," as Cooper phrased it, and Myron Towne was the father of the unborn child. Since Jessie Cooper was barely fifteen, Cooper proposed to charge Myron Stewart Towne with statutory rape. Cooper declared he had been to a lawyer who said the case was solid, and there were witnesses to the fact that Myron had bragged of sleeping with the live-in hired girl in the upstairs room she occupied in the farmhouse. Jessie had told her father this had happened several times during the spring, and now the result was becoming evident.[1]

Choking with impotent rage, Towne told Cooper to leave, but also insisted that Cooper take no hasty action. Towne said that he would investigate. Cooper was shrewd enough to sense that he had achieved his real purpose in going to Towne: The old man would buy his son out of trouble.

Towne seethed from a combination of fury at his son, humiliation at the knowledge that Cooper would talk and soon the whole town would know about it, and the thought that this would destroy the last frail hope of a neat retirement income and modest inheritance for his wife and sons when he was gone. At the same time, reason asserted itself, and Towne recognized he was to blame. He had from the child's early years largely ignored the younger son, who had never suited his father in any way. Towne had permitted the foolishly infatuated mother to rear her favorite as she pleased. Myron was indulged and allowed to get by with any behavior, no matter how bad. He became hopelessly immature, self-indulgent, and irresponsible. Here was the fruit of that combination of neglect and spoiling. Towne took part of the responsibility for hiring the girl to work for his wife. She was too young, although Towne in all honesty had not inquired about her age. She was large for her years and mature enough in appearance, so he had simply thought that he could help the Cooper family to improve its economic status and thus pay for the lots. As for letting her sleep upstairs near Myron's room while he and his wife were rather far removed in their downstairs bedroom, his wife should have known better. He admitted he had not given the matter any thought so perhaps it was unfair to blame her, but he did. A woman should think of the welfare of her youthful employees, Towne decided. Later, he learned that Mary agreed with him, so he felt that he was not exhibiting an outmoded view of women's roles.[2]

The immediate need was to get to the bottom of the charges. As soon as his son arrived in the late afternoon, Towne summoned Myron to the office. There another scene ensued. Myron did not deny the accusation; he sidetracked the issue by vowing he did not "force her." In other words, his excuse was that she was willing. This in no way mollified his father, who responded that a jury would agree that the twenty-three year old man had taken advantage of the girl-child's youth and inexperience. Elizabeth Towne intervened when she heard the loud, angry tones of her husband directed against her darling. She combined tears with a disorganized defense that her son meant no harm, that the girl trapped him or had charged him to cover up the real culprit, whoever that might be. All of this infuriated Towne and he ordered both of them out of his office. However, there was no doubt in Elizabeth Towne's mind that he would "do something" to save her pet. She felt sure he would not allow the disgrace of a public charge or court case. She was right.

Once he was able to compose himself enough to think coherently, Towne plotted his course along the only line that seemed open to him. He cancelled the sale of the farm for he would need it for security against further loans. Next, he notified Cooper that he was ready to negotiate with him. Towne offered to buy back the three lots that Cooper had been trying to pay for in the Fairview Addition and assume all other indebtedness on them. This would amount to purchasing the lots at the price Towne had originally asked for them, plus interest. Further, Towne would add a sum to cover all expenses for the Cooper family to move out of the state.

All of this was subject to Cooper's agreeing to drop all charges against Myron Towne, "Jr." and leaving Missouri forever. Cooper agreed. Towne, acting as his own lawyer, drew up a formal contract in which he itemized all the notes and interest he would assume. He headed it "Agreement made this 14th day of September, 1912." He immediately went to the recorder's office and had the warranty deed recorded.[3] Whether this unwitnessed contract would have been valid in the eyes of a court was never tested. Cooper was not above capitalizing on his daughter's misfortune, but he was no more anxious than Towne to publicize the sorry story. Hence, he used the money as Towne had stipulated, to leave Missouri and go "out West," or so gossip put it.

Gossip was an item Towne could not "buy off." Fortunately, he did not have to bear the brunt of it. His son and daughter-in-law did, and it caused them to leave Unionville. For some time, Mary Towne had suggested on various occasions that her husband should get a job in a larger community, where he would have more opportunities for work in the specialized printing that he did so well and to make considerably higher wages. From 1907 to 1912, Frank had worked as shop foreman on the *Unionville Journal*, edited by Charles Miller.[4] Mary argued that Frank did most of the managerial work, editing, proofreading, and so forth, but Miller retained most of the proceeds and paid low wages. She had kept her campaign low-key, but as gossip swirled around the Towne family in the late summer and early autumn of 1912, Mary announced they must leave as quickly as possible. Frank regarded her wishes as absolute mandates; he would do anything to make her happy, and he believed she wanted only the best for both of them.

It so happened that an advertisement appeared in the publication of the Typographers Union for a foreman with special responsibilities for book publishing at the Journal Printing Company in Kirksville. It intrigued Frank. He applied, and the manager hired him immediately with the request that he report on Monday, October 20, 1912.[5] Mary remained behind for two weeks to pack their belongings for the trip to Kirksville. By election day, Frank came back to vote and supervise the work of the men with a dray who loaded furniture and other items and hauled them to the depot for the trip to Kirksville.[6]

Towne would miss his son and daughter-in-law, but he realized Frank needed to leave Unionville, and Kirksville was a much better location. From Towne's standpoint it had the advantage of proximity and familiarity. It had been more than thirty years since Towne had been in Kirksville, but he still knew a few people there and others who had moved from Putnam to Adair County. With his interest in scientific discoveries, Towne had watched closely the development in Kirksville of the new healing art of osteopathy. It, along with the flourishing normal school, had sparked Kirksville's growth. The book publishing the Journal Printing Company did that occasioned Frank Towne's employment was largely for the School of Osteopathy. Towne now conceded that Unionville lacked growth potential, while Kirksville, although not likely to grow beyond a certain level, would truly become the largest city in north central Missouri. There, Frank could achieve the success that eluded his father.

By 1912 Towne had recognized the futility of the Fairview venture. Two short streets and a few small houses plus some empty, weed-infested lots were all that he had to show for so much work and expenditure. His debts mounted as he borrowed on his properties to pay a loan on something else, like the horse in town or the brick building, the best rental property he owned. After the Monroe Drug Company, which had used Towne's building just east of the square for its printing plant, left Unionville in 1907, rental had been more difficult. In the process of saving Myron, the elder Towne completed his own financial ruin. While he tried to find a way out of the maze of debts, another event occurred which in a sense brought everything to a head.

While his father schemed to ward off Cooper's threats, Myron Towne decided to solve his problems in a typical way for him, that is, create another. He resolved to marry immediately, thereby, he fancied, showing that he had never been seriously interested in the Cooper girl and proving that he was still a desirable match for any girl. He began a whirlwind courtship of Ethel Hinton, the eldest daughter of Lincoln Hinton. There were five younger children and Hinton had a forty-acre farm in the vicinity of Towne's south forty. Ethel had struggled to go to high school. To earn a little money, she had worked for Towne's wife as part-time come-and-go help at special occasions. After a few buggy rides, Myron asked Ethel to marry him, and she accepted so quickly he was amazed. She saw Myron as a good catch economically. The contrast between the meager living she had known on the little hard-scrabble farm and the "nice things" that the affluent Towne family enjoyed proved the point in Ethel's eyes.

That Myron was the subject of ugly gossip did not deter Ethel Hinton. General agreement held that she was a "good girl," but tales had circulated for years about her mother. The truth may never be known at this late time, but Unionville had long laughed or raised eyebrows in horror about how Lincoln Hinton had pursued his wife and a reputed paramour through the cemetery where he had supposedly caught them. He was armed with a shotgun and as they ran he followed threatening to kill her, the man, and himself, but he had relented and taken her back. Whether any or all of this was true made no difference. From that time on, Unionville gossip labeled her a "bad woman." As one might guess, the story resurfaced in the wake of Ethel's precipitate engagement to another subject of gossip.[7]

Towne, his older son, and his daughter-in-law regarded Myron's action as rendering a bad matter worse. They refused to accept a Hinton as an appropriate wife for a Towne and they objected to the bad timing. Only Myron's mother condoned his action and declared it the right thing to do. She immediately adopted Ethel as a daughter in a way she had never treated Mary or that Mary would have accepted. Elizabeth Towne made Ethel's mother a boon companion and took her to a Chautauqua matinee, where she made what Mary Towne regarded as a "scene" by trying to introduce Amanda Hinton to people who did not want to meet her socially, while Elizabeth Towne announced Myron's engagement. Unionville tongues were already wagging assiduously, and Elizabeth Towne's performance added fuel to the fire. It was that occasion which led Mary Towne to insist upon leaving Unionville immediately. As a regular attender of the Chautauqua, she had been an unwilling witness to the ill-bred behavior of her mother-in-law.[8]

The crisis had other wide-ranging consequences. Undoubtedly, the strain weakened Towne's already declining stamina. He was less able to cope with managing of the dairy or with his wife's persistent complaints that he had not done anything for Myron compared to "all" he had done for Frank. He seemed to lack strength to argue with her that her ideas were actually reversed or to ignore her, as had been his wont for years. He consented to permit Myron to take over operation of the farm, but in return Towne insisted that he and his wife move to town to the house he had prepared for their retirement long before. He refused to continue to live with Myron and his wife after their marriage. When he was forced to meet Ethel, he deliberately failed to get her name straight. He called her "Effie" and continued to use that name if he had to speak to her or of her in later years.[9]

However, Myron did not do well with the dairy; he spent more than his receipts. There was a steady stream of requests for money that his mother pushed at her husband. Towne had mortgaged the farm and his other properties to the limit. For the first time since he came to Unionville, he was no longer considered a good risk. He sold the brick building for the debts against it, and he found borrowing on other properties difficult.[10] The pension money did not suffice for their expenses, although he guessed that his wife was giving some of it to Myron each month. Near blindness and increasing difficulty walking precluded Towne from going to the bank and handling business himself. Without Frank, Towne was forced to rely on his wife, who proved either her want of judgment or her gullibility where her favorite son was concerned.[11]

When occasionally Towne did see some old business associates, they would warn him that he was in danger of losing the farm as well as other properties already gone. Finally, A. B. Pratt, who had been the high school principal when Frank and Mary Towne were students and now was in the real estate and loan business, answered Towne's appeal for another mortgage on the farm to pay the interest on the first with a counter suggestion: "Frank is doing well in Kirksville; I have found a buyer for his house in the same block with yours. Why don't you ask him for a loan." Feeling both humiliated and helpless, Towne did just that. With a stubby pencil in handwriting which bore little resemblance to the fine script of his youth or middle age, Towne scribbled a note to his son. This request he would not allow to go through his wife.

Frank replied in his firm, rather angular hand, written extra large so his father could read it. He offered to lend $4,500, taking a second mortgage on the farm, but he would have the deed of trust written so that there would be no interest on the debt. Only the mortgage sum would need to be repaid by January 1, 1921.[12] Towne was moved to tears by his son's generosity. Frank worked through Pratt to arrange the loan, so the real estate man was privy to the secret. Whether Towne told his wife, who in turn would have told Myron, is unclear, but the sequel suggests they knew and acted accordingly.

In 1915 Towne's health suddenly worsened. He suffered a period of extreme weakness, almost total blindness, and clouded mental processes. Later, he reasoned that he had suffered a stroke. While not bedfast, he had to be dressed and half-carried to a chair. Soon after the onslaught of this physical decline, Myron came to the house and he and his mother loaded Towne into the buggy and took him to Pratt's office. There, the wife and son directed Pratt to prepare a deed to the farm to put in Myron's name. Since he knew that Frank not only by right should have a half share in the property after his parents were gone, but that he also held an interest-free mortgage on the farm, Pratt was shocked. He also observed the listless way that Towne sat in the chair to which Myron and his mother had propelled the elderly man. Therefore, so he told Frank later, Pratt asked several times as he prepared the papers, if this was indeed what the senior Towne desired. He did not answer; instead his wife or son separately or in unison declared that was indeed what Towne wanted. They pushed the deed under his hand and Elizabeth Towne guided his hand as he scrawled an almost illegible "M. S. Towne" above the line on which she had already written "Elizabeth Towne."[13] Pratt shivered slightly; this was duress, if he had ever witnessed it, and he hated to be a part of it. Making the matter even worse was his knowledge that Frank would never fight the matter in court. The proper Towne way was never to show the rendered seams of the family in public.

Pratt was right; when Frank received a letter from his former teacher requesting him to come to Pratt's office the first time he was in Unionville, he listened without comment to Pratt's account. Afterward, he said nothing to anyone except his wife. Later, when his father recovered sufficiently to realize he had been duped into doing his elder son a grievous injustice and tried to apologize to Frank, the latter shrugged the matter aside. He was only happy, he told his father, that the latter was now better and more like himself. Although his vision remained very dim, Towne suffered no permanent damage such as paralysis or continued mental confusion. Towne expressed one thought; if he suffered another stroke, he hoped it would be fatal. However, in 1916 and 1917 he seemed better than at any time since the year of catastrophe, 1912.[14]

House at Thirteenth and Washington Streets with Mr. and Mrs. M. S. Towne in the summer of 1916

Chapter Nineteen

The Last Days

ALTHOUGH HE COULD SELDOM LEAVE THE HOUSE, Towne felt stronger in 1917. He affirmed that, considering his age, his health was reasonably good. In June of that year an event occurred which unquestionably buoyed his spirits. After thirteen years of marriage, Mary and Frank had a daughter. The event was a total surprise. They had kept out any hint in their letters; a fact which greatly upset Elizabeth Towne, but her husband thought was a wise decision of the young couple. The second piece of information contained in Frank's call on June 19 was the name given the child, Ruth Warner. This further fretted the new grandmother, who could not see why the baby had not been called Elizabeth. On the other hand, the name thrilled Towne; he began to plan immediately to give the new granddaughter his mother's coin silver spoons in recognition of her initials when the parents brought the infant on their regular late-summer visit.[1]

When the great day arrived, Towne, from his big platform rocker in the bay window at the east end of the long living room, heard the arrival of the Kirksville family. The taxicab which brought the guests from the rail station pulled up to the side door, which led into the dining room adjacent to the living room. Elizabeth dashed out the door and tried to snatch the baby out of her mother's arms as Mary got out of the taxi. Towne heard screams from the baby and Frank's sharp command to his mother to desist.

Ruth had to be won carefully, he said. This brought tears from his mother, but Mary paid no attention and marched into the living room, where she carefully deposited her precious bundle into her father-in-law's lap with a formal introduction, "Daddy Towne, meet your new granddaughter." Whether that did the trick or not, Towne did not know, but there was no repetition of the wails. He sat very still for a moment, then leaned over the baby in his lap to see her better. At that she looked up and spied just above her head a strange object, a short gray beard that necessitated a touch test; therefore, one tiny hand reached upward, grabbed as much of this thing as she could, and gave it a gentle but unmistakable tug. Towne played to her as if they had rehearsed the scene. He wagged his head a trifle, and she tightened her clutch. Then she let out a gurgle which undoubtedly was intended as a baby giggle. She kicked her feet happily and continued to lie there looking at him after releasing his whiskers.[2]

Towne was so happy that he feared he was dreaming, but Frank and Mary continued to exclaim about how unusual their infant had behaved. Up to that point, it had been virtually impossible to get Ruth to look pleasant around those other than her parents. The new grandmother's sniff of disapproval and injured vanity added to Towne's inward amusement. The visitors' short stay came to an end all too soon for Towne, but he understood both Frank's need to get back to his work and Mary's desire to be at home where she could more easily care for her child. He discovered that the care and feeding of infants had become vastly complicated in the years since his children were young. Mary did everything according to the books she had collected prior to her long-desired child's arrival.[3] Before they departed, Towne gave his granddaughter the six coin silver spoons with only one stipulation. He asked that her mother and father tell her about her "old grandfather" with whom she had made friends in their one meeting.[4] Towne assumed that he probably would not be alive by the time the next summer's annual visit came.

Nevertheless, he remained in about the same health for several months. True, he suffered from what he supposed was a normal "let down" after the family from Kirksville returned home. He had tried to appear stronger than he actually was during that short, happy time. He also recognized that he had come to dread winter with its cold, snow, and early darkness, even with the new idea of daylight saving time introduced as in connection with curious war in remote parts of the world.

The winter of 1917–1918 proved to be one of the coldest on record. That fact coupled with the war produced other innovations to conserve coal. Towne and his wife closed the doors to the parlor, its bedroom, and to the upstairs rooms so that they attempted to heat only four rooms. That still left the big high-ceilinged rooms chilly and drafty. Towne looked forward to spring, but it proved to be slow in coming. Cold, dark, rainy days succeeded snows.

It was in that dismal spring that Towne suffered a crippling stroke. It left him unable to get out of bed or even to feed himself. His wife positively reveled in his helplessness. It was as though she again had a baby to care for or perhaps she enjoyed feeling in absolute control for the first time in their thirty-five-year marriage. Now this man, who had been strong and self-reliant and who had made all the basic decisions by himself, was utterly dependent on her. Elizabeth Towne played the role of the loving, martyred wife to the hilt. She claimed that she "never left him."[5] Obviously she did, for she made trips to the grocery store, bank, and so on.

In July, Myron sold the farm or his equity in it. He had accumulated more debts. Earlier he had sold the herd of Holsteins and attempted to engage in row crop production on land that was good for pasture but of little value for tillage. He added a third mortgage to the farm and sold the Fairview lots. In 1917 Myron bought an expensive automobile on credit, which consumed whatever he had obtained from the farm and real estate transactions. In July 1918 he sold the farm to V. T. Altes, proprietor of a mill that dealt in "coal, flour, feed, and hay," according to his letterhead. Altes called the price twelve thousand dollars, but this figure included three mortgages; hence Myron actually received three thousand three hundred dollars.[6]

With his money Myron paid for the car so he could legally take it out of the state. He settled other debts, loaded a few belongings on the car, and he and Ethel left for Chicago. There he got a job in the suburb of Hammond, Indiana, driving a delivery truck for a Chicago dairy.[7]

A. B. Pratt notified Frank of the sale with the wry observation that Altes was attracted by the fact that the second mortgage was interest-free and would not be due until January 1921. Altes, Pratt theorized, would not pay the note until that date.[8]

The sick man in Unionville paid little attention to the departure of his younger son. By midsummer Towne had only one concern remaining: he desired to see Frank once more and then quietly die. The first occurred early in the fall. Frank came hastily in response to his mother's summons following a sinking spell Towne suffered. When he knew Frank was on his way, Towne rallied and exerted every ounce of willpower he possessed to live until his son's arrival. Once Frank was beside him, Towne could say little more than, "So glad you are here. I could not go until I had seen you. Now I am ready."

This was not to be. Later, Frank once more came in response to his mother's call stating that "Papa" was dying. That time Towne could only protest in a feeble whisper that "it is taking so long."[9] Early in December he lapsed into a coma and the end came on December 10, 1918.[10] His long pursuit of success was over.

Had he failed or succeeded? It is difficult for a detached observer blessed with hindsight to answer, and impossible to determine what Myron Smith Towne concluded as he looked back on his long life. One thing is certain: the meaning and nature of success changed as he pursued it. In his youth, Towne had assumed that his goal was to climb above the level reached by his grandfather, Jehiel Warner, and his father, John Smith Towne. That was a major challenge in itself, because they had done very well. By his middle-age years, vast economic changes had reshaped the whole concept of success. It became equated with income sufficient to command an ample share of the vast amount of goods and services available in a rapidly industrializing economy. Status accompanied means. From his strong religious background he viewed both means and status as an avenue to public service. He gave his time and talent freely as a small political official, and he was often the first to put down a dollar or even five dollars to start a church or civic drive for money to be used for some good purpose. After he acquired a permanent family, Towne felt that he must accumulate an estate sufficient to leave to his much younger wife and two sons, who might not be grown when he died. The sons must begin at a level above their father, in terms of formal education, and a start toward greater income.

As he had written about his father, Myron Towne possessed more than ordinary ability, a keen mind, and a higher level of education than most people of his time and rural location. He displayed both talent and leadership in his positions as a teacher, church leader, and army officer. Once established in the Middle West, he did well as proprietor of the Empire House and livery barn and operator of the Fairview Dairy. However, he always strove for more; he was never satisfied. He kept seeing new avenues to greater wealth; his fertile brain hatched projects readily, but he lacked the power to recognize the defects in his plans. He borrowed recklessly, mortgaging properties that were doing well to raise funds for hopeful ventures. All entrepreneurs, great and small, operated on borrowed capital. Towne's problem was that he gambled without good cards in his hand, and he failed to throw them in until too late.

Towne's moves from the East to the Middle West and from Kirksville to Unionville proved major errors. To speculate on the might-have-beens of history is an exercise in futility, but in retrospect one can surmise that had Towne remained in the East, he could have climbed far faster and higher. All he had to do was cross the border into southern New York. Binghamton was a fast-growing city. New immigrants poured in to work in its factories, which were growing larger in number and size. There was a college and law offices to provide real opportunity for advancement. He could have risen to middle management positions in some of the prospering corporations if he had entered early. Professions expanded rapidly, and with his background Towne could have read law in the office of an established lawyer and after admission to the bar by examination moved into partnership in the law firm. Many others did just that.

The other "if only" proposition would have placed him in Kirksville to grow with that small town. It lacked the potential of Binghamton, but it did offer the chance to succeed by way of land in the form of town lots as two colleges aided Kirksville's modest growth. The land also contained coal and timber. Teaching and law also offered means to rise and do well.

Unionville, where Towne spent the last half of his life, provided the least promise. Nonetheless, he did reasonably well there. The hotel, livery stable, and dairy farm in sequence yielded good income, but that was not enough. He sought more. For reasons he deemed sound, he elected to try town lot sales using the dairy as his source of land. He was not wrong in the abstract sense. It worked well in many areas in the late nineteenth and early twentieth centuries. He simply was in the wrong place. That failure, coupled with his younger son's escapade, brought Towne to financial ruin.

In his personal life, Towne's record was blemished despite the fact that he had no vices and was a model of respectability. Of his three marriages only one could be seen as good, and death deprived him of that wife and their two babies so soon that the whole episode faded into vague memory over time. The third marriage lasted the longest and produced two sons, who reached manhood well before their father's demise. This last wife took care of him in his last months with enthusiasm, but that did not disguise their basic incompatibility. Their backgrounds were very different. He could feel a kind of pity for her lack of advantages. He tried to help her improve, but she annoyed him more often. She pretended to view him as a figure to be semiworshipped at the same time that she harassed him with the questions about where he was going, why, and so forth, spiced with acid comments and subtle criticisms. He realized that she betrayed the insecurity stemming from her thirty-five years prior to their marriage; even that vexed him. A Towne, even by marriage, had no reason to feel insecure. They did not need to prove anything to anybody.

No one can depict with certainty what the man who "took so long to die," thought in those months of 1918 when he lay helpless. One can only fancy that Towne, whose mind remained clear up to the last few days, came to a kind of reconciliation in respect to his long search for success. Perhaps he concluded that he had not totally failed. He could rightly claim one success, more meaningful in the long run than fame or fortune, his elder son.

Towne may have, like a historian, toyed with the "what if I had" aspects of his life. Maybe he decided that had he remained in the East or in Kirksville, he would undoubtedly have done better materially, but he would never have met and married the woman by whom he gained a son who meant so much to Towne. Hence, that marriage was not a total failure. He had lavished attention on his older boy. This attention and, he liked to think, innate characteristics, produced an outstanding man. Frank had all the qualities of mind and character of the father only honed to a higher level. In addition, Frank had the steady determination to do his best, stay where things were going well, and rise slowly but surely.

Once Frank Towne reached Kirksville and began to work at the Journal Printing Company, he recognized its possibilities and stayed with it. He bought stock in the company as it became available, and he rose in the printing business. His father did not live to see the steps by which the younger Towne gained the rank of production and personnel manager, handler of the company's book and medical journal publications, and president of the board of directors of the firm. At his death in 1974, it was still a major printing firm in the state.[11] Myron Smith Towne had one thing to illuminate his page in the eternal book of life: he had reared a son who achieved both success and the father's essential goodness of character and kindness to others.

Myron Smith Towne Genealogy Chart

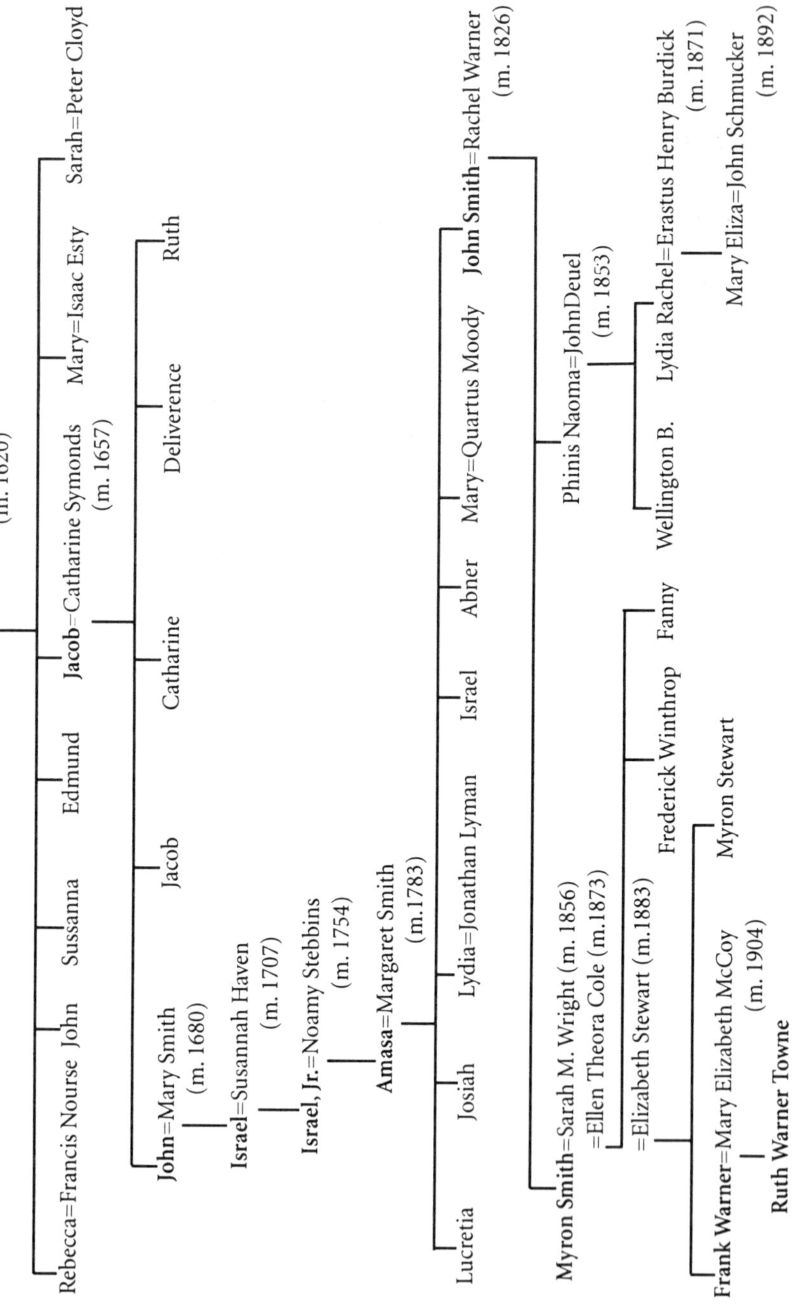

Endnotes

Chapter One: Youth in Pennsylvania

1. Rhamanthus M. Stocker, *Centennial History of Susquehanna County, Pennsylvania* (1887; reprint, Baltimore: Regional Publishing Company, 1974), 481, 491.

2. E. E. Towne, *The Descendants of William Towne* (1901; reprint, Salem, MA: Higginson Book Co., 1989); Towne family genealogy, Towne papers.

3. Stocker, *Centennial History,* 491.

4. Rachel Towne, letters written in her later years demonstrate these points, Asa Warner papers, Susquehanna County Historical Society, Montrose, Pennsylvania.

5. Stocker, *Centennial History,* 481.

6. Deed of Robert H. Rose to John S. Towne, 1828, office of recorder of Susquehanna County, Montrose, Pennsylvania.

7. Towne family Bible.

8. Stocker, *Centennial History,* 492.

9. Books in Myron Towne's library. They were given to him by his aunts.

10. Ari Hoogenboom and Philip S. Klein, *A History of Pennsylvania* (New York: McGraw-Hill, 1973), 214–215.

11. Myron S. Towne delighted in telling his son and daughter-in-law about some of the clever though forbidden things that he and his sister did. In one case in which she was the leader, she secreted a book they were anxious to read behind the big grandfather clock in their Grandfather Warner's dining room so they could crawl away from the circle of Methodists praying fervently and read the book together. Their father spied their absence, came after them, and gave each a spanking following the service.

12. Laurence E. Leamer, *The Vestal United Methodist Church, 1831–1981* (Vestal, N. Y.: private printing, 1981), 26–28.

13. Obituary of John S. Towne, *Carroll County Gazette,* April 5, 1877; clipping, n.d., n.s., Towne papers. It was a precise copy M. S. Towne wrote as his father's obituary and was published in a Montrose paper, but the holdings of the Susquehanna County Historical Society do not include this particular source.

14. Ibid.

15. Leamer, *Vestal United Methodist Church,* 43; Stocker, *Centennial History,* 495.

16. Hymnals, Myron S. Towne library.

Chapter Two: Political Activity

1. Frederick A. Norwood, *Sourcebook of American Methodism* (Nashville: Abingdon Press, 1982), 397–398.

2. Stocker, *Centennial History,* 495.

3. M. S. Towne to Frank W. Towne, who told author. Frank W. Towne quoted his father as saying, "When I was growing up we had fermented fruit drinks and they were good. We drank in moderation as a kind of special treat, but we discovered that others did not so we must set a good example or how could we advocate temperance?"

4. Obituary of John S. Towne, *Carroll County Gazette,* April 5, 1877; clipping of similar obituary, n.d., n.s. in Towne papers.

5. Records of township elections, Towne papers.

6. Donald G. Mathews, *Slavery and Methodism: A Chapter in American Morality, 1780–1845* (Princeton: Princeton University Press, 1965), 165–168; Norwood, *Sourcebook of American Methodism,* chap. 15.

7. Charles Buxton Going, *David Wilmot: Free Soiler* (Gloucester, Massachusetts: Peter Smith, 1966, reprint), chap. 7–9.

8. M. S. Towne to editor of *Unionville Republican,* n.d., Towne papers. The files of the paper are spotty and some copies are missing or partially missing.

Chapter Three: Pennsylvania Schoolmaster

1. Records of schools taught by M. S. Towne, Towne papers.

2. M. S. Towne to Mary E. Towne who told author.

3. School records, Towne papers.

4. M. S. Towne to Frank W. Towne, who told author.

5. M. S. Towne to Mary E. Towne, who told author.

6. School records, Towne papers.

7. Deed, Office of Recorder of Susquehanna County, Montrose, Pennsylvania.

8. *Triennial Catalogue of Harford University* (Montrose, Pennsylvania: Alvin Day, Printer, 1855).

9. Ibid.

10. C. R. Squier, *Franklin Academy, Soldiers Orphan School, Harford University* (Tunkhannock, Pennsylvania: Mulligan Printing Corp., 1989), 129–137; Harford was coeducational. Women were enrolled and attended classes with male students, and three of the six faculty were female. However, female students were required to participate in the only female debating society, and they could not participate in the all-school debates or the elaborate closing exercises that marked the end of the summer term, except to recite a few poems.

11. Textbooks, Towne library.

12. Squier, *Franklin Academy,* 137–154, passim.

13. Ibid.

14. Frank W. Towne to author; author's recollections of her father's interest in observing the sky.

15. Report, Superintendent of Common Schools of Pennsylvania for year ending June 7, 1858, 165–171.

16. Emily Blackman, *History of Susquehanna County Pennsylvania* (1873; reprint, Philadelphia: Regional Publishing Company, 1980), 531–532.

17. Ibid.

18. Music books in Towne's library, many with notes of how he had used them in singing schools.

Chapter Four: Marriage and Divorce

1. *Susquehanna County Register,* October 27, 1853.

2. *Susquehanna County Register,* n.d., clippings, Towne papers.

3. Stocker, *Centennial History,* 481, 491; deeds, Office of Recorder, Susquehanna County, Montrose, Pennsylvania.

4. Stocker, *Centennial History*, 487–488.

5. Records, Appointment of Postmasters, 1832–1941, National Archives and Record Service, vols. 9, 15, 24; Roll 122, 123. Washington, D. C., 1973.

6. Commission, Towne papers.

7. *Montrose Independent Republican*, September 11, 1856.

8. Daguerreotypes, in Towne collection.

9. Stocker, *Centennial History*, 64–65.

10. Census of 1880, Lanark, Carroll County, Illinois; records of Lanark Methodist Episcopal Church, Lanark Public Library, Lanark, Illinois; will of John S. Towne, records of Probate Court, Carroll County, Mount Carroll, Illinois.

11. Records of schools taught by Myron S. Towne, Towne papers; deed of trust, Office of Recorder, Susquehanna County; evidence submitted in *Myron S. Towne v. Sarah M. Towne*, Libel for Divorce, Court of Common Pleas, Susquehanna County, Pennsylvania, 1861.

12. Evidence in Towne v. Towne.

13. Ibid.

14. Sarah M. Towne to Myron S. Towne, July 5, 1859, evidence in Towne v. Towne.

15. Evidence in Towne v. Towne; census of 1860 for Forest Lake Township, Susquehanna County, Pennsylvania.

16. Deeds, Office of Recorder of Susquehanna County, Montrose, Pennsylvania.

17. Records of Susquehanna County Court of Common Pleas.

18. Testimony, Towne v. Towne.

19. Records of Susquehanna County Court of Common Pleas.

20. *Montrose Democrat*, April 1, 1892.

21. Frank W. Towne instantly supplied the name when the author asked him one day not long before his death, "What was the name of grandfather's first wife?"

22. Myron S. Towne to Mary E. Towne who told the author. In retrospect the author added her own evaluation of her mother's reaction.

23. Myron S. Towne, petition for pension filed May 1898, Military Records Service.

24. *Montrose Democrat,* April 1, 1892.

Chapter Five: Enlistment in the Union Army

1. Revisionist historians over the years from a variety of perspectives have attacked anyone who dares to express such "outmoded" views. However, it is hard to deny that Douglas had lost southern support, thereby splitting the Democratic party in 1860 by continuing to offer popular sovereignty, as redefined at Freeport, Illinois, in 1858 as a means to keep slavery out of a territory, if a majority of its voters so determined. Democracy *was* at stake, as Lincoln frequently said during the war.

2. Deed, office of recorder of Susquehanna County, Montrose, Pennsylvania.

3. Stocker, 491.

4. Leamer, *Vestal United Methodist Church,* 62–66.

5. Ibid., 64–66.

6. Ibid., 65, 66.

7. Stocker, 495.

8. A. F. Chaffee, *History of the Wyoming Conference of the Methodist Episcopal Church* (New York: Eaton and Mains, 1904), 428. 493.

9. The house of John Towne still stands, but it has been extensively remodeled. However, at the back, or side in relation to the road, there is clear evidence of the enclosed porch, and local legend still refers to it as the place where people in the neighborhood went during the Civil War to get mail so they could learn the fate of their soldiers at the front. Kathryn Warner to the author, 1988.

10. Record of appointment of postmasters, vols. 9, 15, 24, roll 122, 123.

11. Stocker, *Centennial History,* 242.

12. Enlistment papers, Towne papers.

13. Petition, Towne papers.

14. M. S. Towne, "Speech Before Old Soldiers Reunion, September 18, 1889," *Unionville Republican,* September 25, 1889.

15. Samuel P. Bates, *History of Pennsylvania Volunteers, 1861–5,* vol. 4 (Harrisburg: B. Singerly State Printer, 1870), 487; U.S. Army Military History Research Collection, Carlisle, Pennsylvania.

16. Margaret Leech, *Reveille in Washington, 1860–1865* (New York: Garden City Publishing Company, 1945), 79, 80.

17. Ibid., 204–209.

18. Ibid., 5–7.

19. Commission, Towne papers; Field and Staff Muster Roll, One Hundred Forty-Third Pennsylvania, December 1862, Military Records Service, Washington, D.C.

20. Towne, "Speech," *Unionville Republican*, September 25, 1889.

21. Ibid. Towne was not only opposed to slavery but from his first interest in the issue he was committed to equality before the law.

22. Bates, *History of Pennsylvania Volunteers*, 487.

Chapter Six: Chancellorville and Gettysburg

1. Abner Doubleday, *Chancellorsville and Gettysburg* (New York: Charles Scribners' Sons, 1894), 1–9.

2. Report of Colonel Roy Stone, commanding Second Brigade, *War of the Rebellion: Official Records of the Union and Confederate Armies*, series 1, vol. 25, part 1 (Washington, D.C.: Government Printing Office, 1889), 296–297.

3. Report of Colonel Edmund Dana, One Hundred Forty-Third Pennsylvania Infantry, *Official Record*, vol. 27, part 1, 298.

4. Doubleday, *Chancellorsville and Gettysburg*, 21; report of Major General, John Reynolds, commanding First Corps, *Official Record*, vol. 47, 253.

5. Doubleday, *Chancellorsville and Gettysburg*, 10; Doubleday commented that it was "simply suicidal" for Hooker to delay action until May 2 while Anderson fortified lines and Lee came from Fredericksburg.

6. Ibid., 42–43.

7. Ibid., 53–56; report of Major General Abner Doubleday, commanding Third Division, *Official Record*, vol. 37, 288; Stone, *Official Record*, vol. 37, 296.

8. Ibid., Dana, *Official Record*, vol. 37, 298.

9. Bruce Catton, *The Army of the Potomac: Glory Road*, vol. 2 (New York: Doubleday, 1951), 248–249.

10. Ibid., 258–259; Doubleday, *Chancellorsville and Gettysburg*, 119.

11. Richard Wheeler, *Witness to Gettysburg* (New York: Harper and Row, 1987), 111–113.

12. Doubleday, *Chancellorsville and Gettysburg,* 124–125.

13. Ibid., 130.

14. Ibid., 135–136.

15. Doubleday, *Official Record,* 39: 247.

16. M. S. Towne to editor of *Unionville Republican,* n.d., clipping from Towne papers.

17. Stone, *Official Record,* 39: 331.

18. Report of Major General John Newton, commanding First Corps, *Official Record,* 39: 261.

19. Bates, *History of Pennsylvania Volunteers,* 4: 488–489; M. D. Roche, "Historical Address," *Dedication of Monument and Reunion at Gettysburg, September 11–12, 1889* (Scranton, Pennsylvania: Press of the Sunday News Association of the 143rd Regiment Pennsylvania Volunteers), 5–7.

20. Dana, *Official Record,* vol. 39, 336.

21. Catton, *Army of the Potomac: Glory Road,* 303–304.

22. Doubleday, *Chancellorsville and Gettysburg,* 192–193.

23. Frank W. Towne to author. Doubleday gave the distance as one and a half miles; Doubleday, *Chancellorsville and Gettysburg,* 192.

24. Doubleday, *Chancellorsville and Gettysburg,* 193; Wheeler, *Witness to Gettysburg,* 240.

25. Catton, *Army of the Potomac: Glory Road,* 324–325.

Chapter Seven: Lull in the War in the East

1. Wheeler, *Witness to Gettysburg,* 245.

2. Diary of Asa Warner, Susquehanna County Historical Society, Montrose, Pennsylvania. Warner evidently lost track of time in the confusion of the three-day battle and the long march which preceded it. He failed to mention any fighting, and he records the pursuit of Lee as taking place in June. However, the Muster Roll of the 143rd shows that Myron S. Towne was sick on July 8, 1863.

3. Diary of Asa Warner.

4. Muster Roll for July 10, to September 9, 1863 records Towne "absent" in General Hospital, Washington, D.C. The pension records also give the same dates.

5. Stocker, *Centennial History,* 213–214, 263.

6. Muster Roll, 143rd Pennsylvania September 9, 1863 shows Towne present.

7. Orders from Major General A. A. Humphrey, Chief of Staff, to commanders in field; *Official Record,* vol. 29, part 2, correspondence, 285, 287, 297. Edward Hagerman, "Field Transportation and Strategic Mobility in the Union Armies," *Civil War History* (June 1988): 143.

8. Report of Major General George G. Meade, commanding, Army of the Potomac, *Official Record,* vol. 29, part 1, 9–11; Report of Major General John Newton, commanding, First Corps, 687; Roy Meredith and Arthur Meredith, *Mr. Lincoln's Military Railroads: A Pictorial History of United States Civil War Railroads* (New York: W.W. Norton & Company, 1979), 173.

9. Diary of Myron S. Towne, January 1, 1864; diary in Towne papers.

10. Ibid., January 3, 9, 10, 1864.

11. Ibid., January 12, 13, 15, 16, 19–21, 1864.

12. Ibid., January 24, 25, 1864.

13. Ibid., January 28–31, February 1, 3–5, 9, 10, 13, 14, 1864.

14. Ibid., February 21, 23, 26, March 3–8, 1864.

15. Ibid., March 9, 15, 16, 19–21, 25, 1864.

16. Bates, *History of Pennsylvania Volunteers, 1861–5,* 4: 490.

17. Towne diary, March 29, 1864.

18. Ibid., April 4, 5, 1864.

19. Milton Dana, recommendation for Myron S. Towne, Towne papers.

20. Furlough issued to Commissary Sergeant Myron S. Towne, Towne papers; diary of Myron S. Towne, April 14, 1864.

21.Towne diary, April 15–17, 1864.

22. bid.

23. Statement by J. B. Young that Myron S. Towne had been examined and was to rejoin his regiment, Towne papers.

Chapter Eight: Into the South

1. Towne diary, April 18–21, 23, 30, May 2–4, 1864.

2. Report of Maj. Gen. George G. Meade, commanding, Army of the Potomac, *Official Record,* vol. 36, part 2, p. 189; report of Brig. Gen. Lysander Cutler, commanding, Fourth Division, Fifth Corps, *Official Record,* vol. 36, part 2,

p. 610; Robert Garth Scott, *Into the Wilderness with the Army of the Potomac* (Bloomington: Indiana University Press, 1992), 31–33, 51–61.

3. Scott, *Into the Wilderness,* 61; Towne diary, May 6, 1864.

4. Bruce Catton, *A Stillness at Appomattox,* vol. 3 (New York: Washington Square Press, 1958), 105, 125.

5. Correspondence of Maj. Gen. A. A. Humphreys, Chief of Staff, *Official Record,* vol. 36, part 3, p. 14. Order, Lieutenant General U. S. Grant to Major-General Meade, *Official Record,* vol. 36, part 2, pp. 481–483.

6. Towne diary, May 10, 1864.

7. Ibid., May 11–13, 1864.

8. Ibid., May 24, 1864.

9. Journal of Maj. Gen. Gouverneur K. Warren, commanding, Fifth Corps, *Official Record,* vol. 36, part 1, p. 542; Towne diary, May 20, 1864.

10. Towne diary, May 20, 1864.

11. Ibid.

12. Towne diary, May 23, 30–31, 1864.

13. Ibid., May 22, 27, 1864.

14. Ibid., May 23, 1864.

15. Ibid., June 2, 3, 1864.

16. J. F. C. Fuller, *Grant and Lee: A Study in Personality and Generalship* (1957; reprint, Bloomington: Indiana University Press, 1990), 286–287.

17. Towne diary, June 9, 1864.

18. Ibid., June 13, 16, 1864.

19. Ibid., June 17, 18, 20–21, July 12, 1864.

20. Ibid., July 4, 6, 12–13, 1864.

21. Ibid., July 5, 1864.

22. Ibid., June 26, July 3, 9, 1864.

23. Ibid., July 16, 1864; commission, discharge, and pay voucher, Towne papers.

24. Towne diary, July 16, 1864.

25. Ibid., July 17, 1864.

26. Affidavit of Walter Jenner, application of Myron S. Towne for pension, Towne papers and Bureau of Pensions, Department of the Interior, 1887.

Chapter Nine: Camp William Penn

1. Towne diary, July 18, 1864; Auguste Laugel, *The United States During the Civil War* (1968; reprint, New York: Kraus Reprint Co., 1990), 189–200.

2. Towne diary, July 19, 1864; Stanley B. Warner, medical discharge, September 29, 1864, Military Records Office.

3. Towne diary, July 20, 1864.

4. Ibid., July 21, 1864.

5. Joseph T. Glatthaar, *Forged in Battle: The Alliance of Black Soldiers and White Officers* (New York: The Free Press, 1989), 103–104; Casey, *Infantry Tactics, for the instruction, exercise, and manoeuvres of the soldier, a company, line of skirmishers, battalion, or corps d'armes,* 3 vols. (New York: D. Van Nostrand, 1862). This seemed to prove Towne's point that there was nothing special for colored soldiers; manual in Towne's library.

6. Bates, *History of Pennsylvania Volunteers,* 5: 1106, gives roster of Forty-Fifth Colored Troops.

7. Brooks D. Simpson, *Let Us Have Peace: Ulysses S. Grant and the Politics of War and Reconstruction, 1861–1868* (Chapel Hill: North Carolina University Press, 1991), 56–57.

8. Glatthaar, *Forged in Battle,* 105; Towne diary, July 22, 1864.

9. Towne diary, July 30, 1864.

10. Glatthaar, *Forged in Battle,* 226.

11. Towne diary, July 23–24, 1864; Francis A. Lord, *They Fought for the Union* (1960; reprint, Westport, Connecticut: Greenwood Publishing Group, 1981), 180.

12. Towne diary, July 30, 1864.

13. Ibid., July 9–14, 1864.

14. Ibid., August 4, 1864.

15. Ibid., August 15–17, 1864.

16. Ibid., August 18–20, 1864.

17. Ibid., August 21, 1864.

18. Ibid., August 22, 1864; pictures, Towne family album.

19. Towne diary, August 23–24, 1864.

20. Ibid., August 27–31, September, 1–10, 1864.

Chapter Ten: From Petersburg to Appomattox

1. Towne diary, September 12–14, 16–17, 1864; Special Order, September 19, 1864, Regimental Order Book, 45th U.S. Colored Infantry.

2. Towne diary, September 15, 1864.

3. Ibid., September 18–21, 1864.

4. Pictures in Towne's Civil War picture album, Towne papers.

5. Towne diary, September 21, 1864.

6. Ibid., September 22–23, 1864.

7. Ibid., September 24–25, 28–29, 1864.

8. Glatthaar, *Forged in Battle,* 103.

9. Towne diary, September 27–28, 30, October 1, 3, 7, 1864.

10. Bruce Catton, *Grant Takes Command* (Boston: Little, Brown and Company, 1969) 366–367.

11. Towne diary, October 7, 13, 1864.

12. Brooks D. Simpson, *Let Us Have Peace,* 58–59, 65–67.

13. Catton, *Grant Takes Command,* 375–377.

14. General Order No. 9, October 31, 1864; General Order No. 11, October 28, 1864, Regimental Order Book, 45th U.S. Colored Infantry.

15. Returns of Quartermaster for 45th U.S. Colored Infantry.

16. Bates, *History of Pennsylvania Volunteers,* 5: 1106; Catton, *Grant Takes Command,* 435.

17. Catton, *Grant Takes Command,* 439–447; Bruce Catton, *A Stillness at Appomattox* (New York: Washington Square Press, 1953), 383–384.

18. Souvenirs, Towne papers.

19. Report of Brig. Gen. Robert S. Foster, commanding, First Division, Twenty-Fourth Corps, *Official Record,* vol. 46, part 1, p. 1181.

20. Ibid.

21. Report of Liuet. Dilwyn V. Purington, acting assistant quartermaster, Second Division, Twenty-Fifth Corps, *Official Record,* vol. 46, part 1, p. 1231–1233.

22. *Unionville Journal,* October 13, 1916.

23. Ibid.; Grant to Doubleday, Doubleday in note to Towne, Towne papers.

24. Report of Purington, *Official Record,* vol. 46, part 1, p. 1233.

25. Report of Surg. Charles P. Heischhold, Surgeon Chief, Second Division, Twenty-Fifth Corps, *Official Record,* vol. 46, part 1, p. 1231; report of Brig. Gen. Ulysses Doubleday, commanding Second Brigade, *Official Record,* vol. 46, part 1, p. 1236; report of Brig. Gen. Robert S. Foster, commanding, First Division, Twenty-Fourth Corps, *Official Record,* vol. 46, part 1, 1181. Report of Lieut. Col. James Givin, One Hundred and Twenty-Seventh U. S. Colored Troops, speaking for all of the U. S. Colored Troop regiments, *Official Record,* vol. 46, part 1, 1241.

Chapter Eleven: The Texas Border

1. *Official Record,* vol. 47, part 3, p. 99.

2. William L. Richter, *The Army in Texas during Reconstruction, 1865–1870* (College Station: Texas A&M University Press, 1987), 17.

3. Simpson, *Let Us Have Peace,* 102.

4. Ibid., 102–103.

5. Catton, *Grant Takes Command,* 489–490.

6. General Order no. 13, October 24, 1864; General Order no. 3, December 8, 1864; General Order no. 39, May 3, 1865; Regimental Order Book, 45th U. S. Colored Infantry, 1864–1865.

7. Ibid., General Order no. 28, May 17, 1865.

8. *Official Record,* vol. 47, part 3, p. 1199; vol. 43, part 1, pp. 139, 141; series 3, vol. 5, pp. 228, 289.

9. Ibid.

10. Report of Quartermaster, Myron S. Towne, 45th U. S. Colored Troops, June, 1865, Towne papers.

11. *Official Record,* vol. 43, part 1, pp. 140, 142–143.

12. Glatthaar, *Forged in Battle,* 219.

13. Quartermaster's report, June 1865, Towne papers.

14. Ibid.

15. Ibid., May 1865; see chapters 9, 10, passim.

16. Glatthaar, *Forged in Battle,* 219–223.

17. General Order, no. 47, August 12, 1865, Regimental Order Book, 45th U.S. Colored Infantry.

18. General Order no. 47, August 12, 1865, Regimental Order Book of 45th U.S. Colored Infantry.

19. James W. Daddysman, *The Matamoros Trade: Confederate Commerce, Diplomacy and Intrigue* (Newark, NJ: University of Delaware Press, 1984), 17.

20. Special Order no. 3, July 10, 1865, Towne papers and Regimental Order Book, 45th U.S. Colored Infantry.

21. Testimony in application of Myron S. Towne for pension in 1887, copies in Towne papers.

22. General Order no. 6, September 22, 1865, Towne papers.

23. Testimony in pension application, Towne papers.

24. Glatthaar, *Forged in Battle,* 221.

25. General Order no. 46, July 16, 1865, Regimental Order Book, 45th U.S. Colored Infantry.

26. Accounts of Myron S. Towne to his son Frank W. Towne, as the father showed the son pictures Myron had brought home of Mexican scenes.

27. Daddysman, *The Matamoros Trade,* 20–23; pictures of Mexican and Brownsville scenes, Towne album, Towne papers.

28. See chapter 12.

29. Towne album, Towne papers.

30. *Official Record,* series 3, vol. 5, p. 158. Quartermaster's reports for October 1865, Towne papers.

31. Application for pension, 1887, Towne papers.

32. Ibid.

33. Testimony of Myron S. Towne in pension application explaining why Morris could not give testimony; Hamilton had also died prior to Towne's application for a pension in 1887; Towne papers.

34. Quartermaster's reports for November 1865, Towne papers.

35. Receipts for items delivered by Lt. Myron S. Towne to Schuylkill Arsenal, December 8, 1865, Quartermaster's reports for December 1865, Towne papers.

36. Quartermaster's special report, January 1867, Towne papers.

Chapter Twelve: Starting a New Life

1. Photograph in Towne papers and enlargement in walnut frame hung on wall in living room of Towne's home in Unionville and now in author's home.

2. E. E. Gordon to Myron S. Towne, September 21, 1867, Towne papers.

3. Obituary of Eli Warner, *Carroll County Gazette,* October 2, 1879.

4. A. H. John, *Sketch of Adair County and Missouri in 1800s,* photocopy made by Elizabeth Laughlin for Adair County Historical Society, 1979.

5. Deeds, Office of Recorder, Susquehanna County, Montrose, Pennsylvania.

6. Deed, Office of Recorder, Adair County, Kirksville, Missouri.

7. Ibid.

8. Ruth Warner Towne, *From These Beginnings: A History of First United Methodist Church, Kirksville, Missouri* (Kirksville: Journal Printing Company, 1984), 9–10.

9. John S. Towne to Myron S. Towne, May 1870, Towne papers.

10. Chaffee, *History of the Wyoming Conference of the Methodist Episcopal Church,* 428–429.

11. Photograph, Towne collection.

12. Deeds, Office of Recorder, Susquehanna County, Pennsylvania. John S. Towne deeded the church building and its land to the Fairdale Circuit of the Methodist Episcopal Church for one dollar.

13. Record of Appointment of Postmasters, 1832–1941, Archives and Record Service, vols. 9, 15, 24, Roll 122, 123. (Washington, D. C., 1973).

14. Addition made to Towne family genealogy by M. S. Towne.

15. Ibid.

16. M. S. Towne regaled his new daughter-in-law, Mary E. Towne, with this story soon after her marriage to Towne's son; the latter had heard the story previously and was always amused by it.

17. Clipping, n.d., n.s., Towne papers, but it clearly came from a Montrose or Binghamton paper. The Susquehanna County Historical Society assisted the author in trying to locate the source, but its collection of Montrose papers is spotty and it has none from Binghamton.

18. Photographs, Towne collection. Nellie's portrait hung with others on the wall of the living room in Unionville where Towne lived with his third wife, and she left it there after his death. Now in author's possession.

19. Deed, Office of Recorder of Adair County, Kirksville, Missouri.

20. Affidavit of Charles Decker, M. D., pension application of Myron S. Towne, 1876, copy in Towne papers.

Chapter Thirteen: Death

1. Clipping, n.d., n.s., Towne papers; *Montrose Democrat,* June 3, 1874.

2. Picture, Towne's album of family photographs.

3. Towne family Bible.

4. Clipping, n.d., n.s., Towne papers.

5. E. M. Violette, *History of Adair County, Missouri* (1911; reprint, Kirksville: Journal Printing Company, 1979), 954.

6.,Kirksville-Adair County Bicentennial Committee, *A Book of Adair County History* (Kirksville, MO: Kirksville-Adair County Bicentennial Committee, 1976) 51–53.

7. Deeds, Office of Recorder of Adair County, Kirksville, MO; Deeds, Office of Recorder, Putnam County, Unionville, MO.

8. *Unionville Republican,* December 2, 1875; pictures, Towne album.

9. Putnam County Atlas, 1877.

10. Deed of trust and chattel mortgage, Towne papers.

11. Galusha Grow to Myron S. Towne and enclosed reference, June 13, 1876, Towne papers.

12. *Unionville Republican,* January 13, 1876.

13. Chattel mortgage and promissory note, Towne papers.

14. Towne family Bible.

15. Photograph, Towne album. An enlargement in an ornate frame hung on the wall of the living room in Towne's last home as apparently it had done in other dwellings.

16. Account written by Towne in his addendum to the Towne genealogy.

17. Mary E. Towne to author.

18. Clipping, n.d., apparently taken from Binghamton paper, Towne papers; *Carroll County Gazette,* April 5, 1877.

19. Will of John S. Towne, Probate Court Records, Carroll County, Mount Carroll, Illinois.

20. Deeds of trust and quit claim deeds, Office of Recorder of Carroll County, Mount Carroll, Illinois; in November 1879 Phinis N. Deuel lent $400 to James A. Montgomery of Putnam County; deed of trust, Office of Recorder of Putnam County, Missouri, Unionville, Missouri.

21. *Montrose Democrat,* May 2, 1877; *Carroll County Gazette,* April 12, 1877.

22. M. S. Towne to "Dear Aunt and Cousin" (Bertha Warner and her son, Asa), September 8, 1879, Asa Warner papers, Susquehanna County Historical Society, Montrose, Pennsylvania.

23. Ibid.

24. Rachel Towne to Asa Warner, April 23, 1878, Asa Warner papers.

25. Towne to Bertha and Asa Warner, September 8, 1879, Asa Warner papers.

26. Deed, Office of Recorder, Susquehanna County, Montrose.

27. M. S. Towne, addendum to Towne genealogy.

28. Ibid.

29. Invitation to funeral, Towne papers; *Unionville Republican,* September 8, 1880.

30. M. S. Towne, addendum to Towne genealogy; Towne papers. Unfortunately, the "nice monuments" were totally destroyed by vandals in the 1960s, who raided Forest Cemetery, as the old "City Cemetery" is now named, and pulverized the monuments in the area of the Towne lot. A decade or so later a committee of townspeople formed a cemetery association and with assistance from the city council cleaned up the cemetery and erected fencing to prevent future damage; however many graves were already obliterated. Markers of wood were placed on the lots ,which are now simply covered by grass. The author was contacted as old cemetery records were searched and used to identify the three graves in the lot belonging to M. S. Towne and Phinis N. Deuel. A book prepared by Elizabeth Laughlin for the Adair County Historical Society lists the three names and the information on each monument as furnished by the author from her memory of when her parents took her to view the cemetery before the vandalism.

Chapter Fourteen: A New Family

1. Ledger of the Empire House, Towne papers.

2. Stewart family Bible, Towne papers.

3. M. S. Towne to his daughter-in-law, Mary E. Towne, soon after she married his son. She heard him make similar remarks on other occasions, on one of which his wife rushed into the room to add, "I just wanted a house to keep."

4. Photograph of "Lizzie Stewart," Towne papers.

5. Marriage license and affidavit, pension application of M. S. Towne, Bureau of Pensions, Department of the Interior.

6. *Unionville Republican,* June 19, 1883.

7. Frequent complaint of Elizabeth Towne to daughter-in-law, Mary E. Towne.

8. Story told by M. S. Towne at different times to his son, Frank W. Towne, and later to his daughter-in-law, Mary E. Towne, who repeated the story to the author.

9. Photographs with names and dates, M. S. Towne's album of family pictures.

10. M. S. Towne to his son and daughter-in-law as he gave the spoons to their baby daughter, in whose possession they now are. See chapter 19.

11. *Unionville Republican,* December 13, 20, 1883.

12. Elizabeth Towne to Mary E. Towne. Baby pictures of Frank W. Towne only slightly support such an idea and certainly as an adult there was no indication.

13. Towne family Bible.

14. Ibid. After accepting the awkward name for his second son, Towne dropped "Myron" from his name and became M. S Towne except for some legal transactions.

15. Mary E. Towne's conclusions based on her observations after she married Frank W. Towne. Although she was fond of her father-in-law and did not particularly care for her mother-in-law, she was critical of his nineteenth-century style of being the decision maker in the family and precluding his wife from having anything to say. Mary Towne, a liberated twentieth-century woman, asserted more than once that she would not have accepted such treatment. She had a tendency to exaggerate when aroused, so Towne perhaps did not simply say, "Sign here," to his wife in his business dealings where the spouse's signature was required. Elizabeth Towne's judgment turned out to be so flawed that when she did seize the reins Towne seems to have been justified in not consulting her. Mary Towne also defended the younger Myron as having been ruined by his mother's indulgence and his father's refusal to do anything about it.

16. Pictures in Towne collection, particularly Frank's grade school pictures.

17. Frank W. Towne to his daughter as a youngster. He was giving her the same lessons, only emphatically without any denigration of her mother, whose diction was also that of a person with more education than simply a high school diploma.

CHAPTER FIFTEEN: Life on the Dairy Farm

1. Plat Book of Putnam County, Missouri (Missouri Publishing Company, 1897) 17, 24; deeds, Office of Recorder, Putnam County, Unionville, Missouri.

2. Author's memory of the house in Unionville, which Towne had remodeled along the same lines, she was told, as the farm house.

3.Frank W. Towne to author; picture of Towne's herd of Holsteins grazing on the farm but now lost, Towne papers.

4. Frank W. Towne to author.

5. Mary E. Towne to author commenting on the careless housekeeping of her mother-in-law and the latter's "deplorable" ways with the hired girl.

6. Author's memory of her father's love of fruit and regret that the small lot in Kirksville was not large enough to permit the raising of fruit.

7. Frank W. Towne to author when she was a young child and had her first cat. She heard many stories about Mali.

8. Another Mali story told by Frank W. Towne.

9. Ibid.

10. *Carroll County Gazette,* December 1891, Towne family Bible.

11. *Carroll County Gazette,* May 1891; picture of Mary Burdick, Towne family album.

12. Record in Towne's handwriting of Mary Schmucher's family, which eventually totaled seven sons and three daughters. Twin boys died in infancy, but eight children survived her. *Lanark Gazette,* April 2, 1941. Apparently her family remained Brethren or at any rate her funeral was preached by a pastor of the Church of the Brethren in Lanark where Mary Schmucher's funeral was held when she died in a freak accident in Arizona at age 68. *Lanark Gazette,* op cit.

13. M. S. Towne, "Bells," manuscript of talk given at Unionville Methodist Episcopal Church, January 27, 1892, Towne papers.

14. Ibid.

15. Ibid.

16. Ibid.

17. Frank W. Towne to author as she worked on her biography of William J. Stone, who as governor of Missouri, led a fight on the railroad lobbyists in 1895. *Unionville Republican,* March 15, 1972, described Carroll's mansion. Also, see Ruth Warner Towne, *Senator William J. Stone and the Politics of Compromise* (Port Washington and New York: Kennikat, 1979), 22–24.

18. Pictures and souvenir booklets, Towne papers; materials on the association of soldiers from the 143rd Regiment, Asa Warner papers.

19. Asa Warner to Myron Towne, August 4, 1900, and an invitation to Warner reunion, Towne papers.

20. "Territorial Expansion," manuscript of "talk," Towne papers; program and pictures of members of the family outside the Warner homestead, Towne papers.

Chapter Sixteen: Politics and Public Service

1. *History of Adair, Sullivan, Putnam and Schuyler Counties, Missouri* (Chicago: Goodspeed Publishing Co., 1888), 572; *Unionville Republican,* December 22, 1889.

2. *History of Adair, Sullivan, Putnam and Schuyler Counties, Missouri,* 571–572.

3. *Unionville Republican,* October 9, 1889.

4. Ibid., September 25, 1889.

5. "Songs of the Grange," Towne papers.

6. M. S. Towne to editor of *Unionville Republican,* June 20, 1894, clipping, Towne papers.

7. M. S. Towne to editor of *Unionville Republican,* manuscript of letter, Towne papers.

8. Frank W. Towne to author as she began serious study of Wilson, progressivism, etc.

9. Frank W. Towne, "When Unionville Was Featured on the Nation's Front Pages," *Unionville Republican,* March 25, 1969.

10. Frank W. Towne to author.

11. Towne, "When Unionville Was Featured on the Nation's Front Pages."

12. Frank W. Towne to author. Mary E. Towne also told the story with perhaps a few more details.

13. Ibid.

Chapter Seventeen: The Great Venture

1. Walter Williams, ed., *The State of Missouri* (Columbia, Missouri: E. W. Stephens, 1904), 486–487.

2. Sketch of Fairview Addition drawn to scale, Towne papers.

3. Official surveyor's plat, petition to aldermen of the City of Unionville, and notice of their action, Towne papers.

4. Original copies, Towne papers; official copies, Offices of Recorder of Adair and Putnam Counties respectively.

5. Originals, Towne papers; official copies, Office of Recorder of Putnam County.

6. Ibid.

7. Story of Valentine carnations recounted numerous times to the author by her parents, Frank W. and Mary E. Towne. Until his death in 1974, Frank Towne gave his wife red carnations each Valentine's Day.

8. Jewelry in Mary E. Towne's collection that is now in the author's possession.

9. *Unionville Pantagraph,* October 13, 1904; marriage certificate and marriage announcement with "at home" card with the "after November 1," as the time, Frank W. Towne papers.

10. *Unionville Pantagraph,* October 20, 1902; October 27, 1904. Abel McCoy's mother owned the house and her son, daughter-in-law, and their two daughters had always lived with her, until the older daughter, Gertrude's, marriage.

11. Steven Warshaw, editor, *Drawings of Charles Dana Gibson* (Berkeley, California: Diablo Press, 1968).

12. M. S. Towne to Mary E. Towne on Christmas day, 1904, when he gave her the plates. She delighted in telling her daughter the story. Plates in author's possession.

13. Notes, deeds, clippings from newspapers giving times of sales, etc., Towne papers. Deeds, Office of Recorder of Putnam County.

14. Mary E. Towne and Frank Towne to author. As a child she heard many Mali and Tippy stories.

15. Handbill, Towne papers.

16. Original deeds, Towne papers; official copies, Office of Recorder of Putnam County.

Chapter Eighteen: Shattered Dreams

1. Mary E. Towne to author. Apparently Myron Towne confessed to her about the time Cooper assailed the elder Towne.

2. Mary E. Towne to author based on what Myron had told her in his effort to win her sympathy and support. She did not condone his actions; indeed, she was quite incensed, but she always declared that he was not "bad"; he had simply been ruined by his family.

3. Cooper contract, Towne papers.

4. Frank W. Towne's employment record in his papers.

5. *Kirksville Journal*, October 31, 1912; *Kirksville Daily Express*, October 18, 1962.

6. Mary E. Towne to author.

7. Ibid.

8. Ibid.

9. Ibid. Both Frank W. and Mary E. Towne understood that this was M. S. Towne's way of putting Ethel down. The latent Towne snobbish streak surfaced in this entire episode. The marriage took place November 9, 1912. The couple rented a car and drove to Lancaster, where they were married by the minister of the Christian Church.

10. Deed, Towne papers.

11. Records indicate that Elizabeth Towne signed various notes and deeds as if she were sole owner of the properties, Towne papers.

12. Deed and letters from A. B. Pratt to Frank W. Towne, F. W. Towne papers.

13. Mary E. Towne to author.

14. "Unionville Citizen Is 87 Today," *Unionville Journal*, October 13, 1916. Clipping in Towne papers. No copies of the *Unionville Journal* remain in existence. Report of Lois Letch, Unionville, to author, August 30, 1994.

Chapter Nineteen: The Last Days

1. Frank W. and Mary E. Towne to author. The author heard her grandmother complain more than once about her grandchild not being named after her.

2. Frank W. and Mary E. Towne to author.

3. Mary E. Towne was very proud of how she followed the manuals, as she often told the author. The baby books remained in her possessions until her death.

4. The author possesses the spoons.

5. Mrs. M. S. Towne to Annie Morris, December 25, 1918, Asa Warner papers.

6. Frank W. Towne to V. T. Altes, July 16, 1918; Altes to Towne, July 18, 1918; A. B. Pratt to Frank W. Towne, July 24, 1918; Towne to Altes, November 25, 30, 1920; Altes to Towne, December 1, 1920, Frank Towne papers.

7. Mary E. Towne to author.

8. A. B. Pratt to Frank W. Towne, July 24, 1918, Frank W. Towne papers.

9. Frank W. Towne to author.

10. *Unionville Journal,* n.d., clipping in Towne papers; *Unionville Republican,* December 14, 1918.

11. History of Journal Printing Company of Kirksville, manuscript in author's possession.

Bibliography

Manuscripts

Towne, Frank Warner. Papers. Possession of Ruth Warner Towne. Kirksville, Missouri.

Towne, Myron Smith. Papers. Possession of Ruth Warner Towne.

Warner, Asa. Papers. Susquehanna County Historical Society, Montrose, Pennsylvania.

Federal Records

Appointment of Postmasters, Archives, and Records Service, General Services Administration, Washington, D.C.

Military Records Division, General Services Administration, Washington, D.C.

Pension Records, Pension Bureau, Department of the Interior, Washington, D.C.

Regimental Order Book, Forty-Fifth United States Colored Infantry, Military Records Service, General Services Administration, Washington, D.C.

War of the Rebellion: Official Records of the Union and Confederate Armies. Washington, D.C., Government Printing Office, 1889.

State Records

Deeds, wills, marriage and divorce records. Office of County Recorder, Susquehanna County, Montrose, Pennsylvania; Carroll County, Mount Carroll, Illinois; Adair County, Kirksville, Missouri; Putnam County, Unionville, Missouri.

Plat Books of Susquehanna County, Montrose, Pennsylvania; Carroll County, Mount Carroll, Illinois; Adair County, Kirksville, Missouri; Putnam County, Unionville, Missouri.

Reports of Superintendent of Common Schools of Pennsylvania, 1850–1860, Pennsylvania State Archives.

Newspapers

Carroll County Gazette, Mount Carroll, Illinois.

Kirksville Daily Express, Kirksville, Missouri.

Kirksville Journal, Kirksville, Missouri.

Lanark Gazette, Lanark, Illinois.

Montrose Democrat, Montrose, Pennsylvania.
Montrose Independent Republican, Montrose, Pennsylvania.
Susquehanna Register, Montrose, Pennsylvania.
Unionville Pantagraph, Unionville, Missouri.
Unionville Republican, Unionville, Missouri.

Magazine Articles

Cornish, Dudley Taylor. "The Union Army as a School for Negroes." *The Journal of Negro History*, October 1952.

Hagerman, Edward. "Field Transportation and Strategic Mobility in the Union Armies," *Civil War History*, June 1988, 143–171.

Books

Baritz, Loren. *The Good Life: The Meaning of Success for the American Middle Class.* New York: Harper and Row, 1980.

Bates, Samuel P. *History of Pennsylvania Volunteers, 1861–5.* 5 vols. Harrisburg, Pa.: B. Singerly State Printer, 1870.

Blackman, Emily C. *History of Susquehanna County, Pennsylvania.* 1873. Reprint, Philadelphia: Regional Publishing Company, 1980.

Browning, Robert M., Jr. *From Cape Charles to Cape Fear: The North Atlantic Blockading Squadron during the Civil War.* Tuscaloosa: University of Alabama Press, 1993.

Casey, Silas. *Infantry Tactics, for the instruction, exercise, and manoeuvres of the soldier, a company, line of skirmishers, battalion, or corps d'armes.* 3 vols. New York: D. Van Nostrand, 1862.

Catton, Bruce. *Mr. Lincoln's Army.* Vol. 1 of *The Army of the Potomac.* New York: Doubleday, 1951.

———. *Glory Road.* Vol. 2 of *The Army of the Potomac.* New York: Doubleday, 1952.

———. *Stillness at Appomattox.* Vol. 3 of *The Army of the Potomac.* New York: Washington Square Press, 1953.

———. *Grant Takes Command.* Boston: Little, Brown and Company, 1969.

Chaffee, A. F. *History of the Wyoming Conference of the Methodist Episcopal Church.* New York: Eaton and Mains, 1904.

Cornish, Dudley T. *The Sable Arm: The Negro in the Union Army, 1861–1865.* New York: Longmans Green, 1956.

Daddysman, James W. *The Matamoros Trade: Confederate Commerce, Diplomacy, and Intrigue.* Newark, N.J.: University of Delaware Press, 1984.

Doubleday, Abner. *Chancellorsville and Gettysburg.* New York: Charles Scribners' Sons, 1894.

Dyer, Frederick H. *A Compendium of the War of the Rebellion*, Vol. 3. New York: Thomas Yoseloff, n.d.

Fredrickson, George M. *The Inner Civil War: Northern Intellectuals and the Crisis of the Union.* New York: Harper and Row, 1965.

Fuller, J. F. C. *Grant and Lee: A Study in Personality and Generalship.* 1929. Reprint, Bloomington: Indiana University Press, 1958.

Glatthaar, Joseph T. *Forged in Battle: The Civil War Alliance of Black Soldiers and White Officers.* New York: The Free Press, 1989.

Going, Charles Buxton. *David Wilmot: Free Soil.* n.d. Reprint, Glouster, Mass.: Peter Smith, 1966.

History of Adair, Sullivan, Putnam and Schuyler Counties, Missouri. Chicago: Goodspeed Publishing Co., 1888.

Hoogenboom, Ari, and Philip S. Klein. *A History of Pennsylvania.* New York: McGraw-Hill, 1973.

Ilisevich, Robert, D. *Galusha A. Grow: The People's Candidate.* Pittsburgh: University of Pittsburgh Press, 1989.

Jimerson, Randall C. *The Private Civil War: Popular Thought during the Sectional Conflict.* Baton Rouge: Louisiana State University Press, 1988.

John, A. H. *Sketch of Adair County and Missouri in 1800s.* Photocopy made by Elizabeth Laughlin for Adair County Historical Society, 1979.

Kirksville–Adair County Bicentennial Committee. *A Book of Adair County History.* Kirksville, MO: Kirksville–Adair County Bicentennial Committee, 1976.

Laugel, Auguste. *The United States during the Civil War.* 1968. Reprint, Bloomington: Indiana University Press, 1990.

Leamer, Lawrence E. *The Vestal United Methodist Church, 1831–1981.* Vestal, N.Y.: private printing, 1981.

Leech, Margaret. *Reveille in Washington, 1860–1865.* New York: Harper and Brothers, 1941.

Linderman, Gerald F. *Embattled Courage: The Experience of Combat in the American Civil War.* New York: The Free Press, 1987.

Lord, Francis A. *They Fought for the Union.* 1960. Reprint, Westport, Conn.: Greenwood Publishing Group, 1981.

Mathews, Donald G. *Slavery and Methodism: A Chapter in American Morality, 1780–1845.* Princeton, N.J.: Princeton University Press, 1965.

McPherson, James M. *The Negro's Civil War: How American Negros Felt and Acted during the War for the Union.* New York: Random House, 1965.

Meredith, Roy, and Arthur Meredith. *Mr. Lincoln's Military Railroads: A Pictorial History of the United States Civil War Railroads.* New York: W. W. Norton and Co., 1979.

Neely, Mark E., Jr. *The Last Best Hope on Earth: Abraham Lincoln and the Promise of America.* Cambridge, Mass.: Harvard University Press, 1995.

Nevins, Allan. *The Ordeal of the Union.* 5 vols. New York: Charles Scribner's Sons, 1947.

Norwood, Frederick A. *Sourcebook of American Methodism.* Nashville, Tenn.: Abindon Press, 1982.

Paludan, Phillip Shaw. *A People's Contest: The Union and Civil War, 1861–1865.* New York: Harper and Row, 1988.

Randall, James G., and Richard N. Current. *Lincoln, the President.* 4 vols. New York: Dodd, Mead, and Co., 1955.

Richter, William L. *The Army in Texas during Reconstruction, 1865–1870.* College Station: Texas A & M University Press, 1987.

Roche, M. D. *Dedication of Monument and Reunion at Gettysburg, September 11–12, 1889.* Scranton, Pa.: Press of the Sunday News Association of the 143rd Regiment Pennsylvania Volunteers, 1883. Photocopy, Microfilm International, Ann Arbor, Michigan, 1979.

Scott, Robert Garth. *Into the Wilderness with the Army of the Potomac.* Bloomington: Indiana University Press, 1992.

Shannon, Fred Albert. *The Organization and Administration of the Union Army, 1861–1865.* 2 vols. Cleveland, Ohio: Arthur H. Clark Co., 1928.

Simpson, Brooks D. *Let Us Have Peace: Ulysses S. Grant and the Politics of War and Reconstruction, 18631–1868.* Chapel Hill: North Carolina University Press, 1991.

Skolnick, Arlene. *Embattled Paradise: The American Family in an Age of Uncertainty.* New York: HarperCollins, 1991.

Squier, Charlotte Rhodes. *Franklin Academy, Soldiers Orphans School, Harford University.* Tunkhannock, Pa.: Mulligan Printing Corp., 1989.

Stearns, George A. *The Schools of Susquehanna County, Pennsylvania, 1795–1945.* Montrose, Pa.: Susquehanna Historical Society, 1947.

Stevenson, Louise. *The Victorian Homefront: American Thought and Culture, 1860–1880.* New York: Twayne Publishers, 1991.

Stocker, Rhamanthus M. *Centennial History of Susquehanna County, Pennsylvania.* 1887. Reprint, Baltimore: Regional Publishing Company, 1974.

Taylor, Frank H. *Philadelphia in the Civil War.* Philadelphia: City of Philadelphia, 1913.

Towne, E. E. *Descendants of William Towne: Who Came to America on or about 1630 and Settled in Salem, Massachusetts.* 1901. Reprint, Salem, Mass.: Higginson Book Company, 1989.

Towne, Ruth Warner. *From These Beginnings: The History of First United Methodist Church, Kirksville, Missouri.* Kirksville, Mo.: Journal Printing Company, 1984.

———. *Senator William J. Stone and the Politics of Compromise.* Port Washington, NY: Kennikat Press, 1979.

Triennial Catalogue of Harford University. Montrose, PA: Alvin Day, Printer, 1855.

Violette, E. M. *History of Adair County, Missouri.* 1911. Reprint, Kirksville, Mo.: Journal Printing Company, 1979.
Ward, Geoffrey C., Ken Burns, and Rick Burns. *The Civil War: An Illustrated History.* New York: Alfred A. Knopf, Inc., 1990.
Warshaw, Steven, ed. *The Drawings of Charles Dana Gibson.* Berkeley, Calif.: Diablo Press, 1968.
Welcher, Frank J. *The Eastern Theater.* Vol. 1 of *The Union Army, 1861–1865: Organization and Operations.* Bloomington: Indiana University Press, 1989.
Wheeler, Richard. *Witness to Gettysburg.* New York: Harper and Row, 1987.
Wiley, Bell Irvin. *The Life of Billy Yank: The Common Soldier of the Union.* Baton Rouge: Louisiana State University Press, 1971.
Williams, Walter, ed. *The State of Missouri.* Columbia, Mo.: E. W. Stephens, 1904.

Index

NOTE: *italic* page numbers indicate photographs

Adair County, Missouri, 158-171
  coal mining boom, 177
  Immigrant Aid Society, 158
alcohol, use of, 13, 74, 91
Altes, V. T., 257
Aquia Creek, 85
architecture
  in Brownsville, Texas, 145
  Frank W. and Mary E. Towne house, *239*
  Jehiel Warner house, *2*
  John S. Towne house, 5-6
  Unionville house, 206-207
  Warner homestead, 1801, 2-4

Baldwin, Jeremiah, 37
Baptists, 28
Barry, Joe (brother-in-law of Mary E. Towne), 240
Bates, James T. (Maj.), 101, 108
Baxter, C. J., 178
bell tolling custom, 216-217
Beverly plantation, 86-87
Binghamton, New York, 154-155
Birchardville School, 32
Birney, William (Gen.), 108-109, 114-115, 123
  and U.S. Colored Troops, 117
Bonfoey, B. H., 242
Bristoe Station, 72
Brownsville, Texas, 144, *145*, 146, 147
Bryan, William Jennings, 225-228
Buford, John (Gen.), 59, 60
Burdick, Erastus Henry
  husband of Lydia Rachel Deuel, 162
  move to Kansas, 173
Burdick, Lydia Rachel Deuel
  daughter of John and Phinis Towne Deuel, 27
  death and burial, 172
  in her marriage dress, *163*
  marriage to Erastus Henry Burdick, 162-163
  reburial in Kirksville, 188
Burdick, Mary Eliza. *See* Schmucher, Mary Eliza
Butler, Benjamin (Gen.), 113, 117

Calvinism, 8
Camp Cadwalader, 151
Camp Lincoln, 129
camp meetings, 42-44
Camp Seward, 50
Camp William Penn, 97-107
Campbell, James (Postmaster General), 30
Carroll, John (attorney), 218
Cassandra, troop carrier, 135
cats
  Mali, 210-212, 242-243
  Socrates and Xantippe (Tippy), 243
Catterdon, Allen W. (Sgt.), 108, 110
Chamberlain, Albert (lawyer), 36
Chancellorsville campaign, 53-58
Chase, Amasa, postmaster, 29
Choconut Township, 28
Christian Commission, 70
Church of the Brethren, 214
circulating libraries, 6
City Point, Virginia, 92, 112
  hosts President and Grant, 119
Civil War, 40-52
  Appomattox, 118-125
  Army of the Potomac, 52-67, 68-95, 118
  Bermuda Hundred area, 113
  Chancellorsville, 53-58
  Cold Harbor battle, 89-90
  Gettysburg campaign, 59-68, *64*
  Grant's campaign, 84–97

Civil War (*continued*)
into the South, 82-95
Lee's surrender, 124-126
Petersburg to Appomattox, 108-128
Pickett's charge, 66
Soldiers' Aid Societies, 70
souvenirs, 126-127
Spotsylvania campaign, 84
Union soldiers getting mail, *71*
Warrenton, 72
Wilderness campaign, 82-84
wounded Union soldiers, *50*
Cleveland, Grover, 222
coal mining, 177-179, 232-234
Cobb, George N. (photographer), 106
Cole, Ellen Theodora "Nellie." *See* Towne, Ellen Theodora
Cole, Sally. *See* Warner, Sally
Cole, Winthrop, 166
collectibles
china plates, 240-241
coin silver spoons, 199, 254-255
Company H, 143rd Pennsylvania Volunteers, 217-219, *219*
Confederate States of America, 40
Congregationalists, 5, 28
Conyngham, C. M. (Maj.), 62
Cooper, Charles M., 244
Cooper, Jessie, and Myron Stewart Towne, 244
Crippin, Ben (Sgt.)
and Gettysburg monument, 62, 219
rescues flag, 62
Culpeper, Virginia, 73
Curtin, Andrew (governor), 46

Dairy farming, 208-221
Dana, Edmund (Col.), 55, 58, 83
Dana, Milton (Lt.), 51, 55, 69, 71, 76, 78, 83, 94
Deans, W. B. (daguerreotypist), 31
death, views of, 173, 176-177, 188
deforestation, 177
Democratic Party, 14, 16, 17, 40, 224-226
Deuel, John (husband of Phinis Towne), 26
Deuel, Lydia Rachel. *See* Burdick, Lydia Rachel
Deuel, Phinis Naoma Towne (daughter of John S. and Rachel Warner Towne), 5-7, 37, 74, 104-105, *155*, *214*
housekeeper for M. S. Towne, 35-36
and Lydia's marriage, 161-162
matchmaker for M. S. Towne, 165-166
daughter of John S. and Rachel Warner Towne, 5-7
education of, 6
executor of John Towne's will, 185
marriage to John Deuel, 26
move to Lanark, Illinois, 164
postmaster, 44-45, 164
separation from John Duel, 32
sewing for granddaughter, 175
small loan business, 235
supports granddaughter's family, 215
Deuel, Wellington Bonaparte (son of John and Phinis Towne Deuel), 26
Doubleday, Abner (Gen.), 52, 57, 125, 139
Gettysburg campaign, 61 ff.
Doubleday, Ulysses (Gen.), 101, 118, *140*
and U.S. Colored Troops, 113-115
Douglas, Stephen A., 40, 267n1

Education
American norms, 236
county superintendency established, 24
discipline, 20
European pedagogy, 21
home schooling, 6
journalism, 237
M. S. Towne, 6-8, 29
of colored troops, 133, 143
parochial, 7
Phinis Towne, 6
private, 7
professional (religious), 8
progressivism, 24
public school concept, 6

education (*continued*)
Rachel Warner Towne, 5-6
religious, 8
segregated, in Unionville, 228-230
teachers' associations and institutes, 23, 24
Empire House Hotel, Unionville, *180*, 200
destroyed by fire, 200-201
Essex, troop carrier, 150

Fairview Addition, Unionville, Missouri, 234ff., 248
Fairview Dairy, Unionville, Missouri, 208-221, 233
family planning, by John S. and Rachel Warner Towne, 5, 9-10
fashion, 174-175, 204, 212
Forest Lake Centre Methodist Episcopal Church, 8, 187
and John Smith Towne, 185
established 1848, 9-10
Ladies' Aid Societies, 70
revival at, 44
Forest Lake Centre, McKelvey School, 18, 20
Forest Lake, Pennsylvania, 6, 7
Forest Lake Temperance Society, 13
Forty-fifth U.S. Colored Troops, 75-76, 93-94, 102, 108-128
supplied assistant to Towne, *134*
Texas campaign, 129
Foster, Charles W. (head, Bureau of Colored Troops), 76, 94, 125
Foster, R. S. (cmdr.), 124
France, and Mexican war, 130ff.
Frank, P. (Baptist preacher), 13
Free Soil Party, 17

Garber, Isaac, 235
Gardner, Reuben (guardian of Ellen Cole Towne), 167, 169
German immigrants, 214
Gettysburg campaign. *See under* Civil War
Gettysburg, Pennsylvania, 143rd monument, 217
Gibson, Charles Dana, 240
"Gibson Girl" decorative plates, 240–241
Glazier, Theodore (Maj.), 118
Gordon, R. L., 37
Grant, Ulysses S. (Gen.), 77-78, 84, 88, 90-91
and U.S. Colored Troops, 115-116, 118-119
Griffing, John (Methodist circuit rider), 8
Grow, Galusha (Congressman), 181

Hair-brushing incident between Rachel and Elizabeth, 197-198
Hamilton, Rufus (military surgeon), 141, 150
Harford University, 21
Harford, Pennsylvania, 21
Hartsuff, George L. (Maj. Gen.), 131
Haskell, L. F. (Gen.), 142, 150
health problems
"ill health," 192
consumption, 186ff.
hemorrhoids, 141, 142, 148, 207
hernia, 148
seasickness, 150
typhoid fever, 68-67, 172
varicose veins, 87, 93, 94, 207
Hill, A. P. (Confederate cmdr.), 60
Hinton, Amanda (mother-in-law of Myron Stewart Towne), 249-250
Hinton, Ethel. *see* Towne, Ethel
Hinton, Lincoln (father-in-law of Myron Stewart Towne), 249
Hollister, Fred P. (sheriff), 46
Hooker, Joseph "Fightin' Joe"Gen.r.)
Chancellorsville campaign, 53-58
resignation from Army of the Potomac, 59

Israel and Company, photographer, 110

Jackson, R. H. (Gen.), 124
Jenner, Walter, 94
Johnson, Clement, of Unionville, 179
Journal Printing Company, Kirksville, 247

Kettle Run, 73
Kirksville, Missouri
  Journal Printing Company, 247
  Kirksville Cemetery, 188, 190, 278n30
Knupp, Samuel (Rev.), 215-216

Ladies' Aid Societies, 70, 93
Lanark Methodist Episcopal Church, 158, 185, 215
Lanark, Illinois, 158, 164
Lee, Robert E. (Gen.), surrender, 124
libraries, Middletown, Pennsylvania, 6
Lincoln, Abraham, 40-41
  assassinated, 129
  emancipation proclamation, 51-52
  review of U.S. Colored Troops, 118-119
Lincoln, Levi (sawmill lessee), 42
lumber trade, 177-178
Lutherans, 7
Lyceum lectures, and Harford University, 22-23
Lyman, Lydia. *See* Towne, Lydia

McCoy, Abel (father of Mary Elizabeth McCoy Towne), 237, 239
McCoy, Mary Elizabeth. *See* Towne, Mary Elizabeth
McCullum, Daniel C. (Col.), 72
McKelvey School, Forest Lake, 18, 20
McLean, Wilmer, and Grant-Lee meeting, 124
Mali (family pet), 210-212, 242-243
manufacturing, in Putnam County, 232
marriage, M. S. Towne views on, 165
Marshall, Hugh, 181, 225, 227
Marshall, Neal, 225, 226
Martinstown, Missouri, 163, 189
Maximilian, Joseph, 130
Meade, George G. (Gen.), 123, 124
  Gettysburg campaign, 59-68
  Spotsylvania campaign, 84
Mendota mines, Putnam County, 234
Mercur, Ulysses (circuit judge), 37
Methodist Episcopal Church, 8
  camp meetings, 42
Methodist Episcopal Church (*continued*)
  division over slavery, 14-15
  Kirksville, Missouri, 160
  Lanark, Illinois, 158, 215
  Oneida Conference, 8-10
  and temperance movement, 12-13
  Unionville, Missouri, 215-216
  Vestal Circuit, 42-43
  Wyoming Conference, 43
Mexican War, 15-16, 130ff.
Mexico, home seen by M. S. Towne, *144*
Meyer, Edelmiro (Col.), 148
Middletown, Pennsylvania, 6
military manuals
  Casey's *Manual of Tactics,* 81, 99
  Manual of Instructions for... Confederate States..., 120
  Regulations of the Army of the Confederate States, 120
Miller, Charles, 247
Miller, Valentine, 178
mining, 177-179, 232-234
Missouri
  Kirksville (Adair County), 158-171
  Martinstown (Putnam County), 163
  Unionville (Putnam County), 178
Monroe Doctrine (1823), 130
Monroe Drug Company, 232, 248
Montrose, Pennsylvania, 31
Moody, Elisha (father of Phinis Towne), 2
Moody, Mary Towne. *See* Towne, Mary
Moody, Phinis. *See* Warner, Phinis
Moody, Quartus (husband of Mary Towne), 4
Morris' Studio, Kirksville, 170
Morris, Henry A. (military physician), 150
Morris, John C. (Capt.), 47, 51, 104
Morris, John C. (Union army recruiter), 46
Mott, Orange, Jr., 37
Mott, Orange, Mrs., 70
music. *See* singing

Napoleon III, 130
nepotism, 18

New Orleans, 151
Newton, John (Gen.), 72

143rd Pennsylvania Volunteers
at Gettysburg, 62-68
Company H annual meeting, 217
photograph, *219*
Ord, O. C. (Gen.), 114, 123, 124, 131
osteopathy, in Kirksville, 248

Parker, James M. (Methodist minister), 176
Patrick, Abel H. (purchaser of John Towne's property), 187
Patrons of Husbandry grange, 224
Paul, Josiah (Capt.), hernia, 148
Pennsylvania, public schools, 7
Petersburg, 129
Philadelphia, Pennsylvania, 6-7
photography, 31, 105-106, 110
in Brownsville, Texas, 146, 147
in Kirksville, 170
Pickler, Samuel M., 178
Pierce, Joseph W. (Lt.), 141
Port Royal, 88
Porter, John L., 177-178
Pratt, A. B., 251-252, 257
Purington, Dilwyn V. (Lt.), 125, 127, 128
Putnam County, Missouri, 162, 163, 206
coal mining, 232-234
manufacturing, 232
Putnam Fadeless Dyes, 232

Quartermaster's Department, 84-86

Racism, 130-131, 228-230
railroads, 79, 80, 109, 122, 123, 154, 218-219
and coal mining, 177-179
in Kirksville, 158
lobbyists, 218, 220, 281n17
reading. *See* education
Rebecca Benton, troop carrier, 110-111
Reed, Charles F. (associate judge), 36
religion
and education, 8
religion (*continued*)
Warner family, 5
Wright family, 28
Republican Party, 17, 40, 222, 224
Reynolds, John F. (Gen.), 52, 57, 60, 61
Richardson, Lyman (Rev.) (president, Harford University), 22
Richardson, Maria (niece of Lyman Richardson), 22
Richardson, Williard (nephew of Lyman Richardson), 22
county school superintendent, 23
Richmond *Enquirer,* 120, 122
Roosevelt, Theodore, 226
Rose, Robert (land speculator), 1, 5
Rose, Rodney S. (Methodist preacher), 9

Sanitary Commission, 70, 93
Schmucher, John F.
husband of Mary Eliza Burdick, 213-215, *214*
Schmucher, Mary Eliza Burdick (daughter of Erastus Henry and Lydia Deuel Burdick), 164, 172-175, *174, 198*
marriage to John F. Schmucher, 212-215, *214*
Schuylkill Arsenal, 151
scurvy, on Texas border, 137
segregation, in Unionville, 228-230
Seward, William (Sec. of State), 130
Shepard, D. A. (Methodist preacher), 9
Sheridan, Phillip (Gen.), 121, 124
Sigel, Franz (Gen.), 113
singing
"Ain't I glad to get out of the wilderness," 84
with bass viol, 156
in Chancellorsville campaign, 56-57
"Jesus, Lover of My Soul," 44
"John Brown's Body," 56-57
led by M. S. Towne, 9-10, 224
by Patrons of Husbandry, 224
"Rally 'Round the Flag", 115

singing (*continued*)
teaching of, 25
"There is a Fountain...", 44
by Union troops, 84
by U.S. Colored Troops, 102
at Vestal camp meeting, 44
slavery, 14, 15
abolished in Maryland, 117
and Liberty Bell, 217
emancipation proclamation, 51-52
exchanges between Grant and Lee, 115-116
Smith, A. J., 235
socioeconomic growth, 153-171
Socrates (family pet), 243
Soldiers' Aid Societies, 70
Soldiers' Lodge/Rest/Retreat, 80
Spencer, Ambrose (purchaser of John Towne's property), 164, 187
Stahl, Solomon F., 177
Stanton, Edwin M. (Secretary of War), 45, 93
Stewart, Elizabeth. *See* Towne, Elizabeth Stewart
Stille, George, 236
Stone School, 32
Stone, Roy (Col.), 52, 57, 77, 83
Gettysburg campaign, 61ff.
Strange, John, 13
Susquehanna County, Pennsylvania, 1-4, 21
education, 7
teachers' association, 23-24

Taft, William Howard, and Payne-Aldrich Tariff, 226
Taylor (Maj.), 98
Taylor, Edwin Wallace (cousin-in-law of M. S. Towne), 74
Taylor, Ruth Warner. *See* Warner, Ruth
teachers' associations, 23, 24
temperance movement, 12-13
Teter, I. P. (Rev.), 195
Texas, and Mexican War, 129-152
Thomas J. Sparks, troop carrier, 150
Thorn, Edward (Lt. Col.), 101, 102
Tilden, William C. (purchased Towne property), 159
timber cutting, 177
Tippy (family pet), 243
Towne, Amasa
father of John Smith Towne, 4
father of Josiah Towne, 10
father of Lydia Towne Lyman, 6
father of Mary Towne Moody, 6
Towne, Elizabeth Stewart (third wife of M. S. Towne), 192-199, *205*, 209-210, 250, *253*
Towne, Ellen Theodora "Nellie" Cole (second wife of M. S. Towne), 166-171, *169*
childbirth, 176, 182-183
final illness, death, burial, 186-190
Towne, Ethel Hinton (wife of Myron Stewart Towne), 249-250
Towne, Fanny (daughter of M. S. and Nellie Towne), 182-183, *183*, 185-186
Towne, Frank Warner (son of M. S. and Elizabeth Stewart Towne), 23, 176, *205*
career, 227
Journal Printing Company, 247
at *Unionville Pantagraph*, 236-237
family
relationship with father, 201-203
marriage to Mary Elizabeth McCoy, 237-243
birth of daughter, 254 ff.
illness (measles), 212
personality, 209
love for fruit, 209, 280n6
political affiliations (Democrat), 225
religion (Methodist), 189-190
Towne, Frederick Winthrop (son of M. S. and Ellen Towne), 176
Towne, John Smith (husband of Rachel Warner), 4, 31, 37, 104, *105*
death, 183-184
family, 8, 160–162
collector for M. S., 160-161
goals of, for M. S., 8

Towne, John Smith *(continued)*
family *(continued)*
Lydia's marriage, 161-162
philanthropy/public service
deeds property to M.E. church, 164
establishes library, 6, 187
assists in Forest Lake Centre M.E. Church, 185
justice of the peace, 36, 104, 159
political activity, 12-17
school director, 13-14, 18
photographed, *105,* 106, 107, 110
religion (conversion to Methodism), 8-9
relocation to Lanark, Illinois, 158, 164
vocation
blacksmith, 4
closes blacksmith shop, 156
Towne, Josiah (Rev.) (son of Amasa Towne), 10
Towne, Lydia (Lyman), 6, 10, 104
Towne, Margaret Smith, (mother of John Smith Towne), 4
Towne, Mary (wife of Quartus Moody), 4, 6, 10.
Towne, Mary Elizabeth McCoy (wife of Frank Warner Towne), 38, 237-243, *241,* 280n15
birth of Ruth Warner Towne, 38
Towne, Myron Smith (M. S.), (son of John S. and Rachel Towne) 5, *80, 205*
career/vocations. *See also* military service.
dairy farmer, 206-216
sawmill owner-operator, 27
schoolmaster, 18-25
land venture, 233-236
postmaster, 30
education, 6, 7-8, 29
family
father's death, 184-185
life on the dairy farm, 206-216
new family, 191-205
move to Kirksville, Missouri, 158
postwar, 153-171
Towne, Myron Smith (M. S.) *(continued)*
health problems
hemorrhoids, 141, 142, 148, 207
last days, 254-261
typhoid fever, 68-67
varicose veins, 87, 93, 94, 207
to Sarah Wright, 26, 28-39, 42, 44
to Ellen Cole, 166-171
to Elizabeth Stewart, 192-199
military service
brigade quartermaster, 142
at Beverly plantation, 86-87
and Camp William Penn, 97-107
commands wagon train to Appomattox, 125
commissary sergeant, 51
commission, *96*
at Culpeper, Virginia, 74-81
discharge from 143rd, *95*
discharge from 25th Corps, *149*
in dress uniform, *80*
in Mexico, 143-144
143rd reunion at Gettysburg, 217-219
Petersburg to Appomattox, 108-128
quartermaster (regimental), 102
recommendation petition for, 46-47, *48,* 51
shipwreck, at Padre Island, 150
in Texas, 141, 144-145
Union army service, 44-152
and U.S. Colored Troops, 93-94
orations
"Bells" talk to Old Soldiers Reunion, Unionville, 216
Westward Expansion address, Unionville, 221
personality/talents
animal lover, 210, 223
bass viol player, 147
mischievousness, 168, 263n11
oratory, 223-224
singing skills, 9-10, 25, 44
shattered dreams, 244-261
teetotaler, 13
views on: death, 184-85; marriage, 192-93; religion, 173, 176, 189-90

Towne, Myron Smith (M. S.) (*continued*)
politics and public service, 16-17, 222-231
antisegregationist, 229-230
Anti-Slavery Society member, 81
Democrat, 225
mayor of Unionville, 222-224
Republican, 222, 224
Towne, Myron Stewart (son of M.S. and Elizabeth Towne), *203, 205*
acquires father's farm, 252
and Jessie Cooper, 244-246
move to Hammond, Indiana, 257
personality, 209
Towne, Phinis N. *See* Deuel, Phinis Naoma
Towne, Rachel Warner (daughter of Jehiel and Phinis Warner; wife of John Smith Towne), 4, *105, 197*
and Elizabeth Towne, 196-197
conversion to Methodism, 8
death and funeral of, 212, 215
executor of John Towne's will, 185, 187
move to Middle West, 158
sewing for great-granddaughter, 175
wife of John Smith Towne, 4, 31, 104
Towne, Ruth Warner (daughter of Frank and Mary E. Towne), 254-255
Towne, Sarah M. *See* Wright, Sarah M.
Trigg, Harry, 191, 192
Trigg, Susan Stewart, 192
Turrell School, 20
Turrell, L. M., 13
Twenty-fifth Corps, 129-151

U.S. Colored Troops. *See* Forty-fifty U.S. Colored Troops
U.S. Congress,
Compromise of 1850, 16
freesoil amendments, 16
U.S. Government
Bureau of Colored Troops, 133
Dept. of Ocean and Lake Transportation, 134, 136, 149
military railroads, 79
Sanitary Commission, 70
Union army. *See* Civil War
Unionville Journal, 247
Unionville Methodist Episcopal Church, 215-216
Unionville, Missouri, 23, 178-179, 206
at turn of the century, 232-233
Chautauqua, William Jennings Bryan, 226-228
city directory, *180*
Fairview Addition, *233*
United States Hotel, 97, 99
University of Missouri, 237

Valentine's Day carnations, 237-238, 283n7
Van Valkenburg, Richard (Methodist preacher), 44
Vestal Methodist Church, 9, 42, 44
voting, by Union soldiers, 116-117

Wadsworth, 60
Warner mill, surviving stone wall, *3*
Warner, Asa (son of Azor and Bertha Warner), 46, 47, 69, 164, 185, *219*
and family reunion, 220
in Company H photo, *219*
lay speaker at Methodist Episcopal church, 187
secretary, 143rd Reg. association, 217
Warner, Azor Moody (son of Jehiel and Phinis Warner), 4, 9, 27
Warner, Bertha (wife of Azor Warner), 70
mother of Asa Warner, 185
Warner, Eli (son of Jehiel and Phinis Warner), 4
move to Illinois, 158
Warner, Elisha Hubbard (son of Jehiel and Phinis Warner), 4
Warner, Jehiel (husband of Phinis Moody Warner), 1-4, 7
Warner, Jerub (son of Eli Warner), 158
Warner, Justus Franklin "Frank" (cousin of M. S. Towne), 161, 220
Warner, Kathryn L., 267n9
Warner, Phinis Moody (wife of Jehiel Warner), 2, 4

Warner, Rachel. *See* Towne, Rachel
Warner, Ruth (cousin of M. S. Towne), 74-75
Warner, Sally Cole (wife of Eli Warner), 166
Warner, Samantha C. (cousin-in-law of Rachel Towne), 235
Warner, Seth (son of Jehiel and Phinis Warner), 4
Warner, Stanley (son of Azor Warner), 46, 47, 98, 219
  in Company H photo, *219*
Warren (Gen.), 84, 86, 88
Warrenton, 72
Washington, D.C., during Civil War, 49-51
weather, in Mexican War, 136-137
Weitrzel, Godfrey (Gen.), 117, 130-131, 138
West, Robert, 98
Whig Party, 14, 16
White, Warren T., 36, 37, 42
Wilmot, David (Congressman), 16, 17
Wilson, Woodrow, 226
Wright, Chauncey (father-in-law of M. S. Towne), 28, 36
Wright, Miriam (sister-in-law of M. S. Towne), 28, 31
Wright, Sarah M. (first wife of M. S. Towne), 26, 28
  divorce, 36–37
  farewell letter to M. S. Towne, 34-35
  M.S. Towne's comment to daughter-in-law, 38
Wycof, Samuel (Rev.), officiates Towne-Cole wedding, 169

Xantippe (family pet), 243